REWRITING

SUNY series in Postmodern Culture
Joseph Natoli, editor

REWRITING

Postmodern Narrative and Cultural Critique in the Age of Cloning

CHRISTIAN MORARU

State University
of New York
Press

Published by
State University of New York Press, Albany

Printed in the United States of America

For information, address State University of New York Press,
90 State Street, Suite 700, Albany, NY 12207

Production by Susan Geraghty
Marketing by Mike Campochiaro

Library of Congress Cataloging-in-Publication Data

Moraru, Christian.
Rewriting : postmodern narrative and cultural critique in the age of cloning / Christian Moraru.
p. cm. — (SUNY series in postmodern culture)
Includes bibliographical references and index.
ISBN 0-7914-5107-0 (alk. paper) — ISBN 0-7914-5108-9 (pbk. : alk. paper)
1. American literature—20th century—History and criticism. 2. American literature—Adaptations—History and criticism. 3. Popular culture—United States—History—20th century. 4. National characteristics, American, in literature. 5. United States—Civilization—20th century. 6. Culture in literature. 7. Narration (Rhetoric) I. Title. II. Series.

PS228.P68 M67 2001
810.9'0054—dc21

00-053807

10 9 8 7 6 5 4 3 2 1

Rewriting is a surplus. (Blanchot 34)

By using each other, each other's texts, we keep on living, imagining, making . . . (Acker, *Bodies* 7)

Without understanding the place of the work in literature and its direct dependence on literature, it is impossible to understand its place in the ideological environment. (Bakhtin/Medvedev 27)

CONTENTS

PREFACE

Rewriting . . . the spirit of the times. (Kundera, *The Art of the Novel* 147)

Our culture has been going through an accelerated process of "agonizing revision," of "rewriting everything," as Jean Baudrillard points out in *The Illusion of the End* (12). The stories we tell and write make one think more and more of the original meaning of telling as *re-citare*, "quotation" of former stories (2). Ours is an intractable—some say, typically postmodern—"urge to retell," and "everyone seems to be [yielding to] it" (Schiff, "Contemporary Retellings" 1). One can easily notice the all-pervasiveness of rewriting in fiction by Toni Morrison, Michel Butor, Leonardo Sciascia, Christa Wolf, and J. M. Coetzee, among countless others in various languages. One distinguishes similarly "recitative" protocols in movies by Matthew Bright, Mel Brooks, David Lynch, and Quentin Tarantino; in paintings by Robert Rauschenberg and Carlo Maria Mariani; in mixed-media artifacts such as Larry Rivers's; in the post-Le Corbusier, aggressively "quotational" architecture of Charles Moore and James Stirling; in mainstream, avant-garde, former pop art, and current popular culture alike; in traditionally as well as aesthetically less recognized domains, such as "retro" fashion and automotive design, with the odd-looking Chrysler PT Cruiser and the deceptively advertised "all-new" VW Beetle as prime examples; in commercials, cartoons, music (both "high-brow" and pop), MTV series, in "filmed" books and "booked" films alike, as British novelist Julian Barnes ironically says—in cultural discourse broadly conceived.[1]

This book focuses on rewriting in late twentieth-century America. Specifically, it discusses how postmodern narrative reworks nineteenth-century tales, stories, novels, and novellas. But what drives narrative rewriting? What happens when a story is rewritten? What happens, I mean, to the rewritten and to the "rewrite"? Further, what happens to us, readers—or should I say, *re*readers, confronted as we are, in the rewrite, with the *déjà-lu*? What sort of readerly competence does this "recognition" presuppose? My analyses strive to answer such questions by pursuing the textual transformations obtained through rewriting. As I recount these changes, I also ask, What cultural-ideological issues do the rewriting process and the resulting story cast light on, and how do these issues, and their illumination, bear upon how we understand postmodernism? What formal and cultural mechanisms do rewrites set off while taking up those problems? Which are the ensuing rewriting patterns and the major techniques? How do writers apply them, and what are the broader effects of their use? Last, how does the context of rewriting affect the meaning of the revamped story? Critics from Linda Hutcheon and Brian McHale to Matei Calinescu, Patrick O'Donnell, Marcel Cornis-Pope, Paul Maltby, Susan Suleiman, and Peter Widdowson have stressed the significance of some of these questions. Overall, though, these issues have not been addressed sufficiently. Therefore, I set out to examine systematically the widespread practice of contemporary narrative rewriting.

After taking stock of rewriting's elusiveness as a literary category in the first chapter of Part I, I move on to define the rewriting type that concerns me—and its ties to postmodern discourse. Thus, I acknowledge my interest in *intensive* rewriting—programmatic, thorough, and "overt" ("straight")—as different from the "oblique" or "coded" (Plate, "Visions" 4) reworkings of former narratives. In this light, my inquiry finds insufficient the notion "that all writing"—if not all reading—is rewriting (Trotter 193) or that "every word, phrase or segment is a reworking of other writings which precede or surround the individual work" (Eagleton, *Literary Theory* 119). Furthermore, as a way of reading, organizing, and gauging the force of postmodern rewriting, I turn primarily to *extensive* rewrites, which make a more conspicuous and directly "critical" ("revisionist" or radical) impact on certain notions and representations. In sum, the intensive-extensive rewriting sort I discuss designates a postmodern narrative that, without necessarily showing an "attachment to a single textual precedent" (Connor 80), *(a) reworks in detail one or a few narratives and (b) while doing so, puts forth a critical commentary* on the sociohistorical ambience—values, ideas, formations, cultural mythologies—within which rewriting is undertaken or within which the reworked text was produced. The last segments of Part I's second chapter lay out a certain discourse model that such rewriting both foregrounds and activates. I reconstruct this model through a dialogue with the post-Bakhtinian tradition of intertextual studies, more specifically, with recent work in postmodernism and cultural analysis. In addition, I suggest that this model calls for a germane, indeed "oppositional" (Cornis-Pope, "Ethics" 186) kind of reading, which I analogously build by striking up a polemical conversation with influential, formalist and postformalist takes on literary revisionism broadly understood. My complex—one might say "eclectic"—take on rewriting is befitting, I think, for the rewrites I deal with set in motion both literary and transliterary (social, political, ideological) permutations. These rewrites refurbish *forms*—texts and textual structures—as well as discourse *formations* that critics have usually cut off from the phenomenology of "literariness." Such formations represent, I propose in Part I, cultural or "identity narratives": heavily ideology-laden tales about us as individuals and members of certain communities organized around nuclear terms, discourses, and tropes of nationality, ethnicity, race, social standing, gender, sex, moral-religious beliefs, and so on. I claim that rewriting determines not only a remolding of a certain literary matrix, but, by means of this very retextualization, also a revision—critical retelling—of those cultural tales.

Along these lines, I identify certain "exemplary" authors and ideological areas where they intervene, through specific rewriting strategies, in public discourses of identity turning on the figures and questions above. Thus, Part II focuses on relevant fictions by E. L. Doctorow, Robert Coover, and Paul Auster, explaining how these *re*writers redo former stories to revise what I call the "national narrative." They absorb ethnic, social, and political categories as they engage with romantic and transcendentalist tales by different rewriting techniques: *performative transposition*, *parodic development of certain "micronarratives,"* and "*doubling*" or "*ghostwriting*." Minutely "reenacting" a romantic fable of medieval oppression, Doctorow's 1974 novel *Ragtime*, for instance, recomposes the ragtime chapter of the American narrative around new stories of race and ethnicity. Similarly, Coover's rewrites, chiefly his 1976 novel *The Public Burning*, are eminent examples of how "historiographic metafiction" (Hutcheon, *Poetics* 92) "amends" the literary archive to reconsider—rewrite—the present critically. Certainly, the novel can be, and it has been, read in all sorts of ways. But I reread it here as an elaborate, parodic remodeling of Horatio Alger, to better set forth the scope of Coover's double critique: a critique of the past and the past source, as well as of the present and its ideological tall tales. This Part's last chapter shows how Auster's "antidetective" novels revise Poe, Hawthorne, Thoreau, and others to pinpoint narrative strategies and intertextual ploys that critique the prevailing American story.

History and its polemical retelling also figure as prominent stakes in African American postmodernism. Part III picks out Ishmael Reed, Charles Johnson, and Trey Ellis as culturally distinct examples of black rewriting and its typical method of *cross-fertilization* (Johnson's own term). Possibly more emphatically than anywhere else, it becomes clear here why and how rewriting allows for a critical reconstruction of identity. Black rewriters renarrate to revamp a much wider, less imaginary fable, where their personal stories are enmeshed in a collective and painful history. They rewrite and thereby step across cultural lines, textual, stylistic, and thematic, "rewriting" their way into an exchange as aesthetic as political. Accordingly, the chapter on Ishmael Reed's *outwriting* and *ventriloquizing* tactics demonstrates how Reed's work "purloins" nineteenth-century texts. In Part II, we see how Auster "doubles" Poe; in this Part, I analyze Reed's textual and political rewriterly "appropriation" of Poe's tales and poems. Following this analysis is a discussion of Johnson's phenomenological theory and practice of rewriting. Last, I look at Ellis's related, self-acknowledged method of "hip-hop," *cross-pollinating* reassemblages, which play upon the hypertext model.

Avant-pop rewriting and hip-hop stylistic "mongrels" have a lot in common. This is why Part IV begins with a chapter on Mark Leyner's avant-pop *engrafting* and *plagiarism* and their ironic use of Hawthornian "transplants." In Part III, I indicate how literary "mongrelization" (Ellis's word) takes apart and rebuilds fictional discourse by straddling preset racial divisions; interpreting Leyner's narrative *bric-à-bracs*, I pursue the way they erode inherited distinctions between established and not-so-established cultural materials. By the same token, the Leyner chapter marks my project's deepening interest in culturally "democratic" or "nonelitist" forms of rewriting. From Doctorow's sweeping panorama of the rising modern pop culture in America to Coover's mock apotheosis of mass entertainment to Reed's hilarious cooptation of a whole array of "low-brow" genres to Ellis's dazzling, information-age parodic collage to, finally, Leyner's comic adoption of popular idioms, my inquiry bears out an otherwise unsurprising progress: the history of rewriting over the last twenty years or so traces the increase of popular culture's revisionary presence in postmodern texts. Alongside more prestigious, "high-brow" and "serious" sources, "low-brow," often humorous materials have been worked increasingly into rewrites that have thus acquired superior cultural heterogeneity.

A driving force of postmodern poetics and politics, this heterogeneity also shapes two other Hawthornian rewrites that complement and complicate Leyner's: Kathy Acker's and Bharati Mukherjee's responses to *The Scarlet Letter*. Feminine (and self-avowedly feminist, or "womanist") and postcolonial (and, of late, "transnational") rewriting have been characteristically expanding practices in post–World War II narrative. Seized either separately or in their mutually enriching dialogue, they would certainly deserve individual books. In fact, critics have started to probe the dynamic of gender,[2] ethnicity, and location, on the one hand, and intertextuality and its particular form, rewriting, on the other hand. They have intimated the latter's culturally complex, emancipatory force in writers as diverse as Alice Walker, Maxine Hong Kingston, Joyce Carol Oates, Rebecca Goldstein, Ursula K. Le Guin, Marilynne Robinson, Angela Carter, and Margaret Atwood. As regards my own project, which covers, as I said, chiefly American literature, I had to limit it to two "case studies": Acker and Mukherjee. Yet my choices are anything but arbitrary. These authors engender—in all senses—the narrative "missing link" between avant-pop rewriting à la Leyner and gender- or ethnicity-oriented rewriting at a time new identity elements and practices such as information technology and consumption come to the fore to "interface" with, and "rewrite," sex, gender, ethnicity, location, and other material codes of identity. More than anywhere else in my book, here gender and rewriting betray their illuminating partnership. As Nancy K. Miller comments on Sandra Gilbert and Susan Gubar's analysis of women's "palimpsest" writing, female authors typically write "through the script of the dominant narrative" (87). Leyner plays upon Hawthorne's tale to flesh out, quite literally, a perplexing "supermaleness" while simultaneously cutting open, critiquing the "male" body of language and its underlying fantasies of authority; Acker and Mukherjee revisit Hester Prynne's story to reinvent feminine identity and authorship. As I observe in the second chapter of Part IV, Acker's 1978 work *Blood and Guts in High School* marks out, through rewriting modalities (*theft*, *plagiarism*, *piracy*) that critics have associated with the avant-pop, the redeeming space of a rebellious sexuality. Last, this Part's third chapter focuses on Mukherjee's 1993 novel *The Holder of the World*. Mukherjee uses *apocryphal* rewriting to suggest how gender and sexuality, ethnicity and (trans)nationality, postcolonial "counterwriting" and the revisionist discourse of American postmodernism crisscross to allow the woman subject to overflow stories and representations that have traditionally typecast and reined her in.

Having reconstructed extensive or critical rewriting as an important strain in postmodern literature, I conclude by drawing the ethical and ideological profile of a "certain postmodernism." Critics have taken postmodernism to task for its "formalist" gimmicks and gratuitous "cannibalizing" of the literary past. But rewriting operates selectively, to "un-settle things" (Hassan *Paracriticisms* 42). It sifts through, and retrieves, I argue, the literary archive depending on the rewriter's cultural positioning and agenda. "Rewritten" around the practice of critical rewriting, *this* postmodernism is enmeshed with other discourses of our time and with this time's textual and cultural memory. This kind of postmodern narrative rewrites both the intertextual storehouse of literary history and the intertextual domain of current social and political arenas, where it unavoidably brushes against, and bears upon, formulas and formulations of selfhood.

ACKNOWLEDGMENTS

Over years of thinking and writing about rewriting, I have incurred many debts. To Matei Calinescu my gratitude goes first. My longstanding dialogue with him and his work has been of great consequence to my various endeavors as a student of reading, rereading, and rewriting, as well as modernism, postmodernism, and whatever may be upon us.

Also at Indiana University, where I started to think more systematically about the "intensities" and "extensities" of rewriting, I came across mentors, colleagues, and friends who offered help when it was most needed. Raymond Hedin, Thomas Foster, and Breon Mitchell read an earlier version of this manuscript and gave encouragement and invaluable advice. In addition, I wish to thank the following individuals and institutions that have supported this project at various stages and in various ways: Carolyn Mitchell, James Naremore, Patrick O'Donnell, William Rasch, Henry Sussman, Nicholas Williams, Cary Wolfe; Jeffrey R. Di Leo, gifted scholar of critical theory and dear friend; Heather Price, for insisting that I look at Sena Jeter Naslund's *Ahab's Wife*, and my colleague Joseph Rosenblum, for mentioning Woody Allen's "The Kugelmass Episode" to me; Paul Maltby, himself distinguished student of postmodernism, who has made me aware of theoretical and ideological ramifications I had not foreseen; Marcel Cornis-Pope, Joe Amato, Jerome Klinkowitz, Tyrus Miller, and Brian Richardson, readers at State University of New York Press, for their comments and suggestions; the College of Arts and Sciences and the Departments of Comparative Literature and English at Indiana for financial and other forms of assistance; conference organizers and panel chairs at Harvard; State University of New York Binghamton; University of Louisville; University of Kentucky, Lexington; University of South Carolina, Columbia; Virginia Commonwealth University; University of North Dakota, Grand Forks; and other hospitable places where I gave talks bearing upon my book's topic.

I am very pleased to acknowledge the assistance provided by my home institution, University of North Carolina, Greensboro, in particular by its English Department. James Evans, former Head, and Denise Baker, current Head of the department, have been tremendously supportive. I wish to thank my colleagues for the exceptionally nurturing and challenging environment, without which the bringing to fruition of this enterprise would have been impossible. Keith Cushman, Mary Ellis Gibson, Christopher Hodgkins, Jennifer Keith, Karen Kilcup, Robert Langenfeld, Russ McDonald, Scott Romine, and Yumna Siddiqi, among others, have been especially helpful. Likewise, I thank University of North Carolina, Greensboro, for a 1999 Summer Excellence Research Award and the University of North Carolina Chapel Hill Center for Slavic, Eurasian, and East European Studies for a 1999–2000 fellowship.

To a considerable extent, this book has grown out of my graduate and undergraduate teaching, primarily at UNC-Greensboro. I have learned from the students in my contemporary fiction and theory classes at least as much as I trust they have learned from me. As I was putting the final touches on the manuscript, I found the debates in my Spring 1999 and Spring 2000 graduate seminars, Modern Critical Theory and Contemporary British and American Literature: Postmodern Narrative and Cultural Memory, genuinely stimulating.

James H. Peltz, his assistant at State University of New York Press, Katy Leonard, and Production Editor Susan Geraghty, have provided exemplary professional guidance and timely help. Finally, I thank my wife, Camelia, and my daughter, Maria, for putting up with me and the weekends I have spent chained to my Macintosh.

Earlier versions of a few chapters and sections have appeared in different forms, either reduced or expanded, as follows: "'Dancing to the Typewriter': Rewriting and Cultural Appropriation in *Flight to Canada*." *Critique: Studies in Contemporary Fiction* 41. 2 (Winter 2000): 99–113; "Rewriting Horatio Alger: Robert Coover and the Public Burning of the Public Sphere." *LIT: Literature Interpretation Theory* 10. 3 (1999): 235–254; "Charles Johnson." *Contemporary African American Novelists: A Bio-Bibliographical Sourcebook*. Ed. Emmanuel S. Nelson. Westport CT, London: Greenwood P, 1999. 220–226; "The Reincarnated Plot: E. L. Doctorow's *Ragtime*, Heinrich von Kleist's 'Michael Kohlhaas,' and the Spectacle of Modernity." *The Comparatist* 21 (May 1997): 92–116. I gratefully acknowledge the editors' permission to reprint these materials. Likewise, I thank Gary Hill for letting me use, for the front cover of this book, a detail of his mixed media installation, "I Believe It Is an Image in Light of the Other."

PART I

Rewriting and Postmodernism

CHAPTER 1

Rewriting and Late Twentieth-Century Narrative

> Contemporary fiction seems marked by the imperative of the eternal return. [I]n contemporary fiction, telling becomes compulsorily belated, inextricably bound up with retelling. (Connor 79)

CULTURAL MYTHOLOGY AND THE RETURN OF NARRATIVE

> The mighty dead return, but they return in our colors, and speaking in our voices. (Bloom, *Anxiety* 141)

Poring over John Updike's reasons for redoing *The Scarlet Letter* in *A Month of Sundays*, *Roger's Version*, and other novels, James A. Schiff aptly notes that "attempting to transform Hawthorne's text, Updike is seeking to alter an American myth" (*Updike's Version* 8). Updike himself uses the term *myth* in a letter to his critic. What he means by myth, we discover, is not the more established, anthropological notion Italo Calvino, for example, employs in his essay "Myth in the Narrative" to argue that "fables" (plots) are bound to endure the "repetitive force" (77) of myths and therefore to ever redo their structures. Nor does Updike's concept have anything to do with Joyce's "method," famously described by T. S. Eliot as "mythical." For Updike, myth is also instrumental to narrative rewriting, but as a "story or a pattern of behavior . . . 'linked with a particular culture and dealing with named characters and locations' as generated in a work of literature"; such myths, he adds, build a nation's "bad conscience" (qtd. in Schiff, *Updike's Version* 8).

Schiff's interpretation of Updike and Updike's self-interpretation hit upon an important point. There are highly canonical, widely popular fictions that capture, even give birth to key myths of certain communities. At the same time, they acquire in the long run a communally "mythic" weight through successive editing, teaching, reading, and related institutionalizing acts. The American Renaissance corpus, romance and transcendentalist works, Melville, Hawthorne, Emerson, Thoreau, Poe, Whitman, and other popular figures such as Twain or Horatio Alger are prime examples. They emerge around the same moment and participate in the weaving of a coherent, ideologically and culturally oversaturated "mythology."[1] To recall the Freudian description of myth, their works have become "wish-phantasies of whole nations," "treasure-house[s]" of desires and ideals. It is not surprising that they have been the foremost "ready-made material" to lend itself to "re-fashioning" (Freud 53) and critical rewriting.

The rewrites I discuss are "critical" for they often critique what they rewrite. They rewrite to "transvalue" the values, myths, and other symbolic, "*superlative* objects" (Barthes, *Mythologies* 88) ensconced in the retold tales. Like David Cowart's "parasite"-type "postmodern symbiont," rewriting undermines "the myth or exposes the ideology behind the language of the precursor text" (the "host") (4); in this view, one should probably talk about sabotage rather than symbiosis (Dubrow 116). Terminological squabbles aside, I argue that this ideological critique drives many a contemporary rewrite. Thus, the rewriter is a critical reader in the deepest sense. "The more that I write my own novels," Kathy Acker says, "the more it seems to me that to write is to read" (*Bodies* 66). I will return to this reading-writing dynamic later on. For now, I hasten to stress that to read is, for Acker and others, to read cultural mythologies critically; to read like a "poacher"-reader, to use Michel de Certeau's metaphor. This sort of reading is innovative, polemical, driven by the will to "rewrite history" (*Practice* 168). When explicitly "married with writing" in "the binomial set writing-reading" (168), "reading as poaching" (165) leads to critical rewriting of the writer-as-reader's readings (169). It is in this particular case, I believe, that "writing and reading are not separate, reading is a part of writing. A real reader is a writer. A real reader is already on the way to writing" (Cixous 21). It is so that reading becomes an "activity of production" enabling us to "re-write"—again, critically (Barthes, *Image* 157–64).

True readers are *rewriting-bound*. They are ready to "rewrit[e] the text of the work within the text of [his or her] lif[e]" (Barthes qtd. in Scholes, *Protocols* 1). Such readers "read merely to find a starter for their own performance" (Hartman, *The Fate of Reading* 272). And Joseph Heller does find a "starter" in Washington Irving's sketches in the witty apocryphal plays of *Catch-22*; Coover and Marilynne Robinson (*Housekeeping*) in Alger's tales; Paul Auster, Kathy Acker, Mark Leyner, Toni Morrison, Samuel R. Delany, and Bharati Mukherjee in *The Scarlet Letter*, *Fanshawe*, *The House of the Seven Gables*, and other texts by Hawthorne; Reed in Poe, Stowe, but also former slaves such as Frederick Douglass and Josiah Henson; Kurt Vonnegut's *Player Piano*, David Carkeet's *I Been There Before*, and Acker's *Empire of the Senseless* in Mark Twain's *A Connecticut Yankee in King Arthur's Court*, *Life on the Mississippi*, and *Huckleberry Finn*, respectively; Charles Johnson, Paul Metcalf (*Genoa*), Joan Didion (*Democracy*), Louise Erdrich (*Love Medicine*), Thomas King (*Green Grass, Running Water*), Peter Matthiessen (*Far Tortuga*), Philip Roth (*The Great American Novel*), Sena Jeter Naslund (*Ahab's Wife*), and, again, Acker in Melville; Maxine Hong Kingston in Whitman as her "Wittmanian" plays in *Tripmaster Monkey* bear witness; Auster and Pynchon (*Vineland*) in Emerson; once again Auster, Annie Dillard's *Pilgrim at Tinker Creek*, Tim O'Brien (*Going After Cacciato*, "the *Walden* of Vietnam") in Thoreau—and the list could go on and on.

But even in a comparative, transnational context, this critical reaction to the "model" narrative has proven productive. Especially in Part II's first chapter, my project cuts across national boundaries to link up through time and space Doctorow and German romantic writer Heinrich von Kleist. But Doctorow "Americanizes" Kleist and sets in train a rewriting that renders him an ideal if unlikely lens through which one can scrutinize America. Also, recast as Doctorow's novel, Kleist's novella becomes an "adopted," "immigrating" text by which the rewrite "deromances" the "immigration romance," critically looking back on early twentieth-century New York. The fictional form notwithstanding, this is "critical history," which opposes the more orthodox, "monumental" and "antiquarian" kinds, as Nietzsche writes in *History in the Service and Disservice of Life* (*Unzeitgemässe* 95). Some, though, call Doctorow's book "nostalgic" (Jameson, *The Cultural Turn* 9). Yet I sense nothing nostalgic in this look backward. Doctorow's is no struggle to romanticize the past. Nor do late twentieth-century rewrites leave romance—"social romance" (Alger), "racial romance" (Stowe and, we shall note, Poe), "aesthetic" and moral romance (Hawthorne), travel romance (Melville), the "psychological" romance (again, Poe), the individual self's "transcendental romance" (Emerson, Thoreau, Whitman), and so on—unquestioned, undisplaced, and unrewritten against its stylistic or ideological grain. It is not my goal, though, to "romance" rewriting, to paraphrase Diane Elam's exquisite book on postmodern romance (12), by dwelling upon contemporary rewriting's taste for romance. Also, I am not pursuing a "romantic postmodernism" or "romantic rewriting in American fiction"; nor am I arguing for a "neoromantic" revival in the same (Alsen iii) for that matter. I remain, in actuality, intrigued by how rewriting dislodges largely transcendentalist, nineteenth-century-based "myths."

CLASSICAL "UNDERWRITING" TO CONTEMPORARY "COUNTERWRITING"

> The question to be asked, therefore, is whether there is a specifically postmodernist type of intertextuality, whether postmodernism employs intertextuality in a specific way, with specific strategies and functions. (Pfister 210)

> I write . . . to rewrite the stories others have miswritten about me. (Anzaldua 169)

Since antiquity, when rewriting was both an apprentice's routine and a way to mature achievements through *imitatio auctorum*, literary rewriting has been going on continuously. This happened even in nineteenth-century and early twentieth-century realism, which aimed at following a drastically opposite mimetic poetics: *imitatio naturae*, a social, economic, or simply human nature. It was against the tenets of such a desideratum to flaunt the textual body of the "signifier." The latter was expected to achieve "absolute transparency" and thus give the reader "the impression that he is dealing with a discourse whose only rule is to transcribe the real rigorously" [my trans.] (Todorov, "Présentation" 7; *Poétique de la prose* 92–94, passim). But Todorov, Barthes, Philippe Hamon, Philippe Sollers, Claude Duchet, Jean Ricardou, Riffaterre, and other critics, mainly Continental, have uncovered the fallacious nature of this "immediacy." In a number of books and articles, most of which appeared in journals such as *Poétique*, *Tel Quel*, *Littérature*, and *Communications* throughout the late 70s and early 80s, they have shown that historical realism's "effect de réel" ("reality effect") presupposed the "effacing" of realistic works' "textual realism," a recurrent phrase in Ricardou, Hamon, and others. Instinctively yet firmly, realism pushed intertextuality and rewriting in the background, offstage, as it were, since they were undermining such a presupposition. This is why the great realists of the second half of the nineteenth and early twentieth centuries have not gone down in literary history as "rewriters" proper, even though, according to Barthes, realism does not "copy" the "real" but a "(depicted) copy of the real" and its "codes" of representation (*S/Z* 55).

On the other hand, in spite of his "scientific" ambitions, Balzac does rewrite Walter Scott in "Melmoth reconcilié" and E. T. A. Hoffmann in *La Peau de chagrin* (Calinescu, "Rewriting" 244) as much as Lewis Lambert Strether, Henry James's character in *The Ambassadors*, gives away the author's response to Balzac's 1833 novel *Louis Lambert*. Likewise, Upton Sinclair's *The Jungle* adapts Émile Zola's naturalism, specifically reworking the opening of *Germinal* (1888) into its own beginning. And later on, and along the lines that will drift away from realism, Marcel Proust famously rereads and reworks, among many other things, Balzacian passages into his *Remembrance of Things Past*, while his *Pastiches and mélanges* pastiches and blends a wide spectrum of realist and prerealist authors' styles. Further, *Sanctuary* and *Absalom, Absalom!*, to give only two Faulknerian examples of what might qualify as rewriting, are intensely visited by the ghosts of Flaubert's *Madame Bovary* (Bleikasten 36)—and so was, three decades before, Kate Chopin's *The Awakening*—as well as Hawthorne's *The Scarlet Letter* (Matthews, "Intertextuality and Originality" 148). Also, we saw, Updike himself has rewritten Hawthorne's novel (Matthews, "Intertextuality and Originality" 144, 148, passim; Schiff, *Updike's Version*; Calinescu, "Secrecy"). And the list of examples could go on to define rewriting as the "motor" of literary history in the West: from the Homeric epic poems—themselves "re-tellings" (Brewer 12)—to the early modern reinvention of the genre in Cervantes's parody of chivalresque romance to Laurence Sterne's own exploitation of *Don Quixote* in *Tristram Shandy*, to Joyce, modernism, and postmodernism.

Rewriting could be seized as a special form of "cultural recycling" and, by the same token, postmodernism (Yarbrough 60). In a sense, though, recycling is a concept without glory; to simplify matters, I usually avoid it. It smacks, some say, of impotent rumination, routine, superficiality, worthlessness, refuse—and dealing in the waste of our "excremental culture" (Kroker and Cook) is scarcely glamorous. Nor does it hold great promise of creativity. More important still, numerous postmodern rewrites are anything but repetitive ("anastrophic") "face-liftings" (Baudrillard, *Illusion* 12), epigonic-imitative and shallow "recyclings." In any event, if we accept the latter's negative connotations, then a certain category of rewriting, at least, must be rescued from the mechanics of recycling. The way I read them, the narratives I focus on produce themselves by reproducing other narratives—their plots, themes, and styles—with a notable, formal surplus, and an ideological, revisionary difference to boot. Writers such as Pynchon, Octavia Butler, or Maxine Hong Kingston do not borrow from others because they have "exhausted" (Barth 73), in an "unpleasantly decadent"[2] fashion (72), nonliterary sources of inspiration. Borrowing, Stephen Greenblatt reminds us, need not be "evidence of imaginative parsimony, still less a symptom of creative exhaustion" ("Culture" 229). Consequently, contemporary writers do not rewrite because they are no longer able to write—nor do they quote, as Umberto Eco famously says, because they have become unable to "speak innocently" (67–68); they do not rewrite because there is nothing else left for them to do, as Barth replies in "The Literature of Replenishment" to the detractors of his famous essay "The Literature of Exhaustion." Rewriting is, to my mind, hardly the cultural symptom of a "dead end," to recall Barth again, a new Alexandrinism in which compiling librarians palm themselves off as original writers, *inventio* turns out just a matter of *dispositio*, prodigious memory makes up for the ailments of creativity, and plain theft, plagiarism, and all kinds of "borrowings" reign supreme. In fact, David Cowart has gone so far as to conclude that "contemporary writing finds means to make the old new by rewriting it" through intertextual "symbiosis." Putting a positive spin on symbiotic exchanges, he rightly contends that they amount to "more than a parlor game" (15), "naturally further[ing] the ends of contemporary writing," even "'making it new'" all over again.[3]

If rewriters rewrite, they do so also because they do not have use any more for what Barth calls the "aesthetic of high modernism" (206) and, I might add, for the "aestheticist" limitations this aesthetic had set up. Now, if Barth is not very specific about exactly how the "program" of the "Pound era" fails to suit the (re)writers of our time, this is because he actually keeps addressing postmodernism as retelling and recirculation in strictly aesthetic—and therefore modernist—terms. We need, I propose, to break away from these terms if we want to understand why contemporary rewrites are no "footnotes" to available stories and, more generally, to narrative "topoi." Likewise, we need to question the cliché implying that such works, by reconciling "invention," on the one hand, and "rediscovery" and "permutation" (Calvino 77–79), on the other, ever lock themselves and their authors into an obstinate, essentially "reactionary"—because "escapist"—conversation with the past and past textuality. As I will repeat throughout this book, much of contemporary writing works on—and, again, obsessively works through—other bodies of writing, for those bodies have already bodied forth, narrativized and decisively structured core ideas, identities, and existential rites. These are our mythic stories since they "explain" us—they represent our *legends*, literally, the founding texts that, etymologically, we are to *read*. They literally *tell* us. They tell (us) who we are and how we have come to be what we are. Thus, re-telling (re-writing) them is serious business.

Does rewriting bear witness to an entire *Zeitgeist*, to our "culture of the copy" (to quote the title of Hillel Schwartz's book)? Is it a sign of a postmodernity in which feverish reproduction of "originals" ends up reconstructing—or rather "deconstructing," à la Foucault (*The Order of Things* 332)—the repetitive nature of every "origin"? Are our rewriters merely intent upon deflating the "modern myth that authorship consists in an individual act of origination" (Woodmansee 21), which seems to be the function critics like Rosalind Krauss assign postmodernism when they talk about postmodern art objects as "reproductions without originals" (27). Within postmodernism, rewriting in general and rewriting-as-critique in particular play a variety of roles. Let us not be misled, as Gérard Genette (*Palimpsestes* 43) appears to be, by the delusively apish prefix *re*. Rewriting is endowed with multiply transformative functions: textual, as it trans-forms the "model," but also ideological and political, cultural largely speaking—and we shall see that these are attributes to which critics have begun to pay attention.

Rewriting is both a symptom and an active instrument. It does bespeak, in a sense, our age's penchant for serialization, sequels, and reruns most obvious in popular film series like *Rambo*, *Rocky*, *Aliens* (which redoes the 1985 movie, *Creature*), *Terminator*, *Lethal Weapon*, and so on, as Schiff reminds us ("Contemporary Retellings" 369). But since this kind of "serial discourse" had actually originated with the rise of the modern popular press and, relatedly, the *roman-feuilleton* back in the 1830s, this explanation may not be sufficient. In fact, the critic has proposed a second reason for the fairly recent rewriting upsurge. In this latter instance the re-storied story is no longer solely an index for mutations brewing elsewhere in the cultural field but becomes itself a tool the rewriter uses actively to determine cultural change according to his or her "social agenda" (368). Rewriting continues to have "indicial" value and, as such, speaks to the increasingly multicultural positionings of our time's rewriters. From these very locations they "wage" rewriting to polemically "update" a "familiar story."[4] To do so, they usually take on the representation of race, gender, or class in the "model" story and alter it, or—to recall the term Renato Barilli uses to define *riscrittura*'s effects—*other* (13) it from "marginal" standpoints. It is in this sense that rewriting carries out a complex critical rereading of the rewritten narrative, fulfilling interpretive, aesthetic, as well as ideological and political functions.

The rewriting under consideration here both projects the fictions of the present and undertakes this present's genealogy, critiques it. In addition, it often plays upon, and ironically "subverts," the literary masters, their styles, and their ideologies, whereas the neoclassical philosophy of rewriting does not displace the models, let alone replace them. According to this philosophy, *rewriting is underwriting*, support and reduplication of the already-written. By contrast, the postmodern rewriting practices I examine set up a *counterwriting* distance, a "rupture" between themselves and what they redo—the literary past—as well as between themselves and various hegemonic forces active at the moment and in the milieu of "redoing." They break the continuum that, according to the model of rhetorical *imitatio*, runs through Virgil's Homer to Dante's Virgil to, arguably, Joyce's Homer and Dante to Michel Butor's *Portrait of the Artist as a Young Ape*.

A FEW DISTINCTIONS . . .

What is rewriting exactly? What do we mean when we say that Ackroyd's *English Music*, John Irving's *The Cider House Rules*, Peter Carey's *Jack Maggs*, Sue Roe's *Estella: Her Expectations*, and, last, Acker's *Great Expectations* rewrite Dickens's own *Great Expectations*? In what sense do we use the word to account for the relation between Kafka's short story "The Stoker," to become the opening chapter in *Amerika*, and *David Copperfield*? Or between Kafka's "The Metamorphosis," Bruno Schulz's "Cockroaches" chapter of his 1934 Chagallian fantasy *The Street of Crocodiles* (*Cinnamon Shops*), and Philip Roth, who takes on both in *The Breast*, *The Prague Orgy*, and elsewhere? What is Angela Carter up to in *Love*, where we come across characters named Annabel and Lee, and Poe? What links Nabokov's *Lolita* and Poe—and Lee Siegel's *Love in a Dead Language* and works by Nabokov and Roth, for that matter; or, Joyce Carol Oates's short story "The Turn of the Screw" and Henry James; or, similarly, Lauren Fairbanks's *Sister Carrie* and Dreiser's novel? And how does that relation differ from, say, Dreiser's own debt to authors such as Balzac and Bertha M. Clay? (Carrie enjoys reading both *Père Goriot* and Clay's 1883 romance *Dora Thorne*.) Need rewriters acknowledge this debt plainly? Hint at it? Hide it? Also, must they divulge the identity of the "model," perhaps through allusive, indeed identical titles such as in Leonardo Sciascia's 1977 novel *Candido*, a transparent rewriting of Voltaire's *Candide*? And who is supposed to do all this? The writer, in a prefatory note or "tell-all" interview, such as Pia Pera, author of *Lo's Diary*, a controversial rewriting of *Lolita*? The narrator maybe, à la Milan Kundera's in the 1995 novel *Slowness* (*La Lenteur*), whose main storyteller discloses the book's use of Vivant Denon's 1777 novella *No Tomorrow* (*Point de lendemain*)? Or, can it be a character, such as in Cynthia Ozick's 1997 novel *The Puttermesser Papers*, where, aside from a memorable reworking of the Golem tradition, the main dramatis personae reenact various moments from George Eliot's life and work?

Also, is rewriting a genre proper? If so, a literary genre only? Further, if this is the case, how are we to distinguish it from other intertextual forms such as parody and potpourri, from intertextuality in general? Trouble is, the notion has been employed in a dismayingly wide variety of contexts. Let me review some of those and thus possibly set the stage for a redefinition.

Philology: "Textual Mechanics"

For a long time, rewriting has been taken rather literally to designate a fundamentally textual and markedly *mechanical* operation. Originally, it had almost nothing to do with the conceptual overhaul or with the redoing of the object (text, book, manuscript) being rewritten. In a somewhat cognate sense, the term lives on in journalism, where the job of a "rewriteperson" is to actually format a reporter's raw materials ("the news") as publishable newspaper story. But, roughly speaking, rewriting originated as *formal* revision usually done by the author himself or herself. "Formal" is to be taken literally as stylistic editing, at most, adjustment in size. Rewriting was re-writing in the prevailingly repetitive sense of the prefix. Re-writing as "writing (it) again" came along and is still seized upon as a re-textualizing procedure hardly involving substantial modification. Some still use it to mean literal reproduction, copying, transcribing, and translating.

Translation vs. Rewriting

In this latter sense, André Lefevere maneuvers the concept to equate translation with rewriting. But, in doing so, the critic lays emphasis on both formal and ideological changes. Translation, he argues, "is, of course, a rewriting of an original text. All rewritings, whatever their intention, reflect a certain ideology and a poetics and as such manipulate literature to function in a given society in a given way" (vii). Lefevere's point on rewriting as ideology (re)formation and manipulation through form, subject matter, and the institutional discourses that rewriting acts encroach upon seems to me well taken. However, I have reservations on his practically wiping out the distinction between translation as normally involving the restitution of a foreign language original and rewriting as fictional replica. Laying out his own inventory of translation types, George Steiner seems more cautious. The critic surveys such diverse forms as "literal rewording" (named after Roman Jakobson), *Umdichtung* ("poetic recreation" illustrated by Stefan George's version of Shakespeare's Sonnets), and modern "reprise" (*Ulysses*, "The Waste Land") (466, 404, 490). They entail various "transformations," "substitutions," and "permutations," but the dividing line between the original and its rendition in another idiom remains, as it should, discernable.

History: "Paradigm Shift," Repetition, Rewriting

Lately, rewriting has come to signify virtually any operation of revaluation, emendation, and working over of a subject, image, motif, style, aesthetic or political model, author or authors in more or less coherent series; a work or set of related works; a cultural period, narrowly or broadly defined; even "life" and "reality" (Cornis-Pope, "Self-Referentiality" 258). Recognized and acclaimed by some, denied or deplored by others, the cultural-historical passage from modernism to postmodernism has also been seized upon as "rethinking," "re-reading," "reinscription" of modernity (Hugh Silverman, "Introduction" 1), indeed, as its "rewriting." Postmodernism, Bill Readings and Bennet Schaber observe, "is not a break with modernity, but a radical rewriting, asking what phrase to link to modernity, what to put next" (13). Their claim openly draws upon Lyotard's article "Rewriting Modernity." There, the French philosopher elaborates on his former refusal to conceive of the binary modernity-postmodernity (postmodernism) in sequential terms (*The Postmodern Condition*). Modernity, Lyotard says, "is written, inscribes itself on itself, in a perpetual rewriting" (28). This rewriting has nothing to do with the typically postmodern "use of parodies or quotations," in brief, with "forms and contents." It designates a mechanism of *cultural evolution*. Further, postmodernity (postmodernism) is not so much a "new age, but the rewriting of some of the features claimed by modernity, and first of all modernity's claim to ground its legitimacy on the project of liberating humanity as a whole through science and technology" (34). Thus, rewriting provides a theoretical tool for narrating cultural and epistemological change that breaks its way through "forms" without remaining limited to certain literary genres and subgenres—to intertextuality, more to the point, to intertextuality narrowly understood. But "change" may be a bit out of place here since "rewriting means resisting the writing of that supposed postmodernity" (35). The latter, we gather, refashions modernity by picking up on a "method" at play since long in modernity itself. This ploy is also modernity's own *post*modern sublation—a Hegelian *Aufhebung* of sorts—and postmodernity's paradoxical foe: trying to write itself, postmodernism sets in motion a rewriting that hardly engenders stable, "complete" discourse.

Slavoj Žižek conceptualizes this incompleteness, too, yet differently. "Why is every act a *repetition*," the Slovene critic asks in his discussion of the dynamic of repetition and postmodernity (*Enjoy* 69). And he responds, à la Kierkegaard and Walter Benjamin: we repeat—and history, postmodernity included, "repeats"—because this repetition is never carried through. In this sense, one could claim, à la Danilo Kiš in "The Encyclopedia of the Dead," that nothing in history is "ever repeated." What "returns" by way of this repetition is always "the Same," the "unhistorical kernel" at the core of historicity or the "transhistorical" that remains unchanged, say, in the passage from feudalism to capitalism. Below, I will briefly look at repetition phenomena from a psychoanalytic angle; here, I merely want to place Žižek's notion of "return" in the post-Hegelian, modern, and postmodern tradition that it springs from: the ontological interplay of *difference* and *repetition*. This dynamic originates with Marx (*The Eighteenth Brumaire*), Kierkegaard (*Repetition*) and Nietzsche (*The Will to Power*), running through Heidegger, Maurice Blanchot, Georges Bataille, and then Gilles Deleuze, Jacques Derrida, William V. Spanos, Baudrillard, and other poststructuralist thinkers on both sides of the Atlantic. As J. Hillis Miller comments on Deleuze's *Logic of Repetition* in *Fiction and Repetition*, this line of thought "posits a world based on difference" (6). What drives this world is the "abysmal" retrieval of "the unnameable primordial Ontological Difference" (Spanos 4). Such difference—"differential Sameness"—that repeats itself through "displaced repetition" is a reenactment of a "phantasm," as Michel Foucault notes in "Theatrum Philosophicum" (*Language* 182). And since history-as-repetition can be traced back to no ultimate "source" or "model," Foucault's Nietzsche-modeled "genealogy" is no "search for 'origins'" (140).

Purportedly at loggerheads with classical metaphysics and aesthetics, this ontological paradigm forecloses mimesis, the reiteration through representation of a preexistent reality. "Re-petition," Deleuze maintains, "opposes re-presentation" (57), and it is in this sense that, throughout this book, I place terms such as *origin*, *source*, *matrix*, or *model* within quotations marks, *sous rature*. For many postmodern rewrites do not "copycat" even when they give this impression. True, in his 1997 novel *Timequake*, Kurt Vonnegut does this kind of *reiterative re-writing* by literally "writing again," writing "twice" or for the second time a story written ten years before the world starts its own "rerun" due to a "timequake" of sorts. But Acker, Charles Johnson, and Doctorow attempt something else. Their postmodern "repetitions," we shall discover, fall back on no past model because they are, paradoxically enough, *culturally driven and historically "constructed."* They "produce" and "stage" the "model"—like "mimics" rather than *mimemata*, simulacral copies—to respond to *present* sociocultural contexts. As Lycette Nelson argues apropos of Blanchot's *Step Not Beyond* (x), they generate "repetition[s] without origin."

Blanchot's essay addresses explicitly the relation between repetition and rewriting. Owing to the self's never being identic to itself, there exists, the French writer submits, no present in which presence—including the presence of the "returning" model—may resurface. The "model" is "effaced before being written" (17). Therefore, writing starts an "anxious search for what was never written in the present, but in a past to come" (17). This applies, of course, to our own writing, which "is not accomplished in the present, nor does it present, nor does it present itself," "still less represent[ing]" anything except the mere play of the "repetitive" (32). "To write in this sense," Blanchot details,

> is always first to rewrite, and to rewrite does not refer to any previous writing, any more than to an anteriority of speech or of presence or of signification. Rewriting . . . holds itself apart from any productive initiative and does not claim to produce *anything*, not even the past or the future or the present of writing . . . Rewriting is a surplus, the supplementary relation which, at the limit, could not define itself by anything in regard to which it would add itself—excess of nothing and still excessive. Thus all considerations of influence, of causality, of model, of makes and counterfeits are rendered vain—except in that "plagiarism," such as Lautréamont's irony proposes it to us, could not come after a text given as initial, even to initiate it to itself, but would repeat it as unwritten or would repeat the text about which there is no way to know if it had been produced before, since it is always and in advance reproduced . . . there is no time for writing, if writing has always preceded itself in the form of rewriting. (32–34)

Blanchot rejects the "causality"/"initiation" logic of Platonic mimesis—of a certain level of Plato's mimesis, as I have argued elsewhere (*Poetica* 46–56; "Mimesis" 24–32 passim). I would distinguish, however, between Blanchot's and other critics' generic writing-as-rewriting, which disrupts that logic *in abstracto*, and the postmodern rewriting that intentionally sets off its relation to specific "previous writings," which does not necessarily call for a source-copy sort of model.

Psyche: Wiederholung *vs. Rewriting*

The rewriting sort discussed here is, doubtlessly, a repetitive act only in the above-specified meaning of the repetition concept: a writerly repetition turning out a salient, textual, and political surplus; a *return* in the financial sense, so to speak. Also, I do not approach this act chiefly as a psychoanalytic phenomenon. It should therefore suffice to note that in his 1920 essay *Beyond the Pleasure Principle*, Freud theorizes "repetition compulsion" (*Wiederholungszwang*) as a fundamental unconscious drive. Shoshana Felman points out, for Freud and Freudians such as Marie Bonaparte, repetition repeats, à la Plato, "sameness." But for Jacques Lacan, who wrote extensively on Freud's most "enigmatic *Wiederholen*" in *The Four Fundamental Concepts of Psycho-Analysis* and elsewhere, "repetition is not of sameness, but of *difference*" (Felman 147–48). What "returns" is always the *other* (148), Felman observes with regard to the psychoanalytic "tale" (the story of the unconscious) Lacan famously reads into Poe's "Purloined Letter." In a sense, Lacan rewrites—repeats and simultaneously "others"—Poe. And so have the numerous critics who have responded to Lacan's seminar (Muller and Richardson). More notably, these rewrites, with Lacan's among them, are justified by the fact that "The Purloined Letter" is a rewrite itself, a textual repetition of Crébillon *père*'s 1707 tragedy *Atrée et Thyeste.*

"*Response*": *Reception vs. Production, (Re)Reading vs. Rewriting*

We have already noted—and we shall come back to—the readerly facet of rewriting. Here, I want to touch on this dimension of rewriting from a certain theoretical perspective. In the wake of *Rezeptionsästhetik* and poststructuralism, reading and rereading theorists from Wolfgang Iser to Matei Calinescu have increasingly employed the notion of rewriting to account for the process by which the reader becomes a "mental rereader" and "rewriter" (Calinescu, *Rereading* 214) and thus decomposes and recomposes the work he or she reads. "Implied" as this reader may be, Iser's, for example, plays the role of a "coordinator" of the text's meaning. This role is in effect built-in, in-scribed in a text's "unwritten part"—Iser's famous "vacant spaces" (Iser 210) or "gaps" (280), which, whenever we act like "creative readers," we fill in successfully. Thus, we write in(to) the text, practically finalizing it by fully writing out, "formulating" the "unformulated text" (289). For, rather than a rounded-off product, a text is a "blueprint" for its completion through rewriting, presenting us with a set of "rewrite rules"[5] whose activation yields more elaborate structures.

Two years before Iser published *Der Implizierte Leser* (1972), Roland Barthes had advanced a somehow similar if more seducing and consequential hypothesis in what would become the manifesto of poststructuralist reading theory, *S/Z.* Here, the border between reading and writing—especially when we read what Barthes calls "writerly works"—gets blurred almost entirely. Writing turns into a metaphor for reading, and its terminology applies, in Barthes's view, to readerly acts more accurately than the traditional vocabulary of reading itself. Also, if Iser's text model is necessarily indeterminate, full of gaps that we fill in through perusal, Barthes's branches off into a two-class typology: the *readerly* and the *writerly.* Ideally, reading should be writing, recreation, indeed rewriting; it should offer us opportunities to make use of, and develop, our creativity and inventiveness by rewriting the texts we read. Even critics such as Terry Eagleton admit that "all literary works . . . are 'rewritten,' if only unconsciously, by the societies which read them; indeed, there is no reading of a work which is not also a 're-writing'" (*Literary Theory* 11). For Barthes, however, rewriting has a different meaning. It cannot be applied, for instance, to "readerly" texts. Usually classical, extremely formalized works, they can no longer be rewritten, Barthes claims, although we can *interpret* them, and even brilliantly so, as he himself does with Balzac's "Sarrasine" in *S/Z*. On the contrary, the writerly text can, indeed, requires to be rewritten—provided we locate it. For, with the rare exceptions of some ill-defined "limit-works" (*S/Z* 4), this type of text is hardly a "thing." One cannot find it in a bookstore, for example. This text is rather "*ourselves writing*" (5) before criticism proper reins in the text's plurality by laying some ideological-theoretical grid over it. This is, again, rewriting as "sympathetic" reading. It declines to "consume" what it processes mentally, resists the oversystematization of its object, and thus prevents the "freezing" of "textual productivity."

Robert Scholes declares, though, that "to be a reader" is always to be "outside." A true reader moves "inside" as he or she redoes, re-produces the text in the act of reading as intertextual reading, that is, rewriting: we process a multitude of materials even when we peruse the one book laid open in front of us. "Reading," Scholes states, "consists of bringing texts together. It is a constructive activity, a kind of rewriting" (*Protocols* 10). As I will insist myself, rewriting, especially the rewriting I work with, is being *inside*. It is so because the "reading" it performs is already an "inside job," obtaining in the interstices of other readings and writings, discourses, value hierarchies, representation systems, and cultural formations. To be sure, what we read and "engage" with are not only texts, and merely texts, "forms," but also "paradigms" (Kolodny 104), "formations."

Narratology Meets Anthropology: Rewriting vs. Retelling

Taking aim at the "metacultural" assumptions of structuralist narrative theory and its "misconstruction" of the notion of story, Karl Kroeber discusses how stories "improve with retelling," how they are endlessly retold, indeed, "*told in order to be retold*" (1). The critic's grasp of retelling is predominantly anthropological. He seizes it, like Derek Brewer (26), as an intertextual process involving less *essentially distinct* stories and more "versions," even though he describes in detail how a novel such as Tom Wolfe's *The Bonfire of the Vanities* replies to Thackeray's *Vanity Fair*. Overall, Kroeber expatiates on the importance for an audience to hear the same story time and again (80). Following Walter Benjamin's essay "The Storyteller," Kroeber contends that stories are "intended" to be retold as much as they are meant to be told (55), this repetition being crucial to narrative communication as "social transaction" (11). Therefore, narrative repetition is genuinely embedded in the "principles of narrativity" (3) at play in painting, folklore, mythology, or modern novels. All of them tell, one way or another, a story, which story is bound in its turn to expand on previous narratives and patterns. Clearly, on this level of generality and from the viewpoint of a folkloric analysis that must take into account oral delivery—*transmission* rather than genuine *creation*—retelling and telling cannot be told apart anymore, so to speak. Further, if all telling is retelling from a folkloric-anthropological standpoint, not all writing is rewriting. As I state repeatedly, I see rewriting as a "flagrant" retelling of identifiable literary tales (texts), which is *not* the general case. Moreover, unlike oral literature and particularly the folktale (Brewer 12), there are written stories that do *not* retell. The advent of written, and then print, culture is largely responsible for this situation. The printed text gave rise to the "romantic notions of 'originality' and 'creativity'" by introducing the physical notion of "closed" work, "set off from other works" (Ong 133).

To sum up, rewriting and retelling are *not* synonyms. Whenever I use the term retelling as an equivalent of rewriting, I mean a precise, detailed, deliberate, and ideologically driven retelling of former written narratives. Along these lines, let me also indicate that I do not deal, like Kroeber—or J. Hillis Miller in *Fiction and Repetition*—with internal repetition, that is, with the "recursiveness" of identic or slightly modified events *within* the same narrative. Hillis Miller argues that "any novel is a complex tissue" of "repetitions within repetitions, or of repetitions linked in chain fashion to other repetitions" (2–3), while I look at novels that "repeat" *other* novels.

Rewriting vs. Intertextuality

In *Palimpsestes: La littérature au second degré*, a milestone of structuralist poetics, Gérard Genette employs the term *rewriting* (*récriture*) only by exception. He prefers to talk about "transtextual transformations" and, accordingly, to pinpoint "transtextuality" as the object of his inquiry. Theorizing transtextuality as "a relationship of copresence between two texts or among several texts" (8), Genette maintains that his concept is more restrictive than Julia Kristeva's "intertextuality": transtextuality is confined to literature. Nor is it equivalent to intertextuality à la Riffaterre, whose *Text Production*, *Semiotics of Poetry*, and related works posit an "implicit (sometimes entirely hypothetical) presence of the intertext" (Genette, *Palimpsestes* 9) traceable in a text's dormant memory of tropes, clichés, and phraseologies.

The next chapter will address intertextuality both as literary and cultural discourse. Here, I only offer a bird's-eye view of Genette's transtextual taxonomy. Thus, after sorting out five types of transtextuality, the poetician pins down the one that develops a relation uniting two *literary* texts: a "hypertext"—the later work or the *rewrite*, in my terms—and the "hypotext"—the *rewritten*, earlier work. It is hypertextual interplays that furnish the object of his inquiry in *Palimpsestes*. Additionally, within "hypertextuality," Genette distinguishes two basic varieties: transformation and imitation. As he exemplifies, through transformation, the *Odyssey* became Joyce's *Ulysses*, whereas it was through imitation that Homer's work had "given rise" to the *Aeneid*. Thus, Genette's "hypertext," to be naturally differentiated from the more recent, "digital" use of the term, arises from transformation processes that also yield that which classical and modern poetics has variously termed *parody*, *pastiche*, *collage*, *potpourri*, bric-à-brac, *bricolage*, pêle-mêle, "*deformation*," *literary pun*, "*joke*," or *play*, *plagiarism* and *literary "poaching," piracy*, or "*theft*," *counterfeiting*, *forgery* (*fabrication*), *apocrypha* (*apocryphal sequel*), *irony*, *caricature*, *burlesque*, *travesty*, *transplant*, *grafting*, "*cross-pollination*," *adaptation*, *parallel*, *analogy*, mise en abyme, *amplification*, *summary* (or *fake summary*). One could also mention here related procedures and devices, traditionally specific to other discursive fields, which, Genette states, fall outside his focus: citation, reference, critical commentary, allusion, and so on.

The Rewrite and the "Parasite"

David Cowart has determined "literary symbiosis" as a leading feature of the postmodern aesthetics that continuously and characteristically produces "reconfigured texts." This production—or reproduction, better put—typically launches a relation of mutual dependence between the "host" and "guest" work rather than of unilateral "parasitism" (4). For instance, classics benefit, Cowart submits, from their rewrites, iconoclastic as those may be—and, I should point out, critics such as Robert Kelly have set out to gauge this Borgesian "benefit."[6] In his book, Cowart lays out a broad "symbiotic spectrum" (6), which covers as diverse examples as Nabokov's *Pale Fire* and David Henry Hwang's rewriting of Giacomo Puccini's opera *Madama Butterfly* in the 1988 play *M Butterfly*. Thus, "literary symbiosis" includes phenomena such as translation and "ordinary intertextuality" (6), even though the critic attends primarily to "symbiotic texts" that "appropriate" specific elements of the "hosts," such as characters. Valerie Martin's 1990 novel *Mary Reilly* rewrites by narrative parallels Robert Louis Stevenson's *The Strange Case of Dr. Jekyll and Mr. Hyde* (Plate, "Negotiating" 169). But *Pale Fire*, Kinbote's and Shade's puns and parodies aside, is less of a full-dress, step-by-step rewriting of a particular plot. Thus, Cowart's suggestion that all writing results from "symbiotic" exchanges (15) recalls

Bloom's notion that "all poems can be read as rewritings of other poems" (Eagleton, *Literary Theory* 159).

The arborescent transtextuality Genette organizes has been intensely explored by himself and other critics, such as Laurent Jenny, Elizabeth Marinheiro, Michael Riffaterre, Jonathan Culler, Owen Miller, Göran Hermerén, and Thaïs Morgan, to name a few. It is beyond my scope to trace rewriting back to its parodic, ironic, satiric, and other "transtextual" roots. In a general sense, as Matei Calinescu explains, "major concepts of traditional poetics . . . can be easily subsumed under the rubric of rewriting: they include imitation, parody, burlesque, transposition, pastiche, adaptation, and even translation. Critical commentary, including description, summary, and selected quotations from a primary text, also falls under this heading" ("Rewriting" 243). Solid, exhaustive scholarship of various methodological allegiances, from classical scholars' learned studies of influences, posterities, and legacies to Robert Scholes's, Larry McCaffery's, Margaret A. Rose's, and Linda Hutcheon's more recent studies of metafiction, "surfiction," literary "narcissism," parody, and irony have addressed these forms and concepts persuasively.

AND A DEFINITION: FOCUS AND TERMINOLOGY

Similar to Genette's "palimpsest," Michael Davidson's "palimtext," or Cowart's "symbiosis," rewriting is *not* a literary genre. More likely, in it we are dealing with an *archigenre* or *hybrid practice*. It is, certainly, an intertextual and "inter-discursive"[7] phenomenon, a writing process that may absorb any of the canonical genres, textual relations, and techniques listed above, while showing off this absorption by means of specific references, allusions and, more important, as far as stories and novels go, *elaborate narrative parallelisms*. Yet the rewriting I look at does not overlap with writing, literature, literariness, or intertextuality for that matter. To me, these terms are not synonymous. Rewriting does not equal intertextuality, let alone "'general' intertextuality" or "unlimited semiosis" (Godard 569) as variously conceptualized by Barthes, Derrida, Eco, Riffaterre, and others. Nor is all intertextuality rewriting. For the purposes of this study, I define rewriting as an intertextual form that entails a strong tie to "chronologically prior works," the "trace" of which is discernible in the text (Owen Miller 28, 31) and is marked by the author as an "intentional" presence rather than as an elusive, faint "echo" (Hollander 64). This rewriting is usually—and strikingly—*there* in various degrees of obviousness and thus relates to self-referential/self-reflexive literature in general and metafiction in particular.

In fact, the narrative rewriting I attend to might be determined as a metafictional—"hyperfictional" (Sukenick), "surfictional," or "critifictional" (Federman)—and by the same token a postmodern "subgenre." If metafiction is "an extended prose narrative that draws attention to its status as fiction" (Stonehill 3), rewriting could be seized as a metafictional form that plays out its intertextual, "rewriterly" nature. But unlike most criticism on intertextuality, rewriting, and postmodern revisionism in general, I focus essentially on a rewriting sort that comes about and presents itself essentially as *renarrativization*; again, it is in this sense only that retelling can be its synonym. This renarrativization effects a *developed* narrative transposition[8] of a previous prose text, which *the critic has to pursue, and prove*, by reconstructing in detail the more or less analogous storytelling structure visible, first, as plot or plot segments, characters, and motifs, and then, more broadly, as aesthetic doctrine, style, or ideology. A few intertexts, insufficiently developed or not pivotal enough to the work, do not make it a rewrite per se, that is, full-blown renarrativization. Sukenick's 1999 novel, *Mosaic Man*, often refers to "Ron"'s "work-in-progress," *Great Expectorations*, but that does not make it a Dickensian rewrite proper. Likewise, his 1994 collection *Doggy Bag*, while nicely playing upon Poe, Henry James, D. H. Lawrence, Mary Shelley, and Chaucer, does not actually redo any of these. Pynchon's "cultural references" (Moraru, "'Zonal Ethics'" 268) to "Byron the bulb" and "metal-ebonite-and-plastic young Marcel" in *Gravity's Rainbow*, or to Humbert Humbert in *The Crying of Lot 49* do not turn the two novels into rewritings of Byron, Proust, or Nabokov. Nor do Philip Roth's ironies on Rip Van Winkle render *Sabbath's Theater* a rewriting of Washington Irving.

In good self-reflective, postmodern tradition, rewriting flaunts its "hypotextual" genealogy. But it does more than just lay bare its own techniques, linguistic apparatus, fictionality, and, in relation to this, intertextual makeup. True, *rewriting re-writes*: methodically, deploying detailed narrative analogies to a previous work. But not only does Morrison's retelling of Uncle Remus's "The Wonderful Tar Baby" in *Tar Baby*,[9] for instance, prove that postmodern rewrites do not necessarily imply a "literature which lacks parenthood" (Newman 87). While unmasking its "intertextuality with a vengeance" (Cunningham 8), a rewrite like Morrison's wants to be intertextuality with a conscience, as it were, radical literary practice. In fact, Jerry Varsava, Larry McCaffery, Linda Hutcheon, Marcel Cornis-Pope, and others have salutarily stressed the "sociocultural import" of self-referential texts. They have insisted that "these stories suggest ways in which fiction can rewrite reality" through "unwriting" and similar "revisionistic" procedures (Cornis-Pope, "Self-Referentiality" 259, 258, 260; "Innovative" 10;

"Narrative Innovation" 226). Thus, fiction takes on certain ideologies—or "mythologies"—to become "cultural *rewritin[g]* in the fullest sense of the word" ("Self-Referentiality" 261). The rewrites that preoccupy me take to a higher level such "cultural" work. Of intertextual, metafictional nature, they query the notion that all "intertextuality is finally a conservative theory and practice" (Morgan 272). However, *much as not all intertextuality, metafiction, or surfiction is rewriting, not all intertextual rewriting (renarrativization) engages in equally well-marked and effectively revisionist work*. Below, I offer the "extensive" or critical/revisionist rewriting model as a way of reading the marks of this work in postmodern narratives that appear to rehash a former story while in fact polemically revising that story along with the cultural stories underlying it.

Due to this twofold criticist/reconstructionist component, I normally steer clear of a whole terminological paradigm: remake, duplication (reduplication), copy (simulacrum), update, recuperation, reformulation, remolding, refurbishing, refashioning, recasting, restyling, and so on. For better or worse, this series has supplied our main postmodern vocabulary in general. In particular, this lexical spectrum conveys even to critics like Barthes "'lustreless' repetition of the same" (Morgan 259), along the lines of the insubstantial, purely formalist recycling—and lately, cloning—Jameson and others talk about. But, as already suggested, this is not what I discern in the delusively reiterative prefix of *re*writing. Whenever I have to resort to a synonym to rewriting, I either imply my reader's awareness of this distinction or rehearse it in context to stress the literary and social, re-formative and trans-formative nature of postmodern rewriting. If cloning and recycling are signs of our time, this rewriting is an "untimely" statement. It trades upon this time's recuperating logic to reconstruct and critique, *create* a "surplus," as Blanchot would say. On the production of this surplus I want to concentrate now.

CHAPTER 2

Renarrativization, Revision, Critique

> Re-vision—the act of looking back, of seeing with fresh eyes, of entering an old text form a critical direction . . . (Rich 35)

> The term 're-vision' deploys a strategic ambiguity between the word *revise*: 'to examine and correct; to make a new, improved version of; to study anew,' and *re-vision*: to see in another light; to re-*en*vision or perceive differently; and thus to recast and re-evaluate the original. (Widdowson 164)

INTENSITIES AND EXTENSITIES

> [Rewriting fosters] certain ways of thinking about the world . . . , [is] a site of uneasy cultural struggle and a catalyst for change whose implications are ineluctably moral, ideological, and political (Gerli 8)

Let me say it once more: I attempt to locate, theorize, and assess a rewriting model involving predominantly, albeit not exclusively, critique, revision, and dissent;[10] fractured and retraced lineages; discontinuity and disruption; hardly a systematic attempt to absorb the rewriting process into a larger operation whose goal is the production of totalizing, "grand" narratives, philosophical, epistemological, political, or otherwise. The rewriting that intrigues me queries rather than reveres the "source" and the past overall. By and large I differ with critics that claim the "reenactment" of history is "motivated by an effort to recover [the present's lost] integrity in symbolic form" (Kuspit 64). This sort of rewriting is critical of its own ambiance, the present, and the past alike. As the Epilogue will argue more pointedly, one could dwell upon this component of renarrativization to isolate a powerfully polemical strain in postmodern rewriting and distinguish it from previous moments in Western tradition when rewriting also played an important role—from classicism and neoclassicism, through romanticism and realism, to the modern and "high-" (or "late-) modern" reactions to realism such as Joyce's.

Ulysses may very well be, in effect, the stumbling block of any effort to sift out modern from postmodern forms of renarrativization. The novel could be defined as the *Urtext* of modern rewriting—and a modernist epitome in all respects. Yet, by and large, modernism's antirepetitive "make it new" hardly places rewriting at the core of its aesthetics. Thus, Patricia Waugh may be right to seize *Ulysses*'s parodies and language games as the defining techniques of an author "postmodern before his time" (*Practising* 152). Others, though, have identified the book as a "high-modernist" badge and have set it apart from an earlier stage of literary modernism illustrated by Joyce himself in *Dubliners*' use of Dickens and Ibsen. Finally, Brian McHale has suggested that *Ulysses* is a "literary-historical scandal," "at one and the same time a founding text of 'High Modernism' and a postmodernist text, a 'demonstration and summation' of modernist poetics and a parody of modernist poetics" (*Constructing* 55). Certain chapters of *Ulysses* revolve, McHale submits, around the modernist notion of psychological perspectivism, juxtaposing different "streams of consciousness" to obtain various views of the world. Other parts agglutinate "disparate discourses" by using stylistic mimicry, bricolage, and similar procedures. Coming out of the latter modality is "ontological perspectivism, the parallax of the discourses and the worlds they encode," which is not, as McHale tells us, "a characteristic structure of modernist poetics; yet it *is*," the critic adds, "characteristic of postmodernism, where it may be traced through a whole sequence of carnivalesque, collage, and cut-up or fold-in texts, from Queneau and Burroughs to Barthelme, Puig, Goytisolo, Sorrentino, Acker and others" (55). But critics have pointed out that bricolage is a technique that registers historical and stylistic fluctuations from realism to modernism to postmodernism. Jameson has argued that *Ulysses* and modernist collage/bricolage in general typically "quote" "low-brow" materials and genres. Consequently, they tend to maintain the "line between high art and commercial forms" (*The Cultural Turn* 2), whereas postmodernism "somehow incorporate[s these forms] to the point where many of our older critical and evaluative categories (founded precisely on the radical differentiation of modernist and mass culture) no longer seem functional" (31). Similarly, Jim Collins insists that postmodern narratives "differ from the popular and literary texts produced during the Modernist stage in that they replace 'poetic' stylization with a *bricolage* of diverse forms of already well-established discourses" (75).

In a sense, *Ulysses* brings to fruition a culturally "totalizing" project. It appears to embody, to quote Haines addressing Stephen Dedalus, "the Father and the Son idea" (18). It inserts itself smoothly as a new chapter into the great narrative of tradition, its pastiching furor, formal originality, and brutal realism notwithstanding. Joyce's self-acknowledged "oversystematization"[11] of *Ulysses* and in general the aestheticism or "aesthetic turn" (Scholes, *Protocols* 30) the book marks in his career render rewriting in *Ulysses* fairly different from the rewriting at play in conspicuously "polemical" rewriters such as Coover, Reed, or Mukherjee. Needless to say, I am far from implying that Coover and others like him are more "innovative" or culturally more "revealing" than Joyce. Nor is *Ulysses* wholly "unrevisionist" in its use of ancient Greek, Italian, English, or, in particular, Irish intertexts.

Thus, I hope it is clear—and I shall make it clearer in the last chapter of this Part—that what I am arguing for is *one way of reading—and legitimating, aesthetically as well as politically—rewriting in general and postmodern rewriting in particular*. The distinction this reading model is setting up between playful, repetitive, less "revisionist" rewriting, on the one hand, and ideologically extensive, "transformative" rewriting on the other is not absolute. The types that obtain, much like Paul Maltby's "dissident" versus "introverted" postmodern fiction, are anything but "hard and fast categories." The critic is right: "[A]lmost any literary text may be read as addressing, however marginally or obliquely, some political implications of language" (37). Therefore, the contrast between my two classes or tendencies is also "best thought of as one of degree," where one kind arguably manifests a "*heightened perception*" of the "politics of language" (37). In my turn, I notice that the politics of rewriting is more evident—and more consequential—in, say, Samuel R. Delany, Octavia Butler, and Acker than in such post-Joyceans as Barth, Gass, Gaddis, Sorrentino, and Abish. In addition, this literary and cultural "obviousness" of rewriting raises an important literacy issue: to whom, one might ask, is such obviousness . . . obvious? What kind of reader do such reading and, by the same token, rewriting call for? This is, I think, a cultivated, albeit not necessarily "academic," reader, the type Joseph Pucci calls "full-knowing" and "powerful" (28–29). This is a "caring" reader, too, able to "perceive" the "double mode," intertextual and social of rewriting, a reader capable of "rewriting" his or her own positioning in the cultural environment in which reading takes place.

The reading model I am offering reveals how some postmoderns practice rewritings that overall are simultaneously more *intensive* and *extensive* than modern (let alone premodern) forms of rewriting, as well as other postmodern rewrites. By intensity, I mean the methodically carried out and consistently marked textual operation of *re*writing (re-narrativization) as such. To adapt here one of Manfred Pfister's observations, rewriting as "intertextuality" is not "just used as one device amongst others." In a significant area of postmodernism, it "is foregrounded, displayed, thematized and theorized as a central constructional principle" (214). Postmodern rewriting, and especially the postmodern rewriting that intersts me, is usually more "intensive" in that it deploys and flaunts itself more systematically, often ironically and self-ironically. Still more important is, I believe, the superiorly *extensive* (critical-ideological, political) character displayed by rewrites such as Coover's *The Public Burning* and Reed's *Mumbo Jumbo*, which are *ostensibly and programmatically* intent upon displacing and replacing more than literary intertexts and textualizing manners.

In sum, I limit, on the one hand, rewriting to *intensive*, recurrent, and fairly detailed reworking of a past text. On the other, I wish to see how *this* sort of rewriting engages with, *extends* into various cultural, ideological, and political narratives and issues in the present. This is the specimen of narrative rewriting that fascinates me: the narratively "intensive" and ideologically "extensive" rewriting, whose "critical" or "revisionistic" propensities can be noticed more easily than in otherwise remarkable artists such as Peter Ackroyd, Julian Barnes, John Fowles, John Barth, or John Irving. Again, as suggested above, *fictional rewriting* and *sociocultural revisionism* are *not* synonymous. To paraphrase Adrienne Rich, a most original theorist of rewriting, the former may be conceived as critical "re-vision"; but it is not always its full equivalent. The kind of rewriting I tackle here—rewriting *as* critique and revision—is also a powerful and more often than not self-acknowledged vehicle for ideological criticism in the largest sense possible. Thus, I openly recognize that my reading privileges, within a body of literature largely labeled "postmodern," a certain lineage of *engagée* rewriting—Doctorow, Coover, Roth, Auster, Reed, Acker, Kingston—over another tradition running through the "playful" Joyce, Nabokov, Borges, the Nouveau (Nouveau) Roman, and the OULIPO group (primarily Georges Perec) to peak, on the American soil, in some of the jocular metafiction of the late 60s and 70s.

There are, as I said, important exceptions to this classification, and here is, again, where the critic's "perception" can make a difference. Take Ronald Sukenick's work, for instance. The self-reflective stories from *The Death of the Novel and Other Stories* strikingly interlace formal games and political reflection, invoking (quoting, recapitulating) Beckett to put forth a critique of realist aesthetics ("Roast Beef: A Slice of Life"), as well as to point to the "problematic concept of personal identity" (91) in the Vietnam years. Similarly, Federman's "real fictitious discourse," multiply experimental *Double or Nothing*, rehashes Defoe and Beckett, "beckettianizing" the former in an experiment that closely welds together the aesthetic and sociological tenets. The protagonist, a "Robinson Crusoe of the Noodles" (14), performs "a cross section of America" (154), a cultural and existential space where the personal experience of immigration, colored by literary memory—Kafka

(*Amerika*), Céline (*Voyage au bout de la nuit*)—and Holocaust memories alike, translates into unbearably Beckettian yet artistically redeemable loneliness. Likewise, Barth's novella "Dunyazadiad" (to name just one of his rewrites), Barthelme's absurdist *Snow White*, and Guy Davenport's "neo-pastorals" (*Eclogues, Da Vinci's Bicycle*) rework *The Arabian Nights*, the Grimm brothers, and various cultural anecdotes, respectively, to parodically[12] test out new narrative forms; but they also query the inherited gender structure of the "models."

Having said this, I submit that the focus on the more recent, multicultural, criticist[13] tradition of polemical, powerful[14] rewriting gives us better chances to *(a) uncover rewriting as critique and, based on it, (b) to argue for a rethinking of postmodernism's cultural politics*. I cannot stress enough, in this view, that this kind of rewriting begins with a critical move, a discriminating choice: the rewrite picks out the "model" for the latter's political, ideological, and/or collective significance, for its privileged position in the canon, for the cultural stories that, as I specified, are interwoven with, or shaping it. Therefore, intensive-extensive rewriting is twice a *radical* rewriting. Doubtless, it may—and usually does—promote a radical "surface politics" by openly adopting a certain political stance. Yet at the same time it reaches deep into the body of the reembodied literary model for those "roots" of discourse where literary and transliterary categories—class-, sex-, gender- or race-related—intertwine so closely that rearrangements in either domain spark off displacements in the other. By the same token, revisionist reworking of older works tends to play out the deep-running solidarity between literary and cultural intertextuality more ostensibly than other rewriting forms. What starts out—and frequently appears only—as a refashioning of a literary text ends up as a reordering of collective, ideology-laden figures, languages, mental landscapes.

MODUS SCRIBENDI: DISCOURSE AND INTERTEXTUAL POLITICS

> This emphasis on the primacy of discourse has led to the facile objection that Post-Modernist texts are not interested in the 'real,' but only representation as an end in itself. Since the texts . . . take as their subject matter such 'unreal' topics as the holocaust, sexual repression, political exile, the commodification of human life, etc., any avoidance of the 'real' seems hard to justify. These Post-Modernist texts consistently emphasize that the 'real' is always discursive and that tensions among discourses are not merely formalist squabbles, but have enormous impact on the constitution of individual identity and culture. (Collins 60)

Intensive-extensive rewriting brings to light a model of literary discourse where politics is determined as *textual*, or, even better, *inter*textual politics: a politics that works by means of a particular mechanics of rewriting. Refuting the commonly held view of textual politics as "subject matter effect," Vincent B. Leitch has convincingly pleaded a "poststructuralist manner of understanding the politics of a text." "The system of a text," he says, "including particularly its discontinuities, contradictions, parodies, pastiches, figural aberrations, disunities, and discordant voices, produces textual politics. . . . History pervades the work in the form of heteroglot intertextual traces refracted and revalued within the text's discursive system" (*Cultural Criticism* 98). Earlier in his book, Leitch cites Frank Lentricchia's *Criticism and Social Change*. Lentricchia's argument, in its turn, draws from Kenneth Burke's rhetoric theory of "language as symbolic action" to propose that "the substance of ideology" (44) is "revealed to us *textually* and therefore must be grasped (read) and attacked (re-read, rewritten) in that dimension" (Lentricchia 42). I could not agree more with this injunction. In it, one discerns a timely, "cultural" retooling of the Derridean "il n'y a pas de hors-texte"—"there is nothing outside of the text," or, more accurately, "there is no outside-text." It has been pointed out, such "critique of pure intertextuality," this opening up of textuality as cultural intertextuality, builds on an important, nonformalist tenet of the Derridean textual imaginary. As John Mowitt notes, "The term 'text' here [in Derrida's *Of Grammatology*] is used as a hinge—it serves to name the proliferation and dispersion of literary works, while also reaching around them to designate a structure their plurality presupposes" (93). This hinge belongs to a whole series of metaphors through which Derrida, along with Foucault, Barthes, Kristeva, Sollers, Ricardou, and other members of the *Tel Quel* group, has pumped "materiality" into the romantic, immaterial visions of textuality, authorship, creativity, and originality.

The smorgasbord of Saussurean linguistics, Lévi-Straussian anthropology, Lacanian psychoanalysis, and Althusserian Marxism also known as the "French theory" of the late 60s through the early 80s was grounded in an otherwise relatively unifying recipe of textuality and intertextuality capable, as the manifestoes in the landmark anthology *Théorie d'ensemble* announce, of sounding a text's *profondeur idéologique* (ideological depth) (Foucault et al. 388). To honor its premises, such a model could not develop "outside texts." It had to be uncovered in works—and at work—in certain exemplary writings' *modus scribendi* (Certeau, *Heterologies* 161). It had to be spelled out through a formalization of what specific literary practices already "denuded": their radical protocols of discourse and by implication their opposition to those protocols that had appeared to "efface," discount, or transcend textuality. This explains why writers such as Sade, Rimbaud, Mallarmé, Lautréamont, Raymond Roussel, Proust, Antonin Artaud, Georges Bataille, Francis Ponge, or Joyce, who had been less involved in radical politics than in the revolutionizing of modern discourse, have influenced post–World War II theoretical avant-garde at least as much as Freud, Marx, Nietzsche, Saussure, or Bakhtin.

A comprehensive critical history of intertextual theory, a survey that should naturally chart the modern development of the theory of rewriting, is beyond the scope of this book. Besides, it has already been done satisfactorily by Heinrich Plett, Thaïs Morgan, and others. In her essay, "The Space of Intertextuality," appended to the collection on "intertextuality and contemporary American fiction" edited by Patrick O'Donnell and Robert Con Davis (*Intertextuality* 239–74), Morgan traces the "intertext" back to earlier attacks on nineteenth-century philology and the source-hunting approaches of "influence studies," to Eliot's thoughts on tradition, to conclude with Harold Bloom and the French "intertextual revolution" (Barthes, Kristeva, Derrida, Foucault, and others). She specifies, too, that Bakhtin's deeply intertextual triad—the dialogical (*Problems of Dostoevsky's Poetics*), the carnivalesque (*Rabelais and His World*), and heteroglossia (*The Dialogic Imagination*)—marks from the outset intertextual studies' "culturalism," the tendency to overflow the formalist model.

As is well-known, Bakhtin's/Medvedev's critical revision of late nineteenth- through early twentieth-century Russian poetics has been pivotal to Kristeva's conceptualization of intertextuality in *Le Texte du roman*, *Semeiotike*, and other landmark works. In *The Formal Method in Literary Scholarship* (1928), Bakhtin/Medvedev theorizes the ideological nature of intertextuality and the textual makeup of ideology (27–28). Drawing from Bakhtin, Kristeva famously stresses in *Le Texte du Roman* that "the text is *productivity*," activating "redistributional (deconstructive-reconstructive)" mechanisms, and that it entails "a permutation of texts, an inter-textuality: in a text's space several enunciations, lifted from other texts, intersect and neutralize one another" (12) (trans. mine). We can see, on the one hand, textuality is not restricted to literature; nor does it remain confined to formal discourses for that matter. Further, texts are representation regimes, encoding systems regulating the *formalization* of values, ideas, ideologies, *and* the concrete *forms* coming out of these formalizing acts. On the other hand, textuality, no matter its nature, largely or narrowly defined, is, in good Bakhtinian tradition, always intertextuality. In its domain, there rules something like

Foucault's *convenientia* (*Order of Things* 18–19). This is an ordering principle that opens out the world as a "vast syntax" (18) wherein the "fringes" of objects—the "frontiers" of books (*Archaeology* 23)—are, as we recall, the hinges by which these objects (texts) become "node[s] within network[s]" (23) and articulate with, and transform, one another. It follows that, ever caught in "vaster syntaxes," intertextual acts effectuate, indeed form as ideological displacements.

Extensive rewriting, rewriting as *trans*textual critique, is most thorough and far-reaching among these acts. It steps over the boundaries of literature per se through the very literary apparatus it operates. Let me stress it once more, my approach brings forward the sociohistorical relevance of intertextual permutations by inscribing—rewriting—the rewrite and the literary process of revision it sets in train, within a broader rewrite and rewriting process. Simply put, this is why I find Kristeva's semiotic model still attractive in spite of its underlying "generalized" theory of intertextuality: "rewriting" Bakhtin in (and for) the late 60s, she locates her explorations precisely "at the border between the literary text and its manifold relations to a broad spectrum of other texts, or culture" (Morgan 246). Taking up the Bakhtinian/Medvedevian category of "ideologeme" from *The Formal Method*, she lays emphasis on the intrinsically ideological function of intertextual exchanges, that is, on the sociocultural mutations these exchanges set off. Further, in the *Semeiotike* essay "The Bounded Text," she seizes upon the ideologeme as an "intersection of a given textual arrangement (a semiotic practice) with the utterances (sequences) that it either assimilates into its own space or to which it refers in the space of exterior texts (semiotic practices)." But, importantly, she insists, "by studying the text as intertextuality, [the concept of ideologeme] considers it as such within (the text of) society and history. The ideologeme of a text is the focus where knowing rationality grasps the transformation of *utterances* (to which the text is irreducible) into a totality (the text) as well as the insertions of this totality into the historical and social text" (*Desire* 36–37). Thus, intertextuality becomes, in Jonathan Culler's words, "less a name for a work's relation to particular prior texts than a designation of its participation in the discursive space of a culture: the relationship between a text and the various language and signifying practices of a culture and its relation to those texts which articulate for it the possibilities of that culture" (103). Yet again, the reading model I am using reveals that it is in *systematic or intensive narrative rewriting* of previous writings that intertextuality emerges as *extensive* or "revisionary intertextuality" (O'Donnell and Davis, "Introduction" xvii), wielding its uniquely cultural force, showing that it *does* involve the reordering and reconstruction—deconstruction-reconstruction—of "cultural" texts and paradigms of all sorts: from literature to the "texts" (representations, usages) of "race" and "empire"; from formalized to less formalized narratives; or, as Clifford Geertz says, from written and verbal materials to a domain where the written and the verbal tone down their formalization yet where culture remains "an ensemble of texts, themselves ensembles" (452).

Leon S. Roudiez remarks that, much though the initial concept of intertextuality "has nothing to do with matters of influence by one writer upon another, or with the sources of a literary work" (15), it has been used to denotate almost exclusively a literary sort of "interface." But for all the novels and poems Kristeva picks out as her favorite examples in *Revolution in Poetic Language* and elsewhere, intertextuality characterizes any "signifying practice" (Roudiez 15). As such, it is an interpretive model that has proven its productivity in a wide spectrum of humanistic disciplines ranging from history (Foucault's "archaeology of knowledge"), anthropology (Clifford, Geertz), communication sciences and semiotics (Eco, Riffaterre) to literary history (Paul Zumthor) and criticism proper (McHale, Hutcheon, Maltby, O'Donnell, Frow, Gates, Suleiman, Nancy K. Miller). This has reinforced the notion that intertextuality is both *literary* and *social-cultural* intertextuality, thereby solving the mimetic dilemma of "text" ("intertext") versus "referent" ("reality"). As Mark Currie insists, "intertextuality posits a model of referentiality which cannot distinguish between reference to the world and reference to another text, since textuality is woven into all" (70). Notably, critics have striven lately to incorporate this model more completely and systematically to account for the *cultural intertextuality* of intra-literary interactions. But the extensive, sociocultural revisionism brought forth *through literary inter-textuality* ("intensive" retextualization of prior texts), to wit, the ramifications of "polemical," socially oriented literary rewriting, has been attended to less and less rigorously. This double move has led to what has been persistently dismissed as "formalism" of any talk of "intertext" in literary criticism.

Adding insult to injury, the expansion of the New Historicism and cultural studies since the late 80s has reinforced this perception despite the massive use of the intertextual model and adjacent methodological-terminological repertoires in these areas of critical analysis. Stephen Greenblatt's intertext-based grasp of the "textual trace" (*Shakespearean Negotiations* 3), for example, is a prerequisite, as he makes plain, to the subsequent positing of texts as sites of "ideological contestation" (3). One cannot have the latter without the former—one cannot make the ideological omelette without cracking the textual eggshell and dealing with the textual stuff first. The "politics of culture" makes sense—in and of itself, and of the power relations it seeks to uncover—provided it operates as a Bakhtinian "poetics of culture." Provided, that is, it accordingly values intertextuality in general and intertextual rewriting in particular as a culturally axial phenomenon whose scrutiny helps us glimpse "the institutional negotiations and exchange of social energy" (94), as Greenblatt famously posits. Hence, the abolishing of the textual "isolation" of literature does not toss us up into a realm beyond "forms," beyond books, texts, and discourse. It just means experiencing the social-historical horizon of written bodies as a "larger cultural text" (95). And, significantly, according to Greenblatt, this horizon "cannot simply be set against literary texts as either stable antithesis or stable background, and the protective isolation of those texts gives way to a sense of their interaction with other texts and hence of the permeability of their boundaries" (95). Texts pervade their material horizon because they are material, because their "bodies matter," too. Moreover, as already suggested, they and their con-texts, literature and the "social fabric," share the same organizing principle. Intensive-extensive rewriting, rewriting as renarrativization and sociocultural "intervention," is essentially the same mechanism. Both suggest a *way of writing and living the present world "differently."*

MODUS LEGENDI: AN APPROACH TO REWRITING

> [T]he historicity of the literary text can be theorized most adequately as a relation between two levels of intertextuality: a first level of productive transformation under given conditions of the codes of prior literary and cultural texts; and a second, institutional level at which the text is rewritten in an ultimately political process of valorisation and recontextualisation. (Frow, "Who Shot Frank Hardy?" 23)

German critic Heinrich Plett breaks down the students of intertextuality into two groups:[15] "the progressives" and "the traditionalists." The former, he specifies, turn to Bakhtin, Barthes, Kristeva, Derrida. They combine semiotics, Freudianism, Marxism, and a certain postmetaphysical, radical philosophy to open up the concept of intertext and subsequent practices as to suggest how literary redeployments revisit various paradigms of social life. More analytical, the traditionalists deal with intertextuality—citation, collage, parody, travesty, and the like—chiefly as a literary phenomenon (Plett 4–5). They make use of structural and historical poetics, theory of genres, stylistics, and, not least, comparative literature methodology. They have put together a model for tackling intertextuality as a process shaping *literary* (aesthetic) production and response, have cataloged interliterary transformations, and have traced, with great display of erudition, the historical fluctuations of categories thus identified. So has Genette in *Palimpsestes* and elsewhere; Riffaterre in *Fictional Truth*, *Text Production*, where he discusses the notion of "intertextual semiosis," and in other, shorter pieces; Lucien Dällenbach in his study of *mise en abyme* devices, translated as *The Mirror in the Text*, and in other essays; Paul Zumthor and Laurent Jenny, in a couple of volumes and articles; Karlheinz Stierle, Ulrich Broich, Susanne Holthuis, Hermann Herlinghaus (to list only a few German critics), and even Harold Bloom.

In a series of books back in the 70s and early 80s, primarily in *The Anxiety of Influence* (1973), *A Map of Misreading* (1975), and *Agon* (1982), Bloom has perfected a "revisionist" model of literary history. According to this model, the "strong poet" misreads his (always *his*) "father," and this misreading is a *miswriting in nuce* (*Map* 3) since it leads to the new poet's own writing. Thus, part of "the larger phenomenon of intellectual revisionism" (*Anxiety* 28), the history of Western poetry unveils a "history of anxiety and self-saving caricature, of distortion, of perverse, wilful revisionism" (30). Bloom insists, in a passage marking a major contribution to deconstruction's endeavors to reconceptualize literary history as a narrative of crosstextual traffickings, that "the meaning of a poem can only be a poem, but *another poem—a poem not itself*. And not a poem chosen with total arbitrariness, but any central poem by an indubitable precursor, even if the ephebe *never read* that poem" (70). For "poems rise not so much in response to a present time, as even Rilke thought, but in response to other poems" (99).

True, in *A Map of Misreading* and *Agon*, Bloom somehow takes this latter proposal back. The strong reader/writer, we are told, "also wishes to open received texts to his own sufferings, or to what he wants to call the sufferings of history" (*Map* 4). Responding to this desire, "there is," Bloom concedes, "a referential aspect to a poem, which keeps it from coming into being only as a text, or rather keeps a text from being merely a text" (*Agon* viii). It would follow, then, that miswriting/rewriting does react, after all, to the "present time," to the ambience of rewriting. But this admission remains purely theoretical. In his dealings with "strong misreaders/miswriters"[16] Bloom hardly tells us how history molds the misreading/miswriting process. That is, his literary revisionism is not as revisionary in an "extensive," sociocultural sense. Bloom observes that the ephebe picks out his target carefully but does not specify if this choice carries a relevance other than stylistic, thematic, and so on. Equally important, as the authors I discuss demonstrate, Bloom's "influence" works by extrapolating a masculinist-psychoanalytic and cultural model that no longer applies to our moment. "Anxieties" of authorship have since long been overcome. Nor are influences these days what they used to be. The "parent narratives" are exuberantly resuscitated, sacrilegiously summoned from the past. Marc Chénetier is right: "creative revisitings of the past" have proven more than capable to "transcend" the "anxiety of influence" (*Beyond Suspicion* 204).

In terms Linda Hutcheon uses to distinguish between parody and satire, most critics' explorations of intertextual protocols have been "intramural" (*A Theory of Parody* 39). They have attended, that is, basically to literature-literature encounters. While doing this, they have shown little interest in how such interactions might trade and/or bear upon "texts" largely conceived, in other words, in how *literary* rewriting might come to develop a transliterary, "extramural" impact. No doubt, the reading strategy I am employing in this book benefits from the analytical sophistication of critics such as Genette, Jenny, or Riffaterre. Yet here I also attempt to critique, complete, and "upgrade" their approach. Namely, what I have in mind is fine-tuning their poetics-based method to intertextual/rewriting forms in light of fairly recent, largely Anglo-American developments in critical theory in general and cultural analysis in particular. Thus, I am envisaging a synthetic reading model that integrates respect for textuality narrowly (literarily) conceived, and, to recall Plett, the ability of the "progressives" to insert this type of textuality and the intertextual games generating it, into broader contexts. In other words, I wish to illuminate, as acknowledged at the outset, the culturally transformative role of rewriting operations where, again, whole narratives are retold.

In doing so, I also want to go beyond the typically poststructuralist discourse of intertextuality. While ascertaining the need to look at the wider offshoots of interliterary exchanges, this predominantly conceptual discourse has remained characteristically vague as to exactly where, under which circumstances, by means of what cultural codes, languages, themes, and problematics, and with what consequences these rearrangements come into being. To offset this lack of precision and the oftentimes reckless generalizations of poststructuralism-based intertextual/rewriting theory, I show how recent rewrites engage, as a result (and in the very act) of renarrativization, with "texts" and discourses on race, gender, national self, and similar categories informing the construction of identity in late twentieth-century America. As I have said, rewriting is a literary procedure subordinating literary apparatuses—devices, procedures, "forms"—which activate symbolic mechanisms of identity reconstruction. Extensive—revisionist or oppositional—rewriting rubs up against thematics and styles centering conversation in the public sphere around particular issues and determines reorderings in that arena. Marcel Cornis-Pope, for instance, has repeatedly argued this point in several essays on the "cultural reformulation" ("Systemic Transgression" 87) in Pynchon, Morrison, and "surfictionists" such as Sorrentino, Sukenick, and Federman. His analyses focuses on "revisionistic strategies [that] allo[w] alternative modes of narrative articulation—more fluid, interrogative, multivoiced" (87) and other forms of "revision at the level of narrative poetics" ("Contest" 195). Such "antirealistic"/nonmimetic experiments with language and narrative devices prompt rather than hinder "cultural rewriting" ("Narrative Innovation" 224), which is to say, revaluations of language use, aesthetic and social conventions, and power relations based on sex, gender, race, and so on. Likewise, drawing from Adrienne Rich's notion of writing as re-vision, Peter Widdowson has stressed the "critical" impetus of "re-visionary" writing (164), the features of which are canonical target, conspicuousness of the "source," "denaturalizing" of embedded discourses and ideologies, innovative and "liberating" rereading of the original and its historical context, in which the present becomes oddly "legible." Such "re-visionary" works "have a clearly cultural-political thrust, especially on behalf of the exploited, marginalised and silenced by dominant ideologies." These works demand, he adds, "that the political inscription and cultural complicity in oppression of past texts be revised and re-visioned as part of the process of restoring a voice, a history or an identity to the erstwhile oppressed" (166).

"Extensive," "critical," "re-visionary," or "cultural," rewriting is all the more productive, and spectacular, I remind the reader again, when these sorts of revisions occur alongside *re-writing literally understood*, that is, through actual, methodic ("intensive") retellings of "myth"-laden texts. Thus, the "form" of rewrite and what is actually accomplished culturally—the critical rewriting of certain ideas and hierarchies—make up a dynamic unit. This unit is more ostensible and effective in this *particular* case of rewriting where *literary and ideological intertextuality go hand in hand*. Contemporary rewriters such as Charles Johnson or Kathy Acker set up precisely this type of complex rewriting apparatus. Novels such as Reed's *Flight to Canada* and Octavia Butler's *Kindred* bear out the extensive rewrite's double status: it constitutes a literary goal as well as a means through which the rewriter deliberately joins in a debate *extending* far beyond rewriting's literary territory, in this case the debate around race and gender, how they are represented, and how they could be represented and combined "otherwise." Means (poetics) and ends (politics) go here hand in hand; the revisionist postmodern rewrite splices them tightly together.

Most tentatives to account for rewriting as both literary intertextuality and "interdiscursivity" or "social discourse" (Frow, "Intertextuality" 151; Angenot 107), and to do it in the specific terms of the discourses and formations that rewriting impacts and is impacted by, have been undertaken by postmodern, African American, feminist, and postcolonial and global studies critics. It is primarily in their fields that the highly "existential" or "ontological" (Plate "Visions" 8) stakes of rewriting come to the fore. Throughout my inquiry, I will frequently draw upon trail-blazing works by James Snead, Henry Louis Gates Jr., Robert Stepto, Raymond Hedin, Hortense Spillers, Michael Awkward, David Cowart, Tracy Mishkin, and other African American literature scholars. For they have focused on issues of literary influence, repetition, revision, parody, and other intertextual forms by appropriately contextualizing and historicizing them. Likewise, feminists such as Sandra Gilbert, Susan Gubar, Susan Suleiman, Nancy K. Miller, Molly Hite, Gayle Greene, Susan Stanford Friedman, Elizabeth Langland, Nancy A. Walker, to name only a few, have shown, often in critical dialogue with Hélène Cixous's concept of *écriture féminine*, how women writers rework primarily "masculine literary tradition" (Kilcup 10) to revise both its forms and its discourses of gender, power, and authority. Since femininity shapes, much like race, the rewriter's identity, fictional reformulations of the rewritten work implicitly re-form the author's identity as an individual and an author alike—which also explains, for example, why American feminists are reluctant to discard the notions of authorship, subjectivity, and agency (Susan Stanford Friedman 156–57). Thus, one can conceptualize rewriting as a project to reconstruct, indeed rewrite these categories. Importantly, neither gender nor race is simply "put forward" but rather reworked in its own enunciation, to paraphrase Elspeth Probyn (2). In other words, rewriting declines to "reflect" race and gender, as women rewriters of various racial backgrounds show. It continuously re-produces them in the act of re-textualization. But it is in its turn modulated by already operating discourses of race, gender, sex, and nationality, by upbringing style, philosophical belief, and so on, by how rewriters variously positioned inside "network[s] of inter-textual relations within which texts are inserted as texts-to-be-read" (Bennett and Woollacott 249) have *read* what they are about to redo. These "located," race- or gender-positioned[17] acts of typically "resisting" reading (Fetterley) explain and legitimate the subversive or "disobedient" (Walker) character of most rewritings I work with. Thus, in part, my project further organizes and develops some of the insights surfacing in cultural criticism devoted symptomatically (Leitch, *Postmodernism* 133) to what until recently have been defined as "marginal" forms of literary expression and groups of authors. I will apply, though, my reading model to both "mainstream" and "marginal" rewriters. There is, to my knowledge, no systematic attempt to discuss narrative rewriting in contemporary American literature irrespective of canonical status; nor has there been any rigorous discussion of rewriting that avoids conflating it and overlapping literary or cultural phenomena, especially intertextuality, postmodernism, and the offspring of their incestuous cohabitation, metafiction.[18] Focusing on a series of relevant works, both well established and less recognized, I try to make up for this lack without losing sight of the elements that make critical or "radical" rewrites so intriguingly diverse.

PART II

Rewriting and the National Narrative

> [T]here is no fiction or nonfiction as we commonly understand the distinction: There is only narrative. . . . The development of civilizations is essentially a progress of metaphors. (Doctorow, *Jack London* 160–64)
>
> History is always rewritten backward. (Žižek, *Looking Awry* 157)

In his important study of postmodern "dissenters" such as Coover, Barthelme, and Pynchon, Paul Maltby identifies the target of these writers' critique: "the discourse of 'America.'" He defines this discourse as "the domain of language-use which represents *the idea* of America," more to the point, the "ruling version of this discourse, . . . promoted and reproduced by America's culturally dominant institutions" (103). Revamping "the discourse of America"—or the "American narrative," as I call it—revisiting the "American way," the "American dream," or simply American history, has been a constant objective of rewriting, too. Lately, countless authors have been busy reconstructing the "American narrative" through rewritings of past, "mythic value"–laden stories: Roth's Melvillean replies in *The Great American Novel* and, recently, *American Pastoral*; John Barth's "funhouse" pseudo(hi)stories (*Letters*, *The Tidewater Tales*, *Giles Goat-Boy*); DeLillo's *Americana*, Richard Brautigan's, Reed's, and Doctorow's retellings of the western in *The Hawkline Monster: A Gothic Western*, *Yellow Back Radio Broke-Down*, and *Hard Times*, respectively; Marilynne Robinson's response to Twain and James Fenimore Cooper in *Housekeeping* (Geyh at al. 394–395); Pynchon's megarevisionary games played out in *Gravity's Rainbow* and *Mason and Dixon*. In this part, I propose that we look at how Doctorow, Coover, and Auster reinvent this narrative, as their "counternarratives" are among the most formally intensive and ideologically extensive rewrites of this sort.

CHAPTER 1

Romanticism Reincorporated: E. L. Doctorow and the (Re)Production of America

LITERARY RAGS, HISTORICAL TATTERS

Doctorow's *Ragtime* seizes early twentieth-century American history as step-by-step "revival" of older histories and stories, a time that knits together diverse "rags" and "patches" of culture. Historically dense *because* intertextually "thick," Doctorow's deep-laid rewrite conveys an acute sense of the past and critically scrutinizes it, shows how the past and its texts shape the present and history in general. In this view, I must state my disagreement with Fredric Jameson, who claims that Doctorow's fiction exemplifies postmodern "'intertextuality' as a deliberate, built-in feature of the aesthetic effect and as the operator of a new connotation of 'pastness' and pseudohistorical depth, in which the history of aesthetic styles displaces 'real' history" (*Postmodernism* 20). We shall note that Doctorow does not herald the "waning of history" through "blank" pastiche of the "stereotypical past" (*Postmodernism* 21). Quite the contrary. He grasps history as narrative process, using rewriting to reveal how various (narrative) "body parts" come to form one, albeit plural, body of history: ragtime America. Historical representation is still an objective in Doctorow, yet not as traditional mimesis. As Linda Hutcheon has remarked, he carries out the project transparent in her formula of "historiographic metafiction" (Hutcheon, *Poetics* 137). Along with other postmodern rewriters, he shows that "there seems to be a new desire to think historically, and to think historically these days is to think critically and contextually" (88). Revivifying past stories and the past in light of how our present sees and "pluralizes" it effects a recovery of historicity and a "critical-contextual" meditation on it, on how scattered facts and lives write the ragtime chapter in America's biography.

To narrate this chapter, *Ragtime* rewrites Heinrich von Kleist's 1810 novella, "Michael Kohlhaas." This rewriting is multiply performative. First, the novel as a whole "reenacts" the romantic text, which results in an ample "transposition" of, or parallel to, Kleist's "script." Second, this fictional parallel itself features countless moments, techniques, and tropes of cultural reembodiment, impersonation, and performance. Third, these allegorize Doctorow's relation to Kleist and, more broadly, illuminate the "theater of historicity": on the one hand, Doctorow casts light on the "off-stage" machinery organizing free-floating "occurrences" into a "national" narrative and fictional fragments into "real history"; on the other, he dramatizes history as a theater of recurrence and repetition.

As we may recall, Kleist's hero, Michael Kohlhaas, is a Brandenburg horse dealer. On his way to Dresden, he is stopped by the Junker Wenzel von Tronka's men at the Saxon border and asked to pay a toll as well as to produce a permit stating his right to bring horses across the border. Unable to comply with the latter request, Kohlhaas leaves a pair of horses instead and rides on to Dresden to apply for his "certificate." Finding out that the Junker's demands were illegal, he returns to Tronka Castle only to learn that his well-fed pair of blacks were worked to death in the fields, and the groom he left with them was beaten and driven away. As the law of his time fails to "protect his rights" (Kleist, *Michael Kohlhaas* 27), Kohlhaas sets out to exact his revenge on the Junker. His individual struggle, however, rapidly turns into a violent rebellion that rocks the empire. It takes Martin Luther's intercession to appease Kohlhaas and bring him back into the legal system. Yet, while compensating the horse dealer for his spoiled property, the system puts him to death.

Here, I intend to account in some detail for the strategy of cultural incorporation *Ragtime* employs to absorb "Michael Kohlhaas." I am, in other words, interested in how the romantic text is performed, rewritten and re-encoded, "buried"—yet in order to be "resurrected"—through playful repetition and analogical tran-scription in *Ragtime*'s textual body, the "script" of which "resuscitates" Kleist's text as much as it conceals it like (in) a "crypt." Thus, *Ragtime* appears as a postmodern reincarnation of a major text in the Western canon. By focusing on the performative aspect of critical rewriting in Doctorow, we could illuminate the implications of the Kleistian text's avatars in *Ragtime*: we could show how Doctorow "performs" Kleist, manipulating his obsessions with doubling and revival,[1] intertextuality and repetition in general to stake out a provocative redefinition of modernity as reenactment of transhistorical patterns. For, as Henry Sussman points out, "In a performatively compelling as well as narratively complex and historically 'true' way, . . . 'Michael Kohlhaas' 'reproduces' the aesthetic and subjective conditions of the broader modernity, by invoking, in a multifaceted way, their sources" (133). Doctorow "re-performs" Kleist to take up precisely these conditions and work them into a critique targeting not as much Kleist and the Reformation period—Kleist's historical "referent"—as closer-to-home situations that appear to rematerialize Kleist's.

A number of comparative readings have basically spelled out the similitudes between the two texts; I hope to go a bit deeper. On the one hand, I wish to address the textual reinscription of Kleist Doctorow does through rewriting, which I see as effecting textual transpositions more elaborated than the narrative analogies critics have already uncovered. Thus, I explore the themes of performance, masquerade, representation, repetition, and so on, through which rewriting shapes the novel's form. On the other hand, I look at how performative rewriting also fashions the novel's ideology. For, in rewriting Kleist, Doctorow "performs" him and his very motifs of performance, game, and role-playing to attain more than simply "playful" goals. As I suggested, not only does *Ragtime* mirror its romantic predecessor. It also acts it out in various ways to critically revisit the rise of modern America.

ANTINOSTALGIC DÉJÀ-LU: PERFORMANCE AND MASQUERADE

Peter F. Neumeyer, among the first to note "the Kohlhaas/Coalhouse parallel" (19), claims that "Doctorow's Coalhouse is not central to the book" (20). A startling example of transracial and crosscultural palingenesis—a possibility Kleist himself imagined in "The Engagement of Santo Domingo"—the black man holds in Doctorow a major role. In fact, Coalhouse and the whole rewriting apparatus producing his resurgence tie together the several narrative threads of the novel. If *Ragtime*'s broader conflict lies in "the struggle between stability and change" (Busby 39), then change and the political-ethical questions raised by technological and sociocultural advance meet in the heroic figure of Coalhouse. I find this coincidence ironic because, in a typically postmodern gesture, Doctorow revives a modern and modernizing moment by "resuscitating" a *pre*modern figure, embedding a romantic text in a novel drawing upon apparently *novel* situations and structures. *Ragtime*'s ostentatious "repetition" of the past questions "the main constitutive element" of the "idea of modernity": "unrepeatable time" (Calinescu, *Five Faces* 13), that is, "newness" as the foremost modern myth (Calinescu, "Modernity" 34). In "recasting the "new" as *déjà-vu* or slight "re-novation" of the old, *Ragtime* aligns with recent critiques of "modern temporality" (Latour 69), which, in a Nietzschean vein, place the past's resurgence at the very core of the *novum*[2] as well as "the bitter harvest of progress" (Kolakowski 9). Here, progress is a traumatic moment where the forms of oppression and injustice modernity claims to have "sublimated" come back to haunt it.

The playing out of the new as disguise (masquerade) of perennial, transcultural situations structures Doctorow's whole text. Thus, even before it is actually inserted in the larger narrative—which happens right in the middle of the novel—the story of Coalhouse Walker, Jr., which retells the Kohlhaas tale, gets under way. The startling anatomy of the new, of differential values deconstructed as repetitive phenomena, begins with the first line. In effect, Kleist's shadow visits Doctorow's world starting with the opening chapters. Critics have identified therein subtle allusions to motifs and places from other Kleistian stories, which once again confirms that Doctorow's interest in Kleist stretches far beyond the celebrated novella. Without being revealed as such, the Kleist intertexts undergird the description of "modern times," which thus, ironically enough, set off recognizable patterns of premodern, feudal discrimination. But the reworking of medieval injustice as racial oppression is only the most obvious rewriting of "Michael Kohlhaas" that *Ragtime* accomplishes. As I have maintained, it is not only Kohlhaas's reincarnation in Coalhouse that documents this rewriting, but also the theme and tropes of cultural incorporation, repetition, and performance cropping up throughout the novel. No character of importance, no situation or subplot escapes the impact of these tropes. Kohlhaas's disguise as, or duplication by, Coalhouse is itself duplicated by many other duplications and repetitions, which I will discuss in some detail later on. At this point, an outline of the rewriting undergone by the Kohlhaas tale in the Coalhouse story should help.

Most saliently, this rewriting commences in the hero's name itself. But Marion Faber suggests that *Coalhouse Walker, Jr.* also brings to mind David Walker, a radical African American revolutionary of the early nineteenth century, author of the political pamphlet *Walker's Appeal to the Colored Citizens of the World*, which urges rebellion. The pamphlet's title evokes both Kohlhaas's and Coalhouse's similar manifestoes. Further, the *Jr.* in Coalhouse's name, whether referring to Kohlhaas, to Walker, or to both, highlights a "filial relationship" (149), an "inscription," resurgence or posterity of the "father" in his heir—precisely the ultimate dream of Kleist's hero. To complicate the onomastic filiation issue, Josie P. Campbell has called our attention to George W. Walker, a noted figure in the history of African American performance (the minstrel show) at the turn of the century. In his show,

Campbell reminds us, "George Walker played the 'uppity dandy, immaculately dressed in high style' to the shuffling, loose-jointed satire of the tall, gaunt Williams [Walker's partner]. Ironically, Walker and Williams billed themselves as 'Two Real Coons,' giving the public nothing less then 'a genuine fraud.'" They used the stereotype of the "minstrel character as instrumental satire, to turn the white man's Negro projection into a two-faced mask" (303). To be sure, Walker passes down the polemic and theatrical masquerade outlined in Campbell's genealogy not only to his *Jr.* but to the whole novel, a performative text in its entirety. Mother's Young Brother takes up minstrel show masquerade after joining Coalhouse's group "as an outlaw and revolutionary" (Doctorow, *Ragtime* 254). Booker T. Washington, Martin Luther's "reincarnation" in *Ragtime*, is shocked to find among Walker's companions a man who "was not a Negro but a white in blackface, as if this were some minstrel show" (293). Ironically, the famous African American educator is disturbed by the "unholy company [of] a white who smears himself with color and adds mockery to your [Walker's] arsenal" (294).

But mockery, play, performance in general are already part of Walker's "arsenal" and, as such, inform the novel's plot. If Kohlhaas is a horse trader who travels considerably—he has crossed the border between Saxony and Brandenburg seventeen times before being asked about his permit—Coalhouse is a piano player aspiring to "settle down" and marry Sarah, the black woman sheltered by a New Rochelle family, and who had borne his son. Notably, he is a performer in at least two different senses. He "appears" to us as a skilled musician and a fighter against the prejudices of his time by putting on a witty show of "self-impersonation." "His neat suits, hat and gloves," Duncan Smith maintains, "seem a forgivable parody of himself or an unforgivable parody of the white man" (4). This spectacle brings out, through a combination of mockery and self-mockery, his racial identity, freedom, and pride, which Father finds "reckless" (Doctorow, *Ragtime* 168).

Granted, Coalhouse does not "know his place." Economically, socially, and legally, he is a "border-crosser"—a "Walker." His Model T, "the very symbol of ownership and the badge of white middle-class America" (Campbell 303), amounts to sheer "provocation to many white people" (Doctorow, *Ragtime* 180). Further, his income seems to have already met, if not surpassed, standards once accessible to whites only. And ultimately, his claims test the very limits of the judicial system. Through him, a subject formerly relegated to a well-defined (and well-confined) condition repositions himself socially. His profession, what he does for a living, simply translates his performative motility, his "way of living," morals and politics, into language of explicit performance. Indeed, a prime "trickster" of *Ragtime*, Coalhouse displays impressive "legerdemain" skills (Campbell 302). Though the tragic outcome of his struggle tones down the playful dimension of the novel, he remains a "player," like many other characters of *Ragtime*. Moreover, his performance is part and parcel of the strategy of rewriting by which the narrative assimilates "Michael Kohlhaas" through an interplay of ludic parallelisms and modifications that displace the novella's "serious" epic repertoire onto a sociocultural environment structured by the very themes and figures of reincarnation, impersonation, farce, and duplication. Again, *Ragtime* portrays a period of "musical," "spectacular" transformation that, in a postmodern manner, generates "variations" on old "themes."

BETWEEN THE (RE)ASSEMBLY LINES

One of these major variations reencodes Kleist's feudal class-based plot as racial conflict. Yet Doctorow does not simply adapt a Reformation situation to a modern moment of economic and social reform. He does not solely re-form "Michael Kohlhaas": he per-forms it and renders this performance obvious. From an *inter*textual standpoint, "duplication enters the novel most overtly through the fact that a large chunk of it is carefully based on *Michael Kohlhaas*" (Dawson 206). But this literary palingenesis of sorts, by which the novella is resurrected in the novel, is itself replicated and at times even thematized *intra*textually through a whole symbolic paradigm of rebirth and histrionic impersonation. These two phenomena are in fact inseparable: the materializing or "corporification" of various "models" or (arche)types in their "copies" (new bodies) frequently occurs through performative acts such as imitation, mimicry, impression, and the like. Lying at the core of *Ragtime*'s rewriting of "Michael Kohlhaas," these acts transpose the latter into a jocular-performative register that, paradoxically or not, does not foreclose serious cultural critique.

Thus, Kohlhaas's trade becomes Coalhouse's piano playing. The former's horses change into the latter's Model T, which itself is a paragon of "industrial repetition." As Geoffrey Galt Harpham points out, the Model T, "on whose uniqueness [Coalhouse] paradoxically insists," represents "a case of duplication so utter that there cannot even be said to be an original" (88). The Fordist mode of production, an issue to which I shall come back, sets up a repetitive embodiment that translates the esoteric doctrine of reincarnation into "exoteric" "manufacturing" discourse. Suffice it to observe for now that it is precisely in the middle—and by means—of an account of this doctrine and its sociocultural paraphernalia that Coalhouse is introduced, which insertion gives

Kohlhaas a new (literary) body. As we learn, from the Detroit automotive plants to the Sunday supplements in which mummification is "described in detail" (Doctorow, *Ragtime* 160) to the interior decoration that renders dining a form of "entombment" (161), the whole society participates in a ritual of transmigration, reincorporation, and reinstitution. It is also worth recalling that both in "Michael Kohlhaas" and in *Ragtime* the protagonists ultimately demand the restoration of their property to "its original condition" (220) through absolute (literal) reembodiment. Kohlhaas requests in his manifestoes that his pair of blacks be "fattened" and returned to him as they had been before the incident. In his turn, Coalhouse is given satisfaction by the chief firefighter Will Conklin's rebuilding the "dismantled" Ford out of "body parts" paid for by Morgan, who, we shall see, appears in the novel as another staunch adept of reincarnation theory.

The firehouse lane scene transposes Kohlhaas's predicament at Saxony's border into a gloomy farce with deadly serious upshots. Tellingly, the local police treat it like a "joke." The firefighters "advised [Coalhouse] that he was travelling on a private toll road and that he could not drive on without payment of twenty-five dollars or by presenting a pass indicating that he was a resident of the city" (181). Of course, both the pass and the toll are inventions as much as the "story about the pass was a fable" in "Michael Kohlhaas" (13), a sham of the Junker. Yet while the latter is motivated by greed, Conklin, von Tronka's reincarnation, is looking for racist "fun." Which of course does not mean that the two perpetrators do not become "despised . . . everywhere," as the novel puts it (Doctorow, *Ragtime* 228). Like Wittenberg's inhabitants fearing Kohlhaas's retaliation, the people of New Rochelle dread having Conklin among them. And like the Junker, the fire chief seeks political protection. Developing similarly, Kohlhaas's/Coalhouse's fight for justice moves from individual claims to more general goals. In Kleist, this progress can be traced in the revolutionary texts Kohlhaas authors. In Doctorow, the same phenomenon occurs in Coalhouse's, which boil down the horse dealer's five proclamations to two letters. They constitute the core of the rewriting activity proper as they rephrase Kohlhaas's manifestoes.

Coalhouse's initial writing, a brief epistle addressed to the New Rochelle newspapers, still sets forth personal demands: "I want the infamous Fire Chief of the Volunteers turned over to my justice . . . I want my automobile [which the fire fighters vandalized] returned to me in its original condition. If these conditions are not met I will continue to kill firemen and burn firehouses until they are" (220). The first document Kohlhaas draws up, whether under Hobbesian (Wexelblatt 114) or Protestant influence (Koelb 1102), is a decree in which, "by virtue of the authority inborn in him, [Kohlhaas] commanded the Junker von Tronka, within three days of its receipt, to bring back to Kohlhaasenbrück the pair of blacks he had stolen from him" (Kleist, *Michael Kohlhaas* 31). In his second piece, also to be published in the local newspapers, Coalhouse's requests are of different nature: "One, that the white excrescence known as Willie Conklin be turned over to my justice. Two, that the Model T Ford with its custom pantasote top be returned in its original condition. Until these demands are satisfied, let the rules of war prevail. Coalhouse Walker Jr., President, Provisional American Government" (Doctorow, *Ragtime* 230). The text reads more like a political manifesto, echoing the "so-called Kohlhaas Manifesto" (Kleist, *Michael Kohlhaas* 34). The latter's author "call[s] upon the whole country to give no aid or comfort to the Junker Wenzel von Tronka, against whom he was waging righteous war, but instead required every inhabitant, including relatives and friends, to hand him over forthwith" (34). Shortly thereafter, Kohlhaas composes a "second manifesto" (35), then a third. Both lay down a relevant "contract" between the rebel writer and his potential audience. Kohlhaas summons "all good Christians" and calls the Junker "the common enemy of all Christians," while presenting himself as "a free gentleman of the Empire and the world, owing allegiance to none but God" (36). In his last manifesto, "done at the Seat of Our Provisional World Government, the Chief Castle at Lützen" (40–41), Kohlhaas proclaims himself "a viceroy of the Archangel, come to punish with fire and sword, for the wickedness into which the whole world was sunk, all those who should take the side of the Junker in this quarrel" (40). Dresden's citizens themselves spread "the news of the presence of the avenging angel who chastise[s] the oppressors of the people" (53).

Kohlhaas's individual cause simply disappears at this climactic point. Rapidly expanding his demands from "the particular and parochial to the universal" (Hillis Miller, "Laying Down" 315), Kleist's hero has become a fighter for justice at large "by virtue" of his *individual* right to do so. His is a holy war since oppression is essentially anti-Christian. Appearing alternatively as a "dragon" devastating the land (37) to the feudal authorities and an "angel of judgment" (32) to himself and the humbler citizens, Kohlhaas shapes post-Reformation individualism (Wexelblatt 118) into vindictive Christian imagery and appeals to communal, religious, and ethical values. But this also means that his rebellion is *de facto* already contained by the political system these values and representations underlie. The hero's submission to Martin Luther is quite revealing in this regard. In actuality, Luther's position in the story is contradictory at least, "contribut[ing] to the overall problem even in seeming to (partially) solve it" (Sussman 114). On the one hand, his ideas influence Kohlhaas's thought and actions just as much as Kleist's "shocking" readings from Kant's moral philosophy (Mann in Kleist, *Michael Kohlhaas* 144), Rousseau (*The Social Contract*), and Hobbes (*Leviathan*). Moreover, Luther might very well be Kohlhaas's "spiritual leader" (Koelb 1102). He teaches his followers to be faithful to the "authority inborn in them" and, in translating the Bible, commits an absolute act of insubordination himself. On the other hand, Luther rejects overt opposition, questioning Kohlhaas's right to "take the law into his own hands" (also a recurrent phrase in *Ragtime*).

This may actually explain *Ragtime*'s rather ironic references to Luther. Thus, J. P. Morgan's art collections, which Coalhouse threatens to blow up, contain "a Gutenberg Bible on vellum" (285, 307), "portraits of Martin Luther by Lucas Cranach the Elder" (295), not to mention the "silver tankard with a lid" (286) that "had belonged to Frederick, the Elector of Saxony" (287). Significantly, Coalhouse throws the precious mug into the street after putting in it a piece of paper with a telephone number at which he can be reached by the police. This scene may echo, again playfully, the enigmatic capsule episode in Kleist. The prophetic scroll Kohlhaas swallows becomes, in Doctorow's own incorporation of Kleist, a scrap of paper carrying insignificant information that Coalhouse *expels*. But, to be sure, Booker T. Washington stands out as the most telling intertextual redoubling of the great German reformer. Much like Luther, he opposes "all [Negro] agitation on questions of political and social equality" (291). If Luther calls Kohlhaas an "impious and terrible man" (Kleist, *Michael Kohlhaas* 44) whose "sword has taken the most ferocious revenge imaginable upon the Junker" (46), Washington "smells" in Coalhouse's company "the sweat of rage, the impecunious rebellion of wild unthinking youth" (Doctorow, *Ragtime* 294). His condemnation of Coalhouse reworks Luther's reaction to political disobedience into a conservative doctrine of racial emancipation.

Race comes explicitly into play for the first time in Coalhouse's second text, where the author speaks of Conklin as a "white excrescence." Indeed, it does not turn into a privileged topic virtually anywhere in the novel except for Washington's unsuccessful intervention. Race does generate conflict; but the very scenario of reduplication and impersonation the novel lays out makes the racial plot and the characters involved in it part of a broader political drama. Coalhouse does not merely speak for his racial group. As a rewriter of Kohlhaas's texts and "President" of the "Provisional American Government," he advances from the personal level, a level of social treatment marked by his color, to less and less individual horizons of insurgence; from the outraged individual to race, class, and the "American People." Coalhouse thus challenges the utopian anarchists of *Ragtime*. He shows instinct for the "seat" of "the power of the white world" (280), where the judicial, political, and economic authority are one.

TRANSCENDENT SURPLUS, CAPITAL RESURRECTIONS

Endorsed by anarchist Emma Goldman, Coalhouse's "appropriation of the Morgan property" speaks to his understanding of Morgan's complex power and of the "appropriating" (289) the plutocrat has himself done. A pivotal cultural reincarnation of the novel, Coalhouse symbolically takes on Morgan's art objects as the latter materialize the very philosophy of reincarnation. However, if Coalhouse personifies revolutionary change, Morgan thinks of himself and Henry Ford as conservative epitomes of an atemporal model of control fostering both modernization and stability through technology. He glimpses in Ford's manufacturing model a "projection of organic truth" (152) involving the "interchangeability" (153) of "body parts" as well as of people. According to this truth, individuals are also "interchangeable." What takes place on the assembly line would simply give shape to a historical principle by virtue of which a selected elite rises again at various historical junctures to endow society with leadership and capital control—in all senses. There exist, Morgan claims, "universal patterns of order and repetition that give meaning to the activity of this planet" (154). These patterns supposedly reemerge in people such as Ford and himself, who would thereby "instrumen[t] in our modern age . . . trends in human identity that affirm the oldest wisdom in the world" (154). A beneficiary of modern discoveries like the Fords, Rockefellers, Carnegies, Harrimans, and so forth, Morgan depicts the "mechanistic science of Newton and Descartes" and the modern age in general, surprisingly, as a "great conspiracy, a great devilish conspiracy to destroy our apprehension of reality and our awareness of the transcendentally gifted among us" (156). Nevertheless, he tells Ford, "[T]hey are with us in every age. They come back, you see? They come back! (156). "They" designate the very few possessing the *prisca theologia*, the esoteric wisdom through which "the sufferings of humankind" are being alleviated (155).

The most valuable pieces in Morgan's collections are objects of intense, albeit amateurish, study by which he hopes to acquire this secret knowledge. Among such treasures, he especially values a coffin and a mummy of Seti I, which "the Egyptian government and the entire archaeological community believe it resides in Cairo" (157). The multibillionaire has hired a whole staff of scholars to help him grasp the occult knowledge laid up in "the translated writings of the Egyptian priest Hermes Trismegistus" (156) and in other Egyptian antiquities. He also invites Ford to join him on a scientific trip to Luxor and Karnak. Though the practical Ford refuses to waste his time on "intellectual" exploits and "two-dollar words," the man who "had caused a machine to replicate itself endlessly" (142) confesses that "reincarnation is the only belief [he] hold[s]" (158). Morgan and Ford also founded "the most secret and exclusive club in America. The Pyramid, of which they were the only members" (159).

Morgan's dabbling in "Egyptology," "anthropological" hobbies, and his half-baked theories of afterlife, resurgence, and the like illustrate a characteristic theme in Doctorow. In *The Book of Daniel*, for instance, Grandma visits Daniel after her death. The last pages of *World's Fair* are dominated by the motif of the "Time Capsule" the Westinghouse Company sinks into the "Immortal Well" as a message to people in the year 6939, and, in the same novel, a young boy makes up his own time capsule, which he decides to bury in Claremont Park. Likewise, F. W. Bennett in *Loon Lake* echoes *Ragtime*'s J. P. Morgan. Rich and powerful, Bennett studies primitive monuments and Native American burial practices. Finally, in "The Writer in the Family," a short story in *Lives of the Poets*, the narrator has a dream in which, à la Doctorow's novel *The Waterworks*, his dead, mummylike father comes back to life.

THE IMMIGRATING SCRIPTS AND THE STAGING OF AMERICA

But Doctorow's prime virtuoso of corporeal transgression and on-stage reincorporation is Houdini. The famous escape artist masters techniques of radical negotiation of body boundaries and (re)appearance. Gradually, though, his physical performance based on bodily skills becomes a *figure*—a *schema*—of rising from the dead (*Ragtime* 7–8). As we gather more clearly after his mother's death, his career is a perpetual attempt to regain the maternal body, to regress toward that stage—semiotic, Kristeva would say—prior to the formation of identity as separation from the mother. Following his mother's decease, his "escapes" become more and more suicidal. Houdini's disappearance/reappearance shows bring out a transparent "desire for his dead mother. He was buried and reborn, buried and reborn" (212), unfortunately, in the same body.

Doctorow throws light on Houdini's "passionate" love for his mother early on in the novel and employs this Oedipal suggestion to introduce Freud and his disciples' visit to New York. The visit adds a more general, cultural and historical dimension to the spectacle of alert, dramatic reembodiment of Europe that "uncanny" America displays in the novel. Yet *Ragtime*'s *Unheimliches* itself rehearses an "uncanny" episode in literary history insofar as it recalls the uncanny repetitive patterns embedded in Kleist's text (Kuhns 82–83). Interestingly, the novel introduces its own version of the uncanny right before developing a more elaborate theory on the subject: prior to Freud and Jung's boat ride "through the Tunnel of Love," the founder of psychoanalysis "experience[s] a shock of recognition" in meeting the eyes of Tateh's daughter. Immediately thereafter, the narrator cites Freud's infamous judgment on the American "displacement" of Europe through wholesale "appropriation" that renders a familiar (*heimliche*) tradition a "gigantic "mistake" (Doctorow, *Ragtime* 41).

Mistaken or not, modern America undertakes a big-budget reproduction of Europe. It "produces," or rather *re*produces, the Old World as a (New) "cultural" show. This performance entails Europe's literal "dismantling" (19) and relocation following bulk acquisitions of monuments and antiquities by Stanford White or J. P. Morgan. But this spectacle is part of the inevitable cultural reincorporation and demographic "transmutation" America initiates through immigration. Much as Doctorow turns "Michael Kohlhaas" into an "immigrating" text, *Ragtime*'s immigrants turn American through a complex and traumatic process of adaptation and identity enactment. Tateh and his Jewish family memorably bring into focus this process, as well as the larger theme of "duplication" (Dawson 208) and cinematic representation. The Jewish family undergoes a radical identity reconstruction. If Tateh's wife fails to cope with the process, he and his daughter survive as they acquire impersonating skills. Giving up political illusions, the poor Jewish socialist from Latvia metamorphoses into a rich Baron Ashkenazy continuously putting himself on show in public. In fact, he incorporates in his new social demeanor his recent "incorporation" by the "system." He becomes rich as "the Buffalo Nickel Photoplay, *Incorporated*" (267), which further complicates this game of multiple reincorporations. Starting with paper silhouettes and dramatic portraits suggesting "moods, character, despair" (48), then obtaining a contract on "movie books" (139), composing "photoplays" (269), and finally entering the movie business, Tateh intuits, like Ford in his field, the high value of the "duplicable event" (140). And, in incorporating the widowed Mother into Tateh's family too, Doctorow may hint at the profound changes this value brings on Americans' private life.

One may even read the entire novel as an attempt to identify and critique this value as controlling the modernizing process affecting American society before World War I: the imaginal "event" gestures toward a mesmerizing reality, while in actually it duplicates (keeps unchanged) an unjust world. As I noted, no character or situation of some relevance remains outside the symbolic economy of doubling, rebirth, and intertextual reembodiment. For example, Coalhouse's wife-to-be, Sarah, "plays" the part of Kohlhaas's wife, Lisbeth, sharing her tragic fate but not before the Boy turns her into a character in his own games of impersonation. Likewise, Evelyn Nesbit, former wife of the insane, apish "performer" Harry K. Thaw, "provide[s] the inspiration for the concept of the movie star system and the model for every sex goddess from Theda Bara to Marilyn Monroe" (88). Interestingly, it is Younger Brother's fascination with this erotic icon that first jeopardizes the family bonds. Even though the whole family is in "show business"—Father runs a "manufacture of flags and buntings and other accoutrements of patriotism, including fireworks" (3)—Younger Brother is the only one to take up masquerade and impersonation to break loose from the family. Ironically, his expertise in patriotic shows turns against the "big show" itself after he joins the President of the "Provisional American Government." His are, in fact, the sole (literally) undermining "performances" that a member of the unnamed family ever organizes. This does not mean, however, that the reincarnation tropes or repetitive rituals other members of the family adopt are less relevant. The Boy's role, for instance, seems to be very important in this regard. Apparently incorporating the author's voice, he is a "commemorator." "Treasuring anything discarded" (120), he collects documents, letters, torn papers and drawings, and so on, that the narrator presents as the story's main sources of information. But most remarkably, the Boy is continuously enthralled by stereotypes and recurrent patterns, whether they appear in Grandfather's Ovidian readings from *Metamorphoses* or in baseball games. It is the Boy who tells Houdini to "warn the Duke" (11), before the artist meets the Archduke Franz Ferdinand. Indeed, he is the authorial alter-ego. As such, he personifies the fascination with reincarnation that structures *Ragtime* and sets up its narrative commentary on modern America.

CHAPTER 2

Cold War Fairy Tales: Robert Coover's Social Romance

> [*The Public Burning*] was made up of thousands and thousands of tiny fragments that had to be painstakingly stitched together . . . I was striving for a text that would seem to have been written by the whole nation through all its history. (Coover, "Robert Coover and His Own and Other Fictions" 59)

> History and morality are written and read within the infrastructure of texts (Kristeva, *Desire* 65)

Previously, we examined a revisionary rewrite that "reembodies" its model in great detail. Here, we will deal with a somewhat different kind. While the ideological objectives of revisionism remain fairly unchanged, the rewrite "unfolds" and "dilates" a preexistent "tiny story" without resulting in a minutely worked-out narrative parallel like *Ragtime.* Coover has repeatedly insisted that his technique "consists in thoroughly drawing out the content of a metaphor." "In my writing," he tells us, "I am mostly concerned with the structure likely to allow for the deployment of the metaphor" (Coover, "Les deux amours" 19–20) [trans. mine]. As the novelist acknowledges, his works "typically begin for me as very tiny stories or little one-act play ideas which I think at the time aren't going to fill three pages. Then slowly the hidden complexities reveal themselves" ("Robert Coover and His Own and Other Fictions" 48). Focusing on Coover's model of narrative development, I want to address the intertextual feature of this *modus operandi* in his 1977 novel *The Public Burning.*

The tiny story the novel processes is the narrative of social mobility or so-called social Darwinism, part and parcel of the exuberant rhetoric revolving around the American Dream. Coover locates this scheme in narrative form and in an emblematic fiction: Horatio Alger's Ragged Dick social romance of individual merit and reward. It is this particular story that *The Public Burning* intensively re-stor(i)es while telling its own. In view of this re-storying, I wish, first, to reconstruct the expansion of the Alger "micronarrative," indicating how it unfurls to grow into a sort of "macronarrative"—Coover's meganovel—through a revisionary process involving repeated acts of rereading and rewriting. Second, I want to show how Coover's rewriting of Alger foregrounds a crisis—and a critique—of cold war political discourse and cultural representation by engaging the notions and figures of publicity, public arenas, performance, and spectacle.

THE "DISCOURSE OF AMERICA"

> In what way did this author of juvenile fiction unwittingly put a finger on a form of expression that could define "the rules of the game" of the economic and social order and enter the political discourse about the meaning of America? . . . The appropriation of Alger is a tale about American political culture, discourse, and imagination. (Nackenoff 4)

Certain critics have contended that Alger's famous hero Ragged Dick is a male Cinderella for postbellum America,[3] and what we may take as a more popular version of *Bildungsroman* ("formation novel") or *Erziehungsroman* ("education novel") represents Alger's more realistic, Gilded-Age adaptation of a typical fairy-tale plot. Others have stressed the influence of a national symbol running from Ben Franklin's Poor Richard to Tom Sawyer, Finn, and various Melvillean heroes before attaining its incorporation in the *Ragged Dick* series. Or, one could place the latter in an entire Western lineage, well known to Alger, possibly stemming from the *Odyssey*'s Telemachus journey and Greek romance and peaking in mideighteenth–midnineteenth-century novels of social ascent, poor orphans and rich patrons, boardinghouses, street urchins, and *gavroches*, with Fielding, Dickens, Sue, Hugo, and Balzac as prime examples. But it is also worth noting that the "elite" genre—the nineteenth-century "fame and fortune" novel—overall follows a simple plot germane to popular and folk tales.

The Public Burning is not Coover's first attempt to revisit this narrative form. The 1977 novel marks a climactic moment in a series of texts where Coover renarrates fairy tales and related fables. To give a few examples, "The Magic Poker," a piece from the 1969 anthology of short stories, *Pricksongs and Descants*, recasts the Cinderella story. The title of the 1986 book *Aesop's Forest* is self-explanatory, while the 1980 *Political Fable* reworks the American presidential elections campaign saga as the grotesque exploits of a "Cat in the Hat." Likewise, the 1991 novel *Pinocchio in Venice* retells Carlo Collodi's 1881 *Le avventure di Pinocchio*, whereas *Briar Rose* (1996) refurbishes the Sleeping Beauty story, both tales being also played upon in *The Public Burning*. Considering such a deep-rooted fascination with the genre, it is conceivable that Coover picks the Alger narrative as *The Public Burning*'s core intertext for its fairy tale overtones and mythic structure. He realizes that this "social romance"'s simplicity, its resemblance if not kinship to the fairy tale, and, relatedly, its role of repository for the collective imaginary, memories, and values make the Ragged Dick story widely appealing, moreover, an ideal vehicle for casting—and castigating—a community's self-defining mythology. At the same time, this story falls into a class of its own. This is largely due to its oversaturation with a communal, "political" symbolism. An organizing idea or "monomyth" (Ramage 52) throughout American history, the Ragged Dick parable of socioeconomic achievement has come to define the national self. This image has been determinant in the rise of what I would call, following Paul Maltby, the "Grand American Narrative," or, in Coover's own words, "the Great American Dream" (*A Political Fable* 82). *The Public Burning* critiques the same symbolic narrative, and it does it by a rewriting of the Alger tale as a cold war story.

It is highly relevant that Alger is both the most successful American writer ever—reputed to have sold about 300,000,000 copies of his 135 books—*and* the author who has made the most important contribution to the production and circulation of the American narrative of success through his popular hero, whom Hugh Kenner calls the national "laureate of the paradigm of ascent" (20). Alger's works, especially the six novels in the *Ragged Dick* series (1868–1870), have greatly participated in the formation of the American "discourse" in a precise sense. They have structured this national discourse as a narrative of personal initiative, enterprise, financial responsibility, thrift, equal opportunity, hard-work ethic, education and self-education, and other similar values of Puritan-Calvinist and liberal extraction. True, Alger does not always coat these notions with their original, ethical-religious rhetoric (Lemeunier 128). But his stories do lay down one grand moral legitimation of the "vertical mobility" that other writers already had or would eventually identify as patent arrivism. Alger's stereotypical protagonist always makes it. His Ragged Dick, along with Tattered Tom, Paul the Peddler, Phil the Fiddler, and other street Arabs, bootblacks, and variously employed and self-employed big-city ragamuffins, invariably achieves what Alger's titles and subtitles transparently hint at: *Fame and Fortune*, *Struggling Upward*, *The Progress of Richard Hunter*, *Luck and Pluck*, *Rough and Ready*, *Risen from the Rank*, *Brave and Bold*, *Shifting for Himself*, *Helping Himself*, *Wait and Hope*, and so on. As Carol Nackenoff points out, Alger's heroes and the vocabulary he uses to account for their reenactment of the narrative of accomplishment have become "part of our language of discourse about social mobility and economic opportunity, about determination, self-reliance and success." In brief, Alger "is shorthand for someone who has risen through the ranks—the self-made man, against the odds." He appears "frequently associated with defense of capitalism and conservative values." As such, he supplies a "*form* of discourse" to advertise "strong-willed individuals who . . . triumph rather than engage in collective struggle" (3–4). Ragged Dick's upward move from homeless shoeblack to well-to-do citizen Richard Hunter does not menace the existing social order. His story romances social and economic ascent, cloaking it in a moral vocabulary and justifying it. However, as Dick tells a friend, "readin' and writing'" might help "[i]f my feller-citizens should want me to go to Congress some time" (Alger, *Struggling* 225).

Reading and writing do come in handy as Coover's retelling of Alger's tale takes Ragged Dick/Richard Hunter not only to Congress but also to the White House through *The Public Burning*'s central hero and narrator, Richard Nixon. This is a smooth albeit intertextual transition since Alger's hero personifies "the central myth of upward mobility, the belief that anyone (if not necessarily everyone) can rise from rags to riches, from log cabin to White House" (Beauchamp 324). Quite naturally, Dick Hunter pre-figures Dick Nixon, the "anxious conniver up the ranks" (Poirier 96), as much as Coover's protagonist re-figures Alger's. Both are moments in the incessant American narrative, *loci* of the same public rhetoric, and stages in the development of one dominant desire. They incorporate, we shall see, the same transhistorical Uncle Sam. Again, Alger's Dick is the sociological mold, historical forerunner, and embryonic "tiny story" or "shorthand" for Coover's Nixon and his novel. "Blowing up" the shorthand, *The Public Burning* takes on all values and discursive components enumerated above, using them to narrate a critical episode in the history of post–World War II America.

But why retell the Alger parable to chronicle one of the darkest McCarthyte episodes? Nackenoff's fine reading of the largely conservative annexation of this parable during the Reagan-Bush era (264–271) may again be helpful here. Without mentioning Coover, she suggests that an "Alger-centered discourse" is both a symptom of, and a political response to, times of change, disorientation, and crisis. Drawing from Lévi-Strauss's *Structural Anthropology*[4] and Clifford Geertz's research on "ideology as a cultural system," she contends that the Alger symbolic narrative fulfills a clear sociopolitical function. This narrative sounds reassuring. It purveys, apparently, a model people can supposedly duplicate easily, in their own lives, to overcome economic, cultural, or political frustrations. In fact, politicians have applied it as a kind of discursive balm on the Republic's wounds, scars, and differences in hopes to heal "conceptual contradictions" (265) and create political if not socioeconomic homogeneity. All in all, the Alger story stands out as an eminent consensus ploy of the "hegemonic discourse" (Maltby 103) public institutions have resorted to particularly during trying times—times of less comforting stories. In this view, Coover's choice seems very inspired. His narrative revision of the Ragged Dick tale is a most suitable vehicle for bringing out in bold the deep crisis breaking forth through the Rosenbergs affair. Rewriting *The Ragged Dick*, Coover intervenes, as a novelist and cultural critic, in that "discourse of America" in whose weaving the Alger fable has been so actively involved. After all, his Nixon claims more than once that he is an "Americanist" (LeClair, "Robert Coover" 17): not only a "good American," but also somebody who knows what America really is,[5] what stories "tell" it, and what stories should be "peddled" in its forums. It is at this point that Coover's credo fully makes sense: "[T]he fiction maker's function," he confesses, "is to furnish better fiction with which we can re-form our notions of things" (Gado 149–50). Re-formulating Alger, Coover attempts to re-form our notion of things American.

ALGER'S "WRONG TURN": COOVER'S PERSONAS AND ALEGERSQUE IMPERSONATIONS

Nobody understands *history*! (Coover, *The Universal Baseball Association* 234)

Coover is only a more recent in a long series of writers who have taken up Alger's story. Retracing the venerable history of the Ragged Dick tale's "appropriations," Nackenoff reminds us that the appropriators have almost never respectfully "imitated" it. "The stories of this minor American novelist and story writer," she points out, "have been debunked, maligned, and lampooned." Yet Alger's work keeps fascinating various twentieth-century audiences, from general readers to politicians, televangelists, and writers such as Jack London, Carl Sandburg, Ernest Hemingway, F. Scott Fitzgerald, and others (Beauchamp 325). Steven Weisenburger has completed this list with largely satiric responses by Nathanael West (*A Cool Million*), Charles Wright (*The Wig: A Mirror Image*), Ishmael Reed (*The Freelance Pallbearers*), mentioning Alger in conjunction with Coover's novel by reference to the reviews the novel received right after its publication (*Fables* 286–87).[6]

Coover's book presents us with the most intensive and extensive rewrite of the Alger story in the entire history of American literature. Accordingly, it is worthwhile looking at *The Public Burning* as a detailed amplification and critical revision of what Jackson I. Cope calls the Algeresque narrative "summary" (112) and Coover identifies as "generative" tropes or "stories." We are confronted here with a wholesale, primarily parodic and satiric rewriting that bears upon the entire text, its most significant episodes, characters, and cultural-ideological stakes—not just upon the "Ragged Dick at the White House" analogy. The entire novel may be read as another exemplary and multiple tale of incorporation in that it both gives a new narrative body to the Algeresque text and, equally intriguing, tells a story where bodies are transformed, de-corporated (destroyed, burned *coram populo*) and reincorporated—after all, the famous buggery scene at the end yields an "Uncle Sam (Re)Incorporated" as Nixon. The latter becomes a true "embodiment of the American spirit" (Guzlowski 62) only insofar as he comes to be a "receptacle" (Coover, *The Public Burning* 161) and materialization of the national "Host," to give a new and scarcely more awe-inspiring body to the "comic-book embodiment of the dominant ideology of American society" (Waugh, *Metafiction* 106). The whole novel narrates, I might say, the progress of such an incorporation: Nixon's vice presidency is one long preparation for the final scene, where, ironically enough, Nixon takes in Uncle Sam's spirit through the most physical contact possible.

"[Was] Eisenhower's life in danger? Was the Incarnation to come to me even sooner than I had expected?" (Coover, *The Public Burning* 296), he asks himself around the middle of the novel. By that time, Coover's incorporating design and its critical purpose should have become clear to the reader. Ethel and Julius Rosenberg's arrest and trial, the national debate around them, the main institutions' response to the case, and media reports piece together a story that the author reads as a symbolic chapter of the narrative of "America." The Rosenbergs episode brings forward the latter's language, axial images, and myths. In its own way, the affair is another "incorporating" instance as it violently gives shape and body to an otherwise less substantial if all-pervasive rhetoric. Nixon comes off, in this regard, as both agent and medium, instantiation of, and mouthpiece for a talk, mentality, and culture transcending his individual self. In brief, he is a historical character as much as a storytelling device, but not just because he narrates some chapters in Coover's book. He marks a moment in the Hegelian story of the national spirit's progress, a grotesque yet also all-too-human installment in the teleological unfolding of America's *roman-feuilleton*.

Nixon revisits this *roman* as a "series" of "transubstantiations" going back to the original "crackle of metamorphosis" (83). As we may expect, Uncle Sam's "Primordial Incarnation" was George Washington, to reach a rather frail "transmutation" (83) in Eisenhower. It was, for sure, Washington who opened up the first chapter in the American narrative as secular enactment of a "providential agency" (8). This agency was pleased, Coover's Nixonian voice announces, to throw up, and work "rhetorically" through, figures and patterns which, "as pattern, . . . turn and operate the world" (311). Furthermore, Coover's authorial narrator insists repeatedly that these patterns and their historical embodiments push the Age of Reason's ideology of Enlightenment (8), stressing the also characteristically Algeresque "Doctrine of Self-Determination and Free Will" (8). "Called forth" (8) by God, the "American miracle" assumed the role to carry out modernity's utopian project of giving a body (politic) to these absolute values (8–9).

The Public Burning effects a metanarrative critique of this "inevitable" story by playing Nixon's plural incorporations against each other. Essentially, Coover pits Nixon-as-Ragged Dick against Nixon-as-Uncle Sam to unmask the latter's triumphalist- national(istic)-"imperialist" narrative and ideology as a national narrative constituted around more cynical albeit less apparent notions such as greed, power thirst, and arrivism. No doubt, Coover intently rereads the Ragged Dick parable against its rosy, innocent grain. His parody retools Alger's eulogy of honest hard work as manipulative rhetoric blanketing over something like Balzacian heroes' immorality. To be sure, it is a fairly anti-Algeresque Richard Hunter who hunts for power in *The Public Burning*. But, as Nixon's political obsessions belabor issues of power at play in Alger (Nackenoff 8), Coover pins down a political continuity in Sam Slick's, the "Yankee Peddler's" (6), Nixonian heir and in Nixon's simultaneous intertextual reincorporation of Ragged Dick. Thus, we can only infer that the latter is in fact a predominantly socioeconomic facet of the politically full-fledged Uncle Sam and his cold war's favorite "proxy."

While most critics have in passing signaled the parallels Nixon himself draws between his boyhood and Ragged Dick's, it is worth insisting that the Alger story supplies the intertextual lens through which Nixon himself reconstructs his biography in the first-person, flash-back chapters of the novel. If the real Nixon rewrote, as "[an]other Poor Richard," as Uncle Sam calls him (96), Ben Franklin's *Poor Richard's Almanac* in the navy (Poirier 100), Coover's narrating protagonist read Alger avidly as a boy (*The Public Burning* 181–82). That reading was so consequential that the reader has become—has read himself into—a post–World War II Richard Hunter. And now, he chooses the "struggling upwards" narrative as a form for recalling, reshaping, and putting together, in a critical time for himself and America alike, "the reassuring pictures from my own past, my boyhood vibrating in me like an old movie" (174), a film tellingly turning up Algeresque moments of his Yorba Linda years of hard work. Likewise, his childhood readings also fashion his

Vaudevillelike—"soap opera," Nixon says (434)—encounter with Ethel Rosenberg at Sing Sing, where both play Horatio Alger roles (Ramage 60). When Ethel theatrically turns down his invitation to "confess," he suspects her of dramatizing "[s]ome Horatio Alger novel" (Coover, *The Public Burning* 434). "In the Horatio Alger novels," Nixon goes on,

> the heroines were always saved at last by rich uncles. Ethel didn't have a rich uncle. Neither did I, growing up—except for Grandpa Milhaus's money which put me through school, we were as poor as any other middle-class family—but late I got adopted. By teachers, businessmen, Herbert Hoover, eventually Uncle Sam himself. I was successful with old men, she wasn't. Was this it, then? Was this the reason that that serious little curly-headed girl watering an apple seed in a prison exercise yard was going to get 2000 volts bolted through her brain tonight? A missing character, a lost "closing scene"? Or had the story taken a wrong turn somewhere, putting her beyond the reach of rich uncles? (315)

The passage ranks among countless others calling for a rereading of Coover's novel as a rewriting of the Alger narrative. Conspicuously, Nixon measures himself and other characters against the Ragged Dick model. He explains his success through an almost literal emulation of this model, relentlessly striving to fit the "struggling upwards" scheme with a vengeance. "*Time* has said," he tells us, "that I've had a 'Horatio Alger-like career, but not even Horatio Alger could have dreamed up a life so American—in the best sense—as mine" (295). Unlike Nixon's, the "story" of "losers" such as the Rosenbergs has somewhere taken a "wrong turn." Nixon does not mistake, as the Rosenbergs supposedly have, poverty and injustice for the "parents of revolutionary idealism" (182). For him and his family hardship does not lead to "resentment"; following Alger's New York books (181), where the Rosenbergs may have applied *Capital*, Nixon just "gets busy" and embarks upon lifelong endeavors of "self-improvement" through "self-respect, self-regulation, self-restraint, and self-attainment" (182), efforts eventually rewarded by generous patrons and, of course, by his "incarnation" of, and "possession" by, Uncle Sam himself.

An intertextual embodiment in whose concoction the "Emersonian man," Fitzgerald's Gatsby, Faulkner's Sutpen, Dickens's Uriah Heep, Fenimore Cooper's Deerslayer, and Alger's Ragged Dick seem to have pitched in (Poirier 102), the Nixon of *The Public Burning* comes off first and foremost as a clone of the latter. What is more, he judges his cronies, foes, and contemporaries generally by how closely their biographies measure up to the Algeresque/all-American narrative. As above, where Nixon compares his own story to Ethel's, this pattern is all-embracing. Thus, Julius Rosenberg also cuts, in Nixon's account, a potentially Nixonian—because pointedly Ragged Dicklike—figure. "Like all American boys," Nixon tells us, "I used to dream of rescuing a generous millionaire from being robbed and murdered by a thug and receiving a thousand-dollar reward that propelled me into fame and fortune, being named in the rich man's will and perhaps even marrying his daughter, who was disguised as a poor girl selling apples on the street corner" (310). Or, if characters like Jack Kennedy prove unfit to "sell penny candy and rescue millionaires like the rest of us" (345), they are still categorized—and thus delegitimated—through precise allusions and references to Alger texts. Elsewhere, Uncle Sam tells Nixon that Julius was also a reader of Horatio Alger (62, 92). Intriguingly enough, while trying to evade the demonstrators heading for the Supreme Court, Nixon runs down a boy who looks "like the waifs out of those Horatio Alger novels" (209) but whose "haunting" face (210) belongs to Ethel. Also, Harry Rosenberg, Julius's father, was a store owner and, to Nixon, "something out of a Horatio Alger story" (129), head of a "true Horatio Alger family" (304)—and the list can go on and on to include almost everybody and everything in the novel: Julius's and Ethel's voices, which evoke during the trial testimonies "the sour babble of steerage passengers and backpack peddlers" (128); their son, Nixon wonders, possibly "on his way to a Horatio Alger-like career" (297); the rather obscure Wendell, "The Barefooted Boy from Wall Street," former Republican Presidential nominee—another pathetic "loser" (54); Joseph McCarthy, who, like Nixon, worked as a poor boy in grocery stores (56); Irving Kaufman, the "Boy Prosecutor" (118); Alger Hiss, "the millionaire gone sour in the Horatio Alger novels, the nephew trying to con his rich uncle out of his cousin's inheritance, the wily traitor in a plain respectable man's troubled business" (303–4); Eisenhower and Herbert Hoover, who, also much like Nixon, get to incarnate Uncle Sam precisely because their talk of "rags to riches," "free enterprise" (231), "rugged individualism," and "economic liberty" (259) recuperates the Algeresque ideology; the ragged panhandler, an "anti-Horatio Alger figure" that bums about Times Square as to suggest "the inner failure that Nixon struggles to overcome through diligent study and hard work" (Gallo 44), and so on.

But what makes Nixon a more complex fictional incorporation is the interesting authorial function the writer daringly assigns him. As Daniel E. Frick has observed, "Coover casts the most infamous politician in contemporary American history as a version of his authorial persona." It would follow that Nixon "should be understood as the vehicle by which Coover confronts his marginalized cultural status as a writer of politically oppositional texts" (82). But if Nixon is genuinely an authorial mouthpiece, he does more, it seems to me, than just foreground Coover's authorial "powerlessness" (83). To this compound sort of narrative delegation and to the political and cultural-ideological problems with which it seems to be tied up I would like to turn at the end of my discussion of Coover's novel.

THE PUBLIC BURNING OF THE PUBLIC SPHERE

"Unlikely" narrator as he may be (Ross, *No Respect* 40), Nixon partakes in the critique of the same "discourse" he simultaneously bodies forth and upholds. He is the voice within the story itself, the "diegetic" mask under which Coover undercuts the Enlightenment teleology of the "Grand American Narrative." "Enlightenment or not, we still have our roots in the Dark Ages" (*The Public Burning* 58), Nixon blurts out, anticipating the author's interpretation of the Rosenbergs' execution as a dramatic, exorcising ritual symbolically performed—in a truly theatrical sense, I might add—in New York's Times Square, "the "Entertainment Capital of America" (164) and "ritual center of the Western World" (166). Now, Coover uses Nixon's viewpoint to flesh out his own critique of national history and history generally. In terms of this critique, the Ragged Dick tale alongside its political underpinnings and modernity's narrative of emancipation, progress, rationality, and individual agency are covering up, palimpsestlike,[7] a more cynical story where "agents" turn out to be just "actors" who are assigned parts in a far less idealistic and politically neutral "plot" or "script." The Rosenbergs scandal, Coover claims, perfectly illustrates the duplicity of the historical theory implicit in official renditions of the American story. "Not only was everybody in this case," he has Nixon avow, "from the Judge on down—indeed, just about everyone in the nation, in and out of government, myself included—behaving like actors caught up in a play, but we all seemed moreover to be aware of just what we were doing and at the same time of our inability, committed as we were to some higher purpose, some larger script as it were, to do otherwise" (117). The Rosenbergs, too, he goes on, "seemed to be swept up in this sense of an embracing and compelling drama, speaking in their letters of sinister 'plots' and worldwide 'themes' and 'setting the stage' and playing the parts they had been—rightly or wrongly—cast for 'with honor and dignity'" (117). This is just one example of Nixon's lucid moments, where "so-called history" (193) reveals to him as "construct," immanent (191) and "manipulated language" (136), carnivalesque[8] story or "high drama of building a nation and taking over the world" (424). And the Rosenbergs episode cannot but reproduce the dramatic structure of the frame play, again, "the larger drama," with Nixon as "stage manager" (120). Within this spectacle, the Rosenbergs' performance stages its own combination of farce, tragedy, melodrama, soap opera, and stand-up routine.

Not unlike *Ragtime*, almost everybody in the novel is putting on various acts, beginning with Nixon. Coover depicts him as an actor throughout his life. A champion of "calculated self-exposure," his smart "act" is an intensely rehearsed "disavowal of acting" (Poirier 100) whose vocal emphasis on honesty parodically recalls Ragged Dick's obsession with "grow[ing] up 'spectable" (Alger, *Fame* 220). But "Tricky Dick" (Coover, *The Public Burning* 33) is a "player" as much as Ragged Dick's righteousness does not rule out true passion for impersonations, tricks, games, puns, shows, as well as worrying about the "appearances," the "public image" (Nackenoff 8). Coover plays upon this fixation while tackling Nixonite "respectability" (Beauchamp 342) by determining it as "'spectability," as penchant for spectacle, which earns, if not "respect" from spectators, then interest in the performer's self-exposing debauchery. It is this "spectable" self-exposure—which Coover often likes to take literally—that the Checkers speech (*The Public Burning* 317) exemplifies.

But Pat, Nixon's wife, and Ola, former girlfriend from back at Whittier, have also a taste for theatrics (299). Ethel, in her turn, no less dreams of a glamorous life, possibly a Hollywood career. Both Julius and she are addicted to "role-playing" (128), although theirs and their lawyers' is somewhat of an "amateurish," "improvisation theater" (121), pathetically hollow "in the midst of a carefully rehearsed professional drama" (121). All of them, victims and executioners, puppets and the public alike are "forms," episodes, and "parts" (in all senses) of the great national performance of impersonation which *The Public Burning* incorporates. The performance is naturally composed, directed, and acted out by an ever metamorphotic Uncle Sam also known as "the American Autolycus" for his "cunning powers of conjuration, transmutation, and magical consumption" (7).

This popular show and entertainment in general, Coover suggests, erode the "public sphere" where an issue such as the Rosenbergs case might have been handled more responsibly. In this respect, the novel dramatizes not only the public(ized) execution of the "spies." Their "burning" also enacts a public burning of the public sphere, as it were. That is, it enacts the collapse of the public sphere by showing how, in Habermas's words, "the critical reasoning of private persons on political issues" (*Structural Transformation* 29) has been displaced by the popular, fetishizing representation of these issues. Significantly, the novel stresses the public, publicity, public events, people, styles, and reactions, finally the Rosenbergs' hysterically publicized execution. In doing so, it reveals how rational exchange is being superseded by ritualic, carnivalesque mediatization. The novel spotlights Times Square as a mediatic space producing "ready-made" opinions and thereby eroding the very notion of "agora," of the public space understood as a "forum of discussion" (51) where actual public opinion comes forth. In Coover, the public is no longer a communication medium, an arena of collective debate, exchange, and criticism. "Largely an effect of the general structure of communication" (Maltby 121), the public becomes a form of communal "blindness" and good example of what Coover sees as bankruptcy of the Enlightenment's rational discourse.

Habermas has specifically insisted that the emergence of the bourgeois public sphere was a way of "putting reason to use . . . against state-governed publicity" (*Structural Transformation* 35). Coover's novel foregrounds the reversal of the sociocultural process that had led to the rise of the public sphere as a springboard of a "public opinion" capable of "rational-critical debate" (51) and thus of "criticism and control of organized state authority" (Habermas, *Jürgen Habermas* 231). Both Habermas and Coover hold pop culture and its apparatus of commodification, distribution, and consumption accountable for the supplanting of "critical publicity" by a "manipulative publicity" (178) that sells both "public and private mythologies" as natural objects.[9] Resulting from this substitution is a "public sphere" acting as a "platform for advertising" highly instrumental in the "engineering of consent" and its corollary, the "readiness to assent" (201).

This is Coover's point: the Rosenbergs crisis was a crisis of the American consensual narrative and its repertoire of ideas and images of "agreement." The Ragged Dick story has again proven a useful model as Alger instantiates a "rite of passage" from which not only enterprising heroes spring and triumph, but also the Republic itself (Nackenoff 271). Alger's notion of publicness and communality furnishes a "model" for the healing of the wounds inflicted to the body politic by the Rosenbergs' "dissent." Thus, Coover's Nixon amplifies to grotesque proportions Ragged Dick's ongoing show of "virtuous publicity" (Hendler 419), the permanent "theatrical performance" (422) that always takes place before, or implies, an audience, an art of impersonations, ultimately "a public stage" (423). If Alger marks an important point "in the struggle to shape the American public sphere" (416), Coover's revisitation of Alger belongs to another moment: a moment of crisis of this sphere and of the cultural stories shaping it.

CHAPTER 3

Transcendentalist Rewrites: Paul Auster and the "National Machine"

> I almost invariably appropriate scenes and situations from a book and graft them onto my own experiences—or vice versa . . . I learned that books are never finished, that it is possible for stories to go on writing themselves without an author. (Auster, *The Art of Hunger* 272, 358)

THE SOCIAL "OTHER": TRANSPOSITIONS AND DUPLICATIONS

Commenting on Laura Riding's work, Auster proposes that the poem must be "a going-toward, a moving toward the Other" (*The Art of Hunger* 22). This observation applies to Auster himself. His fiction is "a moving toward the Other" in that it uncovers forms of "otherness" the American mythology of success, affluence, and social homogeneity has overshadowed: "the downtrodden, the dispossessed, the underdogs of the social order" (Auster, *Hand to Mouth* 13). Defying this mythology in *The New York Trilogy* (*City of Glass*, *Ghosts*, and *The Locked Room*, published between 1985 and 1986), *In the Country of Last Things* (1987), *Moon Palace* (1989), *The Music of Chance* (1990), *Mr. Vertigo* (1994), and *Timbuktu* (1999), Auster "sanctif[ies] failure" (*Hand to Mouth* 38). "Challeng[ing] the American way," as Marco Fogg, the protagonist of *Moon Palace*, puts it (60), Auster critiques, like Coover, the prevailing narrative of social Darwinism and thus makes a "powerful case against materialism" (*Hand to Mouth* 11). While Coover's characters grotesquely rehearse this narrative, Auster's skew it, embarking on a story that carries them toward the other and a "higher stage of consciousness" (*Moon Palace* 61).

Some of us, Auster avers, are "born into a state of *otherness*" (*The Art of Hunger* 42); others, his own characters among them, need to go through a "spiritual initiation" (*Moon Palace* 61). They take up unusual ways of living: "dangerously" and on the run, on the outside and outside institutions, families, or careers. This is how they become, Fogg tells us, "an instrument of sabotage, a loose part in the national machine, a misfit whose job was to gum up the works." "No one," he goes on, "could look at me without feeling shame or anger or pity. I was living proof that the system had failed, that the smug, overfed land of plenty was finally cracking apart" (61). Jamming the "national machine," people like Fogg thwart the social narrative woven by it: M. S. Fogg turns into a "glitch" type of text, a "MS" of sorts writing itself into—and against—the dominant one (Weisenburger, "Inside *Moon Palace*" 130). As we noticed apropos of Coover's revision of Alger, in this fantasy story a youngster's (American) dream routinely comes true. This tale typically stresses progress, gain, surplus, materialism, accumulation, production (and sustained consumption), domination, "outward," socially aggressive individualism, security, stability, conformism, structure, as well as cultural and ethnic homogeneity. Further, it emphasizes them over deprivation, dinginess, "hand-to-mouth" life, slack, waste, loss, insecurity, haphazard, mobility, rambling, "inward," philosophical individualism, heterogeneity, and resistance. But Auster queries the values privileged by this set narrative. He sheds light on the blind spots of the "master" tale and reveals how it has estranged us from key aspects of life, cutting us off from "others"—from nature, beauty, people, and ultimately even from ourselves. To reestablish this vital bond, he suggests, the tale must be retold.

Auster does retell it, inventing, like Doctorow and Coover, an other to it. His alternative, too, brings into play literary rewriting. Usually, critics have seized rewriting in Auster as postmodern revision of genre conventions. They have pointed out the "re-writing and deconstruction of the traditional detective story" (Herzogenrath 27) in the "antidetective" novels of *The New York Trilogy*; the use of the logbook, the diary, the travel and "quest" narrative (*Moon Palace*, *Leviathan*, *Timbuktu*), the picaresque novel and the *Bildungsroman* (*Mr. Vertigo*, *Moon Palace*); the manipulation of "the bare-bone narrativ[e]" (*The Art of Hunger* 304) of the fairy tale (*Mr. Vertigo*) and, in relation to it, of utopian-dystopian tradition (*In the Country of Last Things*). What I want to discuss, though, is how Auster handles *certain texts* by a fairly homogeneous category of nineteenth-century American writers, primarily Poe, Hawthorne, and Thoreau. For it is through a dialogue with their works that Auster retells the "national narrative" and "retools" the "machine" that produces it.

Doctorow's rewriting yields, we noted, elaborated, "performative" parallelisms; Coover's parodically deploys a transhistorical "micronarrative" or theme and makes plain its source; akin to Doctorow's analogical reembodiments, Auster's rewriting in its turn works chiefly through conspicuous transfers and transpositions of characters and situations. It "doubles" the rewritten, nineteenth-century text—entirely or in part—in contemporary, unwonted settings at the same time that it methodically labors the complex motif of the "double." Further, Auster's narrative sets up a homology of "doubling" as (re)writing form and the double as motif, welds them together and then weaves them into a renarrating mechanism where, showed off or alluded to here and there, the "mirroring" of the original generally steers clear of parodic or ironic treatment. Similarly, while both Coover's and Auster's rewritings sap the Alger parable, the former does it directly; the latter, by "doubling" Poe, Hawthorne, Thoreau, Melville, and others. Let us look at *The New York Trilogy* and see how this rewriting-as-doubling operates.

THE TEXTUAL DOUBLE: (RE)VISITING POELAND

> What interested him about the stories he wrote was not their relation to the world but their relation to other stories. (Auster, *City of Glass*, *The New York Trilogy* 8)

In *Timbuktu*, Willy Christmas, a down-and-out, moribund writer, collapses in front of Edgar Allan Poe's Baltimore house. Our hero will pass away before long. For the moment, though, he is happy to be back "home again"—if not in Poland, where his Jewish parents came from, then in "Poe-land," the country of "the great forebear and daddy of all us Yankee scribes" (45). In *Timbuktu* and earlier novels, Poe-land represents not only the fictional kingdom of Poe, but also the realm of American letters, of literature generally. Auster resembles his hero in that he, the novelist, keeps returning to this place as his writing itself turns to past writings. Conversely, Willy is his author's alter-ego, his double, if not "Auster/(the)author himself," as the autobiographic *Hand to Mouth*, *The Invention of Solitude*, and "The Red Notebook" apparently imply. In fact, as to confirm our suspicion, Willy refers to a former college roommate named Paul "Anster, [or] Omster" (*Timbuktu* 64–65), showcasing a self-referential ploy Auster routinely uses in *The New York Trilogy*.

The first in this series, *City of Glass* starts with an eye-catching inscription of Auster's trademark "double" signature: the "imprint" of Poe and, visibly cross-stitched into a story that unfolds under the sign(ature) of the former Baltimore resident, Auster's own. Resulting from this,

Auster's "glassy" text develops an *emboîtement* structure (Couturier 77): stories embedded within stories and authorial personas alongside authorial personas in an endless, befuddlingly specular play of analogies, reflections, and reappearances of various *Doppelgängers*.

Auster's protagonist, Daniel Quinn, to begin with, is an author of mystery novels and Auster's omnipresent "intrafictional" alias. Auster gives Quinn's name to several characters in *The Locked Room*, *Mr. Vertigo*, *In the Country of Last Things*, and elsewhere, making him an Austerian/authorial index: a "marker" of his fictional territory and the allusive—and self-allusive—games he plays with us. But, again, this signature writes itself over, and across, other authorship marks as the hero's initials point to at least two different—and real—authors. David B. Quinn, a reputed historian, is one. He has contributions on early America, colonialism, and the evolution of navigation, fields and events to which Auster comes back time and again by insistent references to Livingstone, Marco Polo, Phileas Fogg (Jules Vernes's hero in *Around the World in 80 Days*), and, quite obsessively, Sir Walter Raleigh—Auster's characters bear names such as Marco Fogg, Walter Claireborne Rawley (*Mr. Vertigo*), and Mr. Reilly (*In the Country of Last Things*). The other reference is Don Quixote. A major presence in many of Auster's books from *City of Glass* to *Timbuktu*, where Willy and his dog send us to Cervantes's human and animal characters,[10] the *Don Quixote* analogy is a significant intertext in *City of Glass*. After being mistaken for a detective named Paul Auster, Quinn gets to meet Auster only to discover that the private eye is a writer. At the time of the encounter, he works on an essay on *Don Quixote*, which happens to be one of Quinn's favorite books. Auster's essay focuses on "the authorship of the book" (*The New York Trilogy* 116), dwelling upon "the book inside the book Cervantes wrote," the ploy of the "discovered" manuscript (117).

Books inside books and their writers behind (or inside, rather?) other writers; stories tightly swathed in more stories: "the question is the story itself" (3). For what is at issue here, I think, is the story's palimpsestlike architecture and the literary archaeologist or, even better, the learned detective we must become to respond to the story successfully. No doubt, if "the writer and the detective are interchangeable," as Quinn intimates, then the reader, too, must put on the private eye's hat (9–10) because, according to Auster, "it's the reader who writes the book and not the writer" (*The Art of Hunger* 272). But if this holds true, then what kind of "case" are we on when we find out that our writer/detective is not interested in his own cases'/stories' "relation to the world but their relation to other stories" (*The New York Trilogy* 8)? What sort of "lead" is this, and why do most of those "stories" lead us to Poe? Auster is highlighting the Poe connection as he informs us that Quinn himself "plays" both Auster and Poe—plays *the* author and *two* authors—simultaneously. Quinn "imagin[es] himself as Auster," learns how to see his surroundings "through Auster's eyes" (63), indeed, how "to be Auster" (75), at the same time that he practically calls himself Poe by publishing under the pseudonym William Wilson (3). This mix-up à la Philip Roth's *Operation Shylock* may be based on real incidents in Auster's life (*The Art of Hunger* 342, 358–59). Yet it is all the more remarkable that the writer recounts those episodes by recourse to Poe's detective-readers and the ultimate tale of doubling, "William Wilson."

Playing along—playing "Auster-the-detective" and also replaying various Poesque scenarios of pursuit[11]—Quinn tails a former Columbia professor, Peter Stillman, throughout New York. Thus, another double obtains, with Quinn as the professor's shadow. But the doubling games do not stop here. Peter Stillman is an intertextual double in his own right. His name recalls Adelbert von Chamisso's shadowless vagrant from the 1814 novella *Peter Schlemihl's wundersame Geschichte*. In fact, through Poe, all of Auster's twins, aliases, and counterparts—detectives, writers, artists, anonymous drifters—carry on *de facto* the venerable tradition of the double running from Greek tragedy and Plautus's *Menaechmi* through *Don Quixote* and the Don Juan figure to peak with German romantics such as Jean Paul Richter (who coined the term *Doppelgänger*) and continue with late Victorians like Robert Louis Stevenson, moderns such as Wilde, Mann, Beckett, Borges, and their postmodern heirs.

The latter have been no less taken with the theme, and for good reason. Gordon E. Slethaug explains, "In denying spiritual and psychological completeness or transhistorical, permanent meaning, postmodern authors of the double often make assumptions about culture in general, for personal identity is caught up in the relationship between self and culture, self and history, self and language" (5). To illustrate his thesis, Slethaug focuses on Nabokov, Pynchon, Hawkes, Barth, Brautigan, and Federman, and their novels do back up his argument on identity, language, and culture in postmodernism. However, Auster's fiction—which Slethaug does not discuss—takes a slightly different approach to the double theme. The difference, I think, has to do with the social criticism of rewriting in Auster. Doubling Poe's double(s), "wrapping" his stories and characters in other stories and characters, Auster's "fiction of the double" does raise the questions Slethaug mentions. But it goes beyond the deconstruction of the modern notion of selfhood and, subsequently, of the literary character as mimesis. Karl Miller has observed that the double "stands at the start of that cultivation of uncertainty by which the literature of the modern world has come to be distinguished" (viii).

This fully applies to Auster. His fiction of the double outlines a process of intellectual "growth," even "spiritual wholeness," that spurs yet ultimately overcomes initial blindness or uncertainty. Step by step, Auster's protagonists do learn something. They are dragged by their strange counterparts into a new world, and this is Auster's own way of "moving toward" new people and ways of being in the world—on its fringes, to be more precise.

On the fringes of life, Auster's characters have the revelation of the "other" and even turn into this other themselves. It is there that the writing of Auster's revisionist alternative narrative begins, in the provisional space of material disinterest, reserve, indigence, hunger, "social failure." There, the outer layers of life begin to peel away before the eyes of his heroes who become, like Fogg, "monk[s] seeking illumination" (*Moon Palace* 123). For the double is no ubiquous companion in Auster's work: the *Doppelgänger* may help us discover the benefits of solitude. Being by oneself, in an abandoned building or in a garbage-flooded alley, like Quinn, is being-with-one's-self in a very profound and decisive way. Seclusion opens up a meditative "site of inwardness," to use Auster's own phrase, and this alone allows us to come to grips with the meaning of our being. Thus, Auster's entire work could bear the title of his 1988 memoir, *The Invention of Solitude*. But, again, he is a rewriter who "invents" through others, beginning with Poe. The latter's doubles set off the move from self to other, from a literary form—the private eye—to an existentially charged, self-interrogative kind of writing, finally, from a sort of social narrative to its critical other.

Poe's magisterial spirit and his equivocal twins haunt Auster's entire trilogy. In *City of Glass*, Quinn explicitly recognizes Dupin as his master—and master double—when he tries to figure out the mysterious Peter Stillman, his "actual" double, and it is worth noting that *The Locked Room* also features a Stillman, whom the narrator pursues in Paris. For now, though, Quinn and his Stillman meet in New York on the edge of Riverside Park, where "Edgar Allan Poe had spent many long hours gazing out at the Hudson" and where "Quinn had often sat there himself" (*The New York Trilogy* 100). Also, he realizes that Stillman is, ironically, always on the move. His wanderings trace an "urban writing" on the New York City street map, parallel to the words he takes down in his red notebook. This writing reminds Quinn of "the concluding pages of *A. Gordon Pym* and the discovery of the strange hieroglyphs on the inner wall of the chasm—letters inscribed into the earth itself" (85). Following Stillman and his "writing," Quinn himself starts to write in his own "red notebook" (another Austerian/authorial clue), although it is "difficult to write without looking at the page, and he often discovered that he had written two or even three lines on top of each other, producing a jumbled, illegible palimpsest" (77). Quinn's palimpsest may be illegible; Auster's is less so. After all, as we learn in *The Locked Room*, "the distance between seeing and watching" can be "narrow[ed so that] the two acts [become] part of a single, unbroken gesture" (326). This fluid, ever reduplicating gesture tells a "see-through" story, and what we glimpse first through Auster's looking glass is, again, the specter of Poe. Quinn plays Auster as Auster plays—and rewrites—Poe. A pertinent reading of *The New York Trilogy* must account, to quote Quinn again, for "the strictures of that transformation" (75), for the phenomenology of narrative rewriting where authors revisit former authors.

An *être de papier* of sorts, Quinn hints from the outset at this multiply fictional status, at his being "work." "He stopped long ago," Auster writes, "thinking of himself as real. If he lived now in the world at all, it was only at one remove, through the imaginary person of Max Work" (10). Quinn identifies with his own fictional hero, detective Max Work—with his own work ultimately, and we are intrigued to see him become this work itself. Yet we must remember that this work is signed "Poe" (William Wilson). Hence Quinn unveils his derivative, textual—or rather intertextual—status, the part Auster assigns him in the rewriting drama of *City of Glass*. In an important sense, Quinn becomes work by re-working Poe's work, by doing *within the story* what his real author himself does *with the story*. Wherefore, Quinn "works" as both an "operator" and sign of writing and rewriting-as-doubling, through which Auster "transforms" Poe's stories into his own as well as lets us into this transformation. Further, if Quinn and W-/work come to form a single entity, the detective and the writer once again become, successively, simultaneously, and to our confusion, the same person:[12] "Private eye. The term held a triple meaning for Quinn. Not only was it the letter 'I,' standing for 'investigator,' it was 'I' in the upper case, the tiny life-bud buried in the body of the breathing itself. At the same time, it was also the physical eye of the writer, the eye of the man who looks out from himself into the world" (9–10).

This passage is key to grasping the Austerian dynamic of literary rewriting and ideological critique. Not only does the fragment reinforce the analogy of writing and "private investigation"; further, not only does it remind us that "writing is solitary business," as one of the detective-writers of *Ghosts* declares (209). It also underscores the philosophical and "critical" dimension of "detection." Naturally, the "private eye" first awakens to his own self-reflective "inwardness" and learns how to look "inside." But next he turns his eyes—a writer's eyes, Auster insists—to the outside world and asks it "to reveal itself." The two revelations go hand in hand. The question we ask ourselves calls upon us to pose the "world" a similar question. Talking about his hero's dilemma, Auster points out, "The question is who is who and whether or not we are who we think we are. The whole process that Quinn undergoes in that book—and the characters in the other two, as well—is one of stripping away the same barer condition in which we have to face up to who we are" (*The Art of Hunger* 270).

GHOST(S)WRITING

Playing upon the symmetries of the detective genre, Poe provides Auster with the basic *Doppelgänger* narrative "frame." In *City of Glass*, Auster helps us identify this model and its source easily by frequent references and allusions. Less noticeable in the other two novels of the *Trilogy*, the model remains equally determinant. In *Ghosts*, which reproduces more closely than the other two the "whodunit" recipe, characters bearing strange names such as *White*, *Brown*, *Gray*, *Green*, *Blue*, and *Black* form various couples, reflect each other like as many human mirrors, swap places fast so that the pursuer becomes the pursued, and so on. This also happens in the last novel of the *Trilogy*, *The Locked Room*, where the protagonist and Fanshawe restage the drama of the adversarial double from Poe's "William Wilson" (*The New York Trilogy* 317) and take turns in watching and tracking each other down.

Another complex figure and intertextual operator, Fanshawe carries us into a world where Poe's role decreases. To put it otherwise: through Fanshawe, Auster takes us inside the *Doppelgänger* frame. And what Poe's narrative model "enframes" is, we discover, just another intertextual domain: Hawthorne, Thoreau, Emerson, Melville, Whitman, chiefly figures of the transcendentalist canon. Similar to the twin detectives and writers of *Ghosts*, Fanshawe still reminds us of Poe. A beginner writer, he imitates Stevenson and Poe (*The New York Trilogy* 252) and reads before his classmates a "short detective novel . . . infinitely complex, with the outcome hinging on something like the confused identities of two sets of twins" (253). Predictably enough, Fanshawe becomes a rewriter himself, as Auster's narrator makes plain. Fanshawe's "notebooks," the usual Austerian/authorial clue, contain "a constant retelling" of "stories," "parables," and "little anecdotes" (299–300), including one that retells Poe's "The Pit and the Pendulum." As a "mature" (re)writer, though, both in his life and work—and in Auster they are, we know, quite synonymous—Fanshawe emulates Hawthorne. His name "quotes" the title of Hawthorne's *Fanshawe*, and some critics have gone so far as to call *The Locked Room* a "postmodern *Fanshawe*" (Alsen 240). Fanshawe is not only a double of William

Wilson—"There were times," the narrator recalls, "when little scenes would flash through my head—of strangling Fanshawe, of stabbing him, of shooting him in the heart," and so on (*The New York Trilogy* 317). He comes across as a full-fledged Hawthornian double, too, and in several ways. First, the character is a replica of Nathaniel Hawthorne himself. Auster's Fanshawe disowns his work, and in that he resembles Hawthorne,[13] who grew so ashamed of his 1828 romance that, as Millicent Bell reminds us, he forbade his friends to "mention his authorship" (Hawthorne, *Collected Novels* 1244). Second, he is not unlike Hawthorne's romantic recluse Fanshawe. The latter fell unhappily in love with Ellen Langton, and we should note that the sister of Auster's hero is also named Ellen, while Fanshawe's and, later on, the narrator's wife, is baptized Sophie, after Hawthorne's wife. When Fanshawe disappears—a symbolic leitmotif in Auster—Sophie hires one Quinn to find him. Quinn fails, which makes everybody assume that Fanshawe is dead. Before vanishing, Fanshawe designates the narrator, his childhood friend and well-connected penman himself, as his legatee. In this capacity, the narrator starts publishing Fanshawe's "posthumous" novels, poems, and plays, which turn out a success. Engrossed in his efforts to make Fanshawe's genius known, the narrator comes to comprehend that he has identified with—and begun to "double," repeat, in body and spirit—Fanshawe. The latter remains a "ghost I carr[y] around inside me" (*The New York Trilogy* 232).

A writer himself, the narrator had nourished, he tells us, "great hopes, thinking that I would become a novelist. . . . But time went on, and little by little I realized that this was not going to happen. I did not have such a book inside me" (244). Yet he does have something: Fanshawe's "ghost." And so, the ghost of Fanshawe, the ghost of Hawthorne and others alongside and inside him come back to haunt not only Fanshawe's legatee, but also the author and his writing, in an enlightening parallelism: "I realized," the narrator confesses, "that once all of Fanshawe's manuscripts have been published, it would be perfectly possible for me to write another book or two under his name—to do the work myself and yet pass it off as his" (236, 279). And *The Locked Room* does play upon the abysmal, unremittingly specular figure of pseudonymy we came across in *City of Glass*—William Wilson as Quinn as "Auster" as Auster as (a rewriter of) Poe. Actually, the publisher of Fanshawe's manuscripts suspects that the narrator is simply putting out his own work under the *nom de plume* of Fanshawe, signing his books "Hawthorne," much as Quinn signs them "Poe." And in fact, the narrator envisions further "Fanshawe" books based on the style the public has come to identify as Fanshawe's. But he need not be Fanshawe's posthumous ghostwriter—the ghostwriter of a ghost who himself used to do some ghostwriting on the side (241)—much as he agrees to become, before stunned readers and publishers, Fanshawe's "spokesman" (262) and "guardian of his work" (243). It is not necessary for him to rewrite Fanshawe simply because Auster does it himself. *The Locked Room* can be read as a thorough rewriting of Hawthorne—of *Fanshawe*, as I have suggested, but also of "Wakefield."[14]

Auster obstinately reworks the bizarre "disappearance-cum-watching-from-across-the-street" plot throughout his trilogy; but *Ghosts* tackles the Hawthornian intertext head on. Black tells Blue, the detective who is supposed to observe and report back on Black's own moves, about a Fanshawelike writer, "another ghost . . . shut himself up in his room" (208–209), Hawthorne himself, and about his Wakefield tale. This is another *mise en abyme* moment, since Black and Blue repeatedly rehash throughout the novel, together or separately, the Hawthornian story. There is more, though, to this self-reflective episode. There is, I mean, another Russian doll inside it; there are other ghosts inside Auster's ghostly literary references (Alsen 240). What actually prompts Black's minilecture on Hawthorne's "Wakefield" is Thoreau's visit to Whitman, which sets in motion another merry-go-round of the Austerian double. I will not get in all the details here. Suffice it to say that Thoreau comes, in Black's account, to see Whitman at his house in Brooklyn Heights on Orange Street, where the poet "handset the first edition of *Leaves of Grass* . . . in 1855" (Auster, *The New York Trilogy* 163). It is on the same street that Blue watches, à la Wakefield, Black, who lives across the street. Also here, Blue, dressed up like Whitman yet claiming to imitate the garb of a tramp of his boyhood, one Jimmy Rose—a transparent reference to Melville's short story (Alsen 242)—meets Black, while the specter of the Thoreau-Whitman meeting hovers above them. Whitman, we find out, is among Blue's favorite authors, along with Hawthorne (Auster, *The New York Trilogy* 219) and Melville. When Black is struck by the "remarkable resemblance" between Whitman and Blue, Blue replies that "every man has his double somewhere. I don't see why mine can't be a dead man" (205).

The "dead" twins of Auster's characters—their invisible literary doubles—surround and guide them as they guide our reading of Auster's novels. There are, truly, "ghosts all around us," as Blue points out (207), around and inside Auster's books: Poe and Emerson, the tutelar spirit of *Leviathan*; Melville and his Jimmy Rose, Bartleby, Ishmael, and Wellingborough Redburn. Like Quinn in *City of Glass*, Blue follows in the footsteps of Bartleby (63), and so does, incidentally, the learned Black; like Fanshawe in one of his "ghostly"—postdisappearance—letters to his executor, he could tell Blue, in jest, "[C]all me Redburn" (321). Or, like the executor himself, he could just as well go around introducing himself as "Herman Melville, an American sailor" (347). Yes, they are all here: Hawthorne, Whitman, all great spirits of transcendentalist writers, roaming about in Auster's books, pointedly resurrected or "doubled" by his rewrites. This uncanny return of the ghost writers nourishes and defines Auster's rewriting as ghostwriting. Not unlike the narrator in *The Locked Room*, Auster becomes the "ghostwriter" of transcendentalist tradition. If his characters mysteriously disappear, this is just to prompt the reappearance, through Auster's rewriting, of the great literary specters of the nineteenth century.

Auster's ghostwriting—through which the ghosts keep writing, continue, like Fanshawe, their work—entails a rewriting of the ghost, so to speak. Not only does Auster retell particular stories by Hawthorne or Melville. In all of these retellings we come back, again and again, as Eberhard Alsen insists, to one single topic: "self-imposed isolation," "individuals who remove themselves from the company of those closest to them" (244, 242). Now, the critic distinguishes a "romantic" and "idealistic" strain in the recurrent development of this topic. While the transcendentalist references and rewriting "models" crop up in Auster, I argue, though, that seclusion, solitude, meditative, fiercely protected, antimaterialistic anonymity—the whole Austerian problematic of "disappearance"—are themes of a larger, socially and culturally specific critique. Over and over, Auster suggests that this disappearance marks a polemical withdrawal from the social apparatus of mainstream America. Repeatedly reenacting this withdrawal scenario, Auster's novels tell an alternative story, which obtains by "doubling" Poe, Hawthorne, and Melville. But it is *The New York Trilogy*'s recuperation of Thoreau that brings out most forcefully the contestatory politics that drives Auster's spectral duplications.

MANHATTAN TRANSFERS: FROM POE TO WALDEN POND

> No truer American existed than Thoreau. (Emerson, Thoreau 269)
>
> Thoreau was the only man who could read the compass for us. (Auster, *Leviathan* 43)
>
> [A] calculated withdrawal, from the life of the Republic, from its machinery. (Pynchon, *The Crying of Lot 49* 101)

Thoreau's specter reigns supreme throughout Auster's fiction. With each new allusion to, or rewriting of, *Walden*, it becomes clearer that the genre of whodunit and Poe's detectives and doubles appeal to Auster insofar as they draw forth a broader, ideological narrative of withdrawal and self-centeredness as "sabotage" of the social machinery. Thoreau's uncompromising dissidence supplies the lens through which Auster reads the "American story." In *The Music of Chance*, for instance, *Walden*, along with Rousseau's germane *Confessions*, gives Jim Nashe a utopian model for his "separateness" and "loneliness" (201). Oddly enough, *Moon Palace*'s Marco Fogg relocates Thoreau's hermitage in Central Park. Also, *Leviathan*, a fairly intensive reworking of *Walden*, opens with an Emersonian epigraph deploring the "corruption of every State" and has a recluse writer, Sachs, as its protagonist. Either in his room or out in the Vermont woods, Sachs is searching for a "sanctuary of inwardness" (63), with Thoreau's *Walden* and the 1849 essay "Resistance to Civil Government" as guides. One of his books is titled *Leviathan*, alluding to Thomas Hobbes's 1651 political treatise; another is *The New Colossus*, a reference to the Statue of Liberty. Its characters represent, as we may expect in this Austerian book-in-the-book, "figures stolen from the pages of other novels" (41), and I might add that Sachs's book itself has been condemned for its alleged "anti-Americanism" (53).

It is *Ghosts* that chiefly summons the *spiritus rector* of Thoreau. Auster has acknowledged, in fact, "In *Ghosts*, the spirit of Thoreau is dominant. . . . The idea of living a solitary life, of living with a kind of monastic intensity—and all the dangers that entails. Walden Pond in the heart of the city. . . . The determination to reject everyday American life, to go against the grain, to discover a more solid foundation for oneself" (*The Art of Hunger* 271). Within, and building on, the Poesque detective story, on its apparent outwardly projected "watching" of the other, Auster chronicles the *Walden*like growth of critical self-consciousness, the inward turn of the gaze in solitude and outside a society that changes, as Thoreau proclaimed, people into machines (*Walden* 5). This Thoreauvian turn literalizes the self-specular signification embedded in the name of the private eye genre and puts a critical spin on it. As Denis Barone notes, Auster's critique suggests that the society of consumption has become a "consumed society" that "uses up" ("Introduction" 17) its members by forcing them into materialistic, "trivial pursuits." Foreseeing such developments, the "Economy" chapter of *Walden* offers that "[i]t would be some advantage to live a primitive and frontier life, though in the midst of an outward civilization, if only to learn what are the gross necessaries of life and what methods have been taken to obtain them" (11).

This is precisely what Auster's protagonists try to do: invent "primitive" ways of life amidst hectic, wearisome urban America and thus wedge their newly discovered "asociality" into the narrative of participation, progress, success, initiative, and social visibility. Again, most of these stories start out in the "action" mode of the detective genre but surreptitiously change into something else. Their heroes drop out of sight, give up their former routines and identities, move out of their homes to literally become homeless. They live "from hand to mouth" and take up a life of deprivation at the symbolically cynic end of society's "Diogenes Terminal," like Sam in *In the Country of Last Things*. Typically, the search for the missing other touches off a search for one's self. The other returns, according to the Poesque/Austerian logic of the double, the searcher his or her own image so much so that a character from *Ghosts*, Blue, feels that "he need merely look into himself" to know what the "other" is doing (*The New York Trilogy* 186). Detection and "tailing" in open spaces set off self-detection and self-understanding in the "solitude" where Blue understands that "he had nothing to fall back on anymore but himself" (139).

Of course, this greatly complicates the standard *policier*. And, let me stress it one more time, Auster uses Thoreau both to foreground and to bring this struggle to fruition. Allusions, references, paraphrases and unacknowledged quotes do the former; outright rewriting takes care of the latter. This process, through which, as Marc Chénetier writes, the hard-boiled goes very "soft-boiled" ("Paul Auster" 38), is fairly transparent in *Ghost*. In the novel, Blue is given an assignment that promises nothing else than boredom. But Black, whom he is watching, turns out to be an interesting type: a writer and an avid reader of *Walden*. Looking at somebody read, Blue gets sucked into a world different from anything he has experienced, "for," we are told, "to watch someone read and write is in effect to do nothing" (*The New York Trilogy* 166).

But is doing nothing a waste of time? Hardly: "suddenly, with the world as it were removed from him, with nothing much to see but a vague shadow by the name of Black," Blue "finds himself thinking about things that have never occurred to him before" (171). What the unsophisticated Blue discovers is "speculation," a new awareness of things and himself. "To speculate," Auster reminds us of the root meaning of the concept, comes "from the Latin speculatus, meaning to spy out, to observe, and [is] linked to the word speculum, meaning mirror or looking glass. For spying out at Black across the street, it is as though Blue were looking into a mirror, and instead of watching another, he finds that he is also watching himself. Life has slowed down so drastically for him that Blue is now able to see things that have previously escaped his attention" (171–72). Like Quinn living out the sudden revelation of clouds (140), Blue becomes aware of "the trajectory of the light," "the sun at certain hours," and a new pace of life.

These are "feelings" as much as allusions to *Walden*. In fact, only a few pages after this episode, as Blue more and more "mirrors" his double, he himself becomes a reader of Thoreau. In *Walden* Blue feels in an "alien world" at first, but this is because he reads as he used to live (and read): too fast and solely "fast" readings (newspapers, magazines, etc.). But he does not give up and has the revelation of "slow reading," as he has discovered "slow living." "Books must be read as deliberately and reservedly as they are written," Auster writes (*The New York Trilogy* 194) or rather quotes, without crediting, Thoreau's "Reading" chapter of *Walden* (80).[15] Books have to be read in a certain "spirit." What is more important, that "reading spirit"—pace, attitude, disposition, sensitivity—puts us on the way to our own spirit, self and self-understanding, and this is about to happen to Blue, changing his life forever (194–95), making him "essentially free" (200). Blue keeps reading *Walden*, copies down whole sentences in his notebook, where he is supposed to write his report on Black, and searches the meaning of his situation in a Thoreauvian passage such as this one: "We are not where we are . . . but in a false position. Through an infirmity of our natures, we suppose a case, and put ourselves into it, and hence are in two cases at the same time, and it is doubly difficult to get out" (200). Blue writes (down), possibly like Black himself (203), Thoreau; by implication, Auster writes *Ghosts* by rewriting *Walden*, by staging Blue's identity drama as a restaging of Thoreau's social critique. "[E]xud[ing] a sweet indifference to the world around him" (204), making everything, like Black, "part of a determined plan to remain alone" (211), Blue fancies himself another Thoreau, "somewhere else, faraway from here, walking through the woods and swinging an axe over his shoulder. Alone and free, his own man at last" (222). To be sure, Thoreau provides Auster with a way "out"—out of the reigning social narrative..

UNNAMABLE THOREAU

> My name is Paul Auster. This is not my real name. (Auster, *City of Glass*, *The New York Trilogy* 49)

In *City of Glass*, Peter Stillman assumes the name of one of his own "figments" (96), a character in a book he wrote before "disappearing": Henry Dark. Asked about his pseudonym, Stillman replies to Quinn that it refers to Humpty Dumpty, not to Henry David (Thoreau) as Quinn conjectures. Yet the latter's guess is not to be dismissed offhand either. We know that Stillman has published a book, *The Garden and the Tower: Early Visions of the New World*, that deals with utopianism and focuses, among others, on one Henry Dark, a late seventeenth-century Miltonian scholar and Puritan from Boston. Stillman himself implies that Dark and his "prelapsarian" nostalgia foreshadow Thoreau's individualist utopia. We should also recall that Fanshawe, a diehard recluse, lives in Boston under the alias of *H*enry *D*ark, and, finally, that one Denis Walden (249) is among the narrator's and Fanshawe's former friends.

But what does all this mean? What are we to make of Auster's "dark" Thoreau, of the obsessive references to the darkness surrounding Auster's heroes in their anxiety-ridden, half illuminating, half maddening solitude? It means, I propose, that Stillman, Fanshawe, Quinn, Sachs, Marco Stanley Fogg, Sam, and all who dramatize Thoreau's postures from *Walden*'s "Solitude" part embody and develop by recurring acts of rewriting Thoreau's "dark side," so to speak. Auster's is no idealistic return to transcendentalism and the romantic mythology of untainted nature. His Thoreau is, like his Poe, Melville, or Hawthorne, a strange one. He is so because, similar to other postmodern rewriters studied in this book, Auster revisits his transcendentalist "model" through more recent writers and philosophers of solitude and anxiety: Kierkegaard, Knut Hamsun, Kafka, and Beckett.

Auster's reiterated narratives of fasting and abstinence, with their emphasis on indigence and hunger as sources of illumination and models of resistance to the "feasting" society, tap in striking detail Hamsun's 1890 novel *Hunger*, which features a starving young writer wandering through the Norwegian city Christiania, and Kafka's famous short story, "The Hunger Artist." In effect, *The Art of Hunger* specifically expounds the outcasts' refusal to consume and thus participate in society's symbolic production-reproduction cycle. "To eat," Auster says in an essay on Louis Wolfson, "is a compromise, since it sustains him within the context of an already discredited and unacceptable world" (33). Thus fasting equals, the author insists apropos of Hamsun's hero, a refusal of a way of life if not of life simply put; ultimately, it is a political statement (13). Warding off the routine of consumption as self-preservation and preservation of a whole array of values and ideologies, the "art of hunger" is, Auster claims, an "existential art." As such, it brings forth an entire phenomenology of "need" (18), at the end of which, like Kafka, we may have a chance to find ourselves (25).

Kafka's "hungry artistry" (Sussman 284) and his motif of tragic-absurd transformation are profoundly instrumental to Auster's own "existential art." It seems to me, though, that Beckett's discourse of negativity, his characters' loneliness and ceaseless crawl "on [their] face[s]" in the "existential" "mud" of the "dark," to quote from his 1961 fiction *How It Is* (9, 11, 13), not least the illogisms and paralogisms plaguing his dramatis personas' language, have left a more enduring mark on Auster's writing. In actuality, commentators such as Stephen Bernstein have gone so far as to contend that "Auster's intertextual debt to Samuel

Beckett is as great as that he has to the American Renaissance" (100). And, I should add, Auster himself has corroborated this verdict (*The Art of Hunger* 265). Let me stress, though, the correlation between the two categories of models Bernstein mentions. For what rewriting essentially does in *The New York Trilogy* and elsewhere is "beckettianize" Thoreau. This rewriting effect is most visible in *City of Glass*, which, in a way, is Auster's response to Beckett's 1956 novel, *Malone Dies*. Like Beckett's narrating hero, Peter Stillman, son of Peter Stillman (the former Columbia faculty member and one of Quinn's doubles), sits "alone in the dark." His compulsory references to darkness and solitude during his meeting with Quinn—"Dark. Very dark. As dark as very dark. . . . An entire childhood spent in darkness" (19, 31)—when Quinn agrees to play Auster strikingly recall Beckett's themes, language, and the split identities of his characters. Like them, Stillman Jr. makes and succeedingly retracts his statements, names and unnames himself repeatedly: "I am Peter Stillman. This is not my real name" (21). In a manner of speaking, this is true: the son's name is and is not his since it essentially names, points to the father. But through the father—and in his name, as it were—P(eter) S(tillman) becomes Auster's post-scriptum to Peter Stillman as Henry Dark as H. D.'s (Thoreau's) precursor. For we find out that the father has conducted, à la Henry Dark, a most bizarre experiment on his son, forcing him to grow up "alone in the dark" in hopes to make him speak the pre-Babel, perfect language. Yet the son did not grow up in the Thoreauvian, revitalizing solitude, but in its opposite, the Beckettian darkness that shatters mind and language. The son speaks the language of Beckett's heroes, and thus Auster's writing itself, while minutely rewriting Thoreau, speaks in tongues: in the tongue of Beckett, that is. Tellingly, while writing in his "red notebook," Quinn-as-"Auster" reveals the Beckettian authorial identity through which, revisiting Thoreau's, Auster builds his own: "All I can say is this: listen to me. My name is Paul Auster. This is not my name" (49). If Thoreau is Auster's serene double, Beckett is the "dark" one. The former gives hope; the latter breaks it. The transcendentalist and absurdist, angst-ridden specters are locked onto each other and, together, into Auster's ghost-summoning, extensive rewriting of the "American story."

PART III

Rewriting Race: Models of "Cross-Fertilization" in African American Postmodernism

> For a critic of black literature to be unaware of the black tradition of figuration and its bearing upon a discrete black text is as serious a flaw as for that critic to be unaware of the texts in the Western tradition which the black text echoes, revises and extends. (Gates, *Black Literature* 6)

> We must read the texts that black writers inscribed between the lines of America's master texts. (Nielsen 24)

REPETITION, REINSCRIPTION, AND BLACK POSTMODERNISM

> [I]t requires courage to will repetition. (Kierkegaard 4–5)

> [R]epetition is a different form of displacement. (Ehrmann 246)

James A. Snead submits that "one may readily classify cultural forms according to whether they tend to admit or cover up the repeating constituents within them" ("Repetition" 60). Drawing from Nietzsche's *Will to Power*, the critic underscores cultures' inbuilt "cover-up" strategies. The latter have yielded "long-term *coverages*" of—and against, as Snead puts it—repetitions and borrowings. These "policies" have been so effective that oftentimes we forget that culture also means "the *culture* of culture," to wit, "a certain continuance in the nurture of those concepts and experiences that have helped or are helping to lend self-consciousness and awareness to a given group" (60). European cultures,

Snead goes on, tend to overlook or conceal this continuity when it gets in the way of "progress," whereas "black culture highlights the observance" of the repetition that brings about continuity (65). The "progressive" algorithm of repetition-as-accumulation-of-growth versus the nonprogressive model of repetition-as-circulation-and-flow would then make up the binary best contrasting the European and black modes of repetition, the distinctive repetitive mechanisms at play in whites' and blacks' definitions of self-awareness, identity, and sense of belonging.

Snead admits that Stravinsky's use of the "cut" or the whole post-Joycean line of intertextuality and rewriting ultimately bespeaks late twentieth-century European culture's "ongoing reconciliation with black culture" (75). But is Tom Stoppard's refusal to dissimulate his "travesty" of the Shakespearean sonnet truly tantamount to mere "circulation" (67) of Shakespeare? Or, do Ishmael Reed's novels, which Snead singles out as epitomes of black repetition, really body forth the nonprogressive model? If the ultimate upshot of repetition is to produce "difference" (Gates, *Black Literature* 10), then Reed showcases a project at odds with Snead's interpretation. Reed brings about such a difference with a vengeance, demonstrating that "black formal repetition always repeats with a difference, a black difference that manifests itself in specific language use" (Gates, *Signifying Monkey* xxii–xxiii). In so doing, he also participates in the repetition-as-progress cultural scenario because this enables him to imagine change.

Reed offers just one example, though probably one of the most salient, of an entire revisionist strain that has been developing within black literature since the late 60s. Focusing primarily on Reed, Charles Johnson, and younger novelist and cultural theorist Trey Ellis, I want to show how, while drawing upon traditionally African American strategies of appropriation and (re)circulation, their works reconstruct particular texts in both black and white traditions to ferret out narrative possibilities of configuring a new, "postmodern" African American identity. Engendered "as an 'optical' effect by the more profound game of difference and repetition" (Deleuze ixx), identity and its racial-cultural underpinnings are decomposed and recomposed in these works intertextually, through polemical revisitations of the literary past. Reed's, Johnson's, and Ellis's repetition of nineteenth-century narratives is empowering—a purchase of freedom via agonal rewriting of black and white traditions alike. These writers take on white authors, "repeat" them—as much as they revisit former slaves' autobiographies—by adapting traditionally vernacular repetitive/differentiating modes to locate black identity in history and lay down a strategy of *re*location.

This strategy may be seized as postmodern since it envisages this identity's reproduction and repositioning *through discourse*. According to bell hooks's view of "postmodern blackness," "part of our struggle for radical black subjectivity is the quest to find ways to construct self and identity that are oppositional and liberatory" (29). The black writers I deal with have been part of this quest and thus have been playing a major, albeit less conspicuous, role in the ongoing critique and fine-tuning of the postmodern paradigm. Cornel West has noted that this paradigm has been confined often within a solely aesthetic, "Eurocentric," and thereby "parochial" framework (88). By excluding or ignoring certain communities, this paradigm has reduced, West claims, the revisionary potential of postmodernism. Critics such as Phillip Brian Harper also contend that "the experiences of socially marginalized groups," while implicitly "inform[ing] the 'general' postmodern condition," have not been "accounted for in theorizations of it" (4). I hold with Harper's claim that the time has come for theory to acknowledge these experiences fully. I argue, in fact, that rewriting in recent African American literature is a literary-cultural practice that presents us with an ideal opportunity to recover and conceptualize such experiences. In Reed's, Johnson's, and Ellis's fictions and aesthetic concepts, I discern closely related, exemplary fashions of employing rewriting to fulfill the political reinscription of those others whose absence West makes out in the postmodern debate. Such "crossover" texts, along with works by Clarence Major, Toni Morrison, Alice Walker, Octavia Butler, Samuel R. Delany, Darius James, Terry McMillan, and other contemporary African American (re)writers, have marked off "sites of a potentially enabling yet resisting postmodernism" (West 96). These sites, I think, are no longer peripheral. They have taken center stage and force us to rethink postmodern aesthetics and politics.

CHAPTER 1

Outwriting: Ishmael Reed's Critical Reappropriations

MASTER OF THE CROSSROADS: SIGNIFYIN(G), REWRITING

Reed's 1976 novel *Flight to Canada* carries out a critical rewriting of nineteenth-century works, such as slave narratives, Harriet Beecher Stowe's *Uncle Tom's Cabin*, and especially Edgar Allan Poe's texts. Generally speaking, one can seize black rewriting as a particular form of "Signifyin(g)," whose original model Henry Louis Gates, Jr. has identified in Yoruba trickster myths and theorized as the most salient feature of African American literary history (*Signifying Monkey* 124). A method and oftentimes "explicit theme" (89) or trope for "formal revision, or intertextuality, in Afro-American literary tradition" (xxi), Signifyin(g) is truly the inner logic of this history. As such, it defines black writing as *re*writing: black "[w]riters Signify upon each other's texts by rewriting the received textual tradition" (124). Notably, Gates has acknowledged that his Signifyin(g) concept arose from a reading of Reed's novel *Mumbo Jumbo*. "Repeating received tropes and narrative strategies with a difference" (Gates, *Signifying Monkey* 217), Reed systematically Signifies on authors, genres, styles, and motifs. Zora Neale Hurston, Richard Wright, and Ralph Ellison stand out among the favorite African American targets of his "black-on-black" (re)writing. But, while Signifyin(g) "black-on-black," Reed also rewrites, "black-on-white," targeting as he does culturally relevant, symbolic value-laden works and themes in the Western, primarily American canon. It is through this insistent crosscultural revisionism that Reed complicates Gates's Signifyin(g), which the critic has theorized to account for literary exchanges essentially *within* black culture.

Reed's textual-ideological revisionism can be traced back to his first novel, *The Free-Lance Pallbearers*, which ventriloquizes "the confessional mode which is the fundamental, undergirding convention of Afro-

American narrative" (Gates, *Signifying Monkey* 218). The *Flight*'s "method" and its literary targets including the dogma of realism are also here first introduced. Next, *Yellow Back Radio Broke Down* escalates Reed's attacks on "neo-[socialist]realism." His "patarealism," a term he coins after Alfred Jarry's "pataphysics," like Clarence Major's antirealistic experiments, taps into the iconoclastic energies of the historical avant-garde at a time Black Aesthetic proponents such as Hoyt W. Fuller, Larry Neal, and Addison Gayle Jr. imperatively demand that "authentic" Black Art abide by the rules of traditional representation. But as Patrick McGee points out, if *The Free-Lance Pallbearers*, "a rewriting of Ralph Ellison's *Invisible Man*, announces its postmodernism through its declaration of war against the concept of totality," the second novel formulates its "postmodern political aesthetic" (26) by absorbing popular forms such as the western, cartoons, and so on.

A "novel about writing itself . . . , a book about texts and a book of texts" that both "parod[ies] and underscor[es] our notions of intertextuality" (Gates, *Signifying Monkey* 220, 223), *Mumbo Jumbo* marks out among Reed's works probably the place where Legba, the "crossroads master," feels at home most. Dramatizing black resistance to "monocultural" attempts to unify the symbolically "dispersed," "untogether" Text (69) and secretly "mol[d] the consciousness of the West" (25), *Mumbo Jumbo* mounts "as much an attack on the present as on the Harding years" (Hutcheon, *Poetics* 196). The novel plays upon *Invisible Man* and Richard Wright's *Native Son*, as well as upon Goethe's *Faust* and Freud's psychoanalytic model.[1] Reed's rewrites take to task the mimetic pressure of tradition and its "ideologies of domination" (Hutcheon, *Poetics* 130). These ideologies come to the fore, albeit differently, both in Goethe and in Wright. Reacting to the former, *Mumbo Jumbo* questions the political upshots of technological progress (90–92); mocking *Native Son*, Reed challenges Wright's authority in order to break away from the realistic and naturalistic codes that controlled African American writing up until the late 60s.

The Last Days of Louisiana Red keeps interrogating "foundational" texts, cultural forms and myths of Western and African American heritages through an ironic remake of Sophocles, Wright, Hurston, and Chester Himes, as well as Hermann Hesse and Ernest Hemingway. Juggling with genre conventions, Reed rewrites tragedy as detective story, one of his favorite genres. Finally, *The Terrible Twos* retells Dickens to put forth a humorous critique of Christmas's "commodification" at the hands of monopolies and parodies *The Divine Comedy* to refigure Dante's hell as a tormenting place for dishonest politicians. Prefacing her discussion of the Dickens and Dante intertexts in Reed's book, Linda Hutcheon observes that "intertextual parody of canonical American and European classics is one mode of appropriating and reformulating—with significant change—the dominant white, male, middle-class, heterosexual, Eurocentric culture" (*Politics* 130). The revisionist renarration of canonical works is the defining appropriating mode of Reed's rewriting. Let us now look more closely at this mode by focusing on *Flight to Canada.*

IMPROPER APPROPRIATIONS: "STOLENTELLING" AND THE DEROMANCING OF RACE

> American Slavery . . . [n]aturally and necessarily, the enemy of literature. (Matlack, Bibb i)
>
> Never yield a piece of property. (Reed, *Flight* 19)

The *Flight* is a multifaceted story of appropriation. On the one hand, it showcases an impressive "textophagic" apparatus able to digest carefully picked narrative materials. On the other, it tells us several appropriating "tales," thematizing the relationships among writing, literary agency, property, and subjectivity. All these elements are intimately tied together in the figures of Uncle Robin and Raven Quickskill, former slaves and main actors in the novel's vivid dramatization of rewriting. Both characters are writers in their own right. In effect, the book opens with a poem by Raven, which bears the same title as the novel. As we will find out, the poetry piece "liberates" as much as gets its author in trouble. "Flight to Canada" provides us with the necessary context for a reading of the text that follows; but by the same token it acts like a textual "bloodhound" (*Flight* 85), sniffing out its own author and supplying Massa Swille's "Slave Catchers" with the information they need to "read" Raven's "traces" and track him down after his escape from Swille's antebellum Virginia plantation. The latter designates a symbolic place: it is a signifier for slavery as a historical institution as well as for a specific literary and cultural tradition. The two, Reed subtly implies, are interwoven, and his hero does his best to evade both. Through his poem, Raven is relocating himself as a character in Reed's story and as a writer in his own, disobedient style.

In this light, the treatment of generic conventions seems quite telling. The slave narrative is one genre the *Flight* "parasitizes" this time, subverting it as another, apparently paradoxical "master narrative." But the novel offers a second, let us call it "postmodern," response to the midnineteenth-century classical "fugitive" story. A response, namely, that follows the Harlem Renaissance and other modern African American writers' reply to what Robert Stepto has dubbed the "pregeneric myths" or "founding calls" of black literature. Reed's novel echoes both these prestigious calls—autobiographies by Frederick Douglass, Henry Bibb, Josiah Henson, Solomon Northrup, and William Wells Brown—*and* the "response" these calls have received from James Weldon Johnson, Wright, and Ellison. And it is only with radically revisionist authors such as Reed that the slave narrative and its common readings become a new tradition, an unavoidable source of formal and thematic constraints, and thereby a target of rewriting.

Revisiting African American narrative, as well as the history and the politics embedded in it, Reed plays out his "method"—his work and freedom simultaneously. Like his fictive alter-ego, Raven, he is the "bookkeeper" of his tradition (*Flight* 35). He does venerate its books, true "American Bibles" (*Conversations* 140). But this does not stop him from "mucking about" with them and "white" books alike, and, while doing this, from writing his own, the *Flight*, and proclaiming his political and artistic freedom. Raven, whom Swille charges with "writing passes and forging freedom papers" (35), Frederick Douglass, whose figure Raven both performs and critiques, and Reed himself all belong to the same paradigm of "militant," emancipatory authorship. At the same time, Reed-as-Raven suggests that Douglass's model of disobedient writing was not radical enough. This model, he submits, got somewhat contained by the very system it had aimed to evade[2]—ironically enough, Swille's slaves live in the "Frederick Douglass Houses" (56). Molded on the classical pattern of autobiographic narrative, *Narrative of the Life of Frederick Douglass* and the stories of resistance deferentially reiterating it have been unable, as Toni Morrison has also argued, to "destroy the master narrative" (50). Hence Reed doubts that Douglass's work purveys a strategy of truly liberating writing. Moreover, he acknowledges his debt to William Wells Brown, "the greatest satirist of these times," as Raven calls him (*Flight* 121). Further, aside from admiring Brown's *Clotelle*, the first African American novel (1853), "Flight to Canada" imitates Brown's "style," as Raven himself tells Brown, whom, oddly enough, he runs across on a Lake Erie steamer.

Unlike Douglass's 1845 narrative, Reed's writing is set upon openly "writing back." It reaches its goal by turning the "host" style, genre, or intertext against itself, caricaturizing its very claim of "originality." The "copy" writes this pretense off, so to say, through "excessive," pugnacious *re*writing. For, to be sure, "Writin' Is Fightin'," as Reed proclaims in the title of one of his books. The novelist himself and his characters Raven and Robin are brave fighters, "wielding" writing accordingly. In its particular form of intertextual performance and ludic rewrite, writing serves as a political weapon. Appropriating, as much as intervening in, the cultural and stylistic cast of certain texts, the author and his characters-as-writers reappropriate their own identities: they come to be what they are by refusing to perpetuate, and be perpetuated by, a "master" discourse.

The *Flight* consistently thematizes the notion of cultural appropriation and its forms, possession and repossession, expropriation and reappropriation. Symbolically, literary property and property in general—African Americans as property in the first place—dovetail from the outset. When we find out in the novel's first chapter that Stowe's *Uncle Tom's Cabin* is a "steal," the alleged theft suggests more than copyright infringements.

In his essay on twentieth-century "literary symbiosis," David Cowart reminds us of the *Finnegans Wake* wordplay on storytelling, defined as *stolen*telling. What Joyce implies here is, Cowart points out, that "storytelling always involves theft, that all 'telling' is 'stolen'" (2). It is true, an entire line in contemporary philosophy and criticism bases its approach on a "vol-onto-theology" of writing, determining the latter as pure "theft," as Geoffrey Hartman notes in his essay on Derrida's *Glas* and Jean Genet's *The Thief's Journal* (*Saving the Text* 67–95). Property, Hartman insists, is somehow ill-conceived, im-proper. There is no property—just "appropriation." Writing is essentially appropriative, ceasing to be an ethical issue to become an issue of poetics, of "amoral" exchanges and adaptations.

Reed's take on—and intake of—Stowe's book raises some questions about this theory. "Universal" as the "principle of artistic larceny" (Cowart 2) may be, Stowe's narrative "theft" is not an innocent, indeed largely inevitable illustration of the "dynamics of intertextuality" (2). The problem with such a stolentelling, Reed implies, is that in lifting materials from Josiah Henson's *Life of Josiah Henson, Formerly a Slave*, not only did Stowe "borrow" his tale, his *Life*; she also "took" his "life," repossessing the "property" her novel was actually attempting to free. This otherwise not unusual act of "inspiration" appears to Reed as a deadly blow since that story—again, Henson's *Life*, after all—"was all he had. His story. A man's story is his gris-gris. The thing that is himself. It's like robbing a man of his Etheric Double. People pine away" (*Flight* 8). True, "Harriet gave Josiah credit in her *The Key to Uncle Tom's Cabin*."[3] Nonetheless, the narrator claims, this was not enough. The "key" has not quite worked. Despite the acknowledgement, Stowe's source has remained largely ignored: readers do not use *this* key to unlock the narrative and the life (Henson's) locked up in Stowe's text.

The story of Josiah Henson's story, so to speak, bears upon the *Flight*'s rewriting techniques, supplying us with an important reading tool. The "spirits," Reed's narrator intimates, "touched" Harriet Beecher Stowe for having dispossessed Henson of his "property." "When you take a man's story, a story that doesn't belong to you, that story will get you" (*Flight* 9). Significantly, the revenge of Henson's story shapes into vindictive rewriting as Stowe became subject to parody and satire. *Her* story—her work and biography—was being "staged" and undermined on stage, in shows, cartoons, and other "corrosive," because highly performative, genres. "Loa," the African HooDoo (Voodoo) deities of mimic, performance, and, I might add, jocular rewriting also involve future writers in this process of polemical recirculation. As critics from Richard Yarborough to Marva Banks have insisted, Reed is not the first African American writer to take issue with *Uncle Tom's Cabin*. From the "antebellum black response" to Stowe to James Baldwin's 1949 essay "Everybody's Protest Novel" (Banks 212), there has been a long series of responses to the stereotypes and ambiguities Stowe cultivates. Reed's response mounts, I think, the most potent of these critiques as the novel rewrites and "reposses," through the intertextual figure of Uncle Robin, Stowe's stolentale. Thus, the *Flight* opens up a new paragraph of the "HooDoo writing" Stowe unwittingly unleashed when she "took" Henson's story. Through Robin, Reed confronts the racial clichés *Uncle Tom's Cabin* is accountable for. Interestingly, Reed's character declines Stowe's offer to do his biography (*Flight* 173–74). Raven will be the one to "write Uncle Robin's story in such a way that, using a process the old curers used, to lay hands on the story would be lethal to the thief. That way, Uncle Robin would have the protection that Uncle Tom (Josiah Henson) didn't" (11). "Avenging" Henson and his story, Robin's *biography*—"writing of life"—unseats the romancing, "domesticating" representation of blackness Stowe's story set forth. At stake appears to be, here and everywhere in Reed, the problematic "co-optation"—and, again, "theft"—of black culture and its styles and subjects (in all senses). Reed reacts to this symbolic co-optation by using, as James Snead explains, "a narrative principle that will undermine the very assumptions that brought the prior appropriation about" ("European pedigrees" 247).

"Appropriation need not be subversive" (Childers and Hentzi 17). In Reed, though, it really is. As a "textual form" (Hutcheon, *A Theory of Parody* 37), appropriation here is a parodic way of dealing with Stowe's alleged appropriation of Henson's narrative and with human appropriation in general. It foregrounds the literary, political, and economic meanings of the term. Reed ostensibly brings out all these ramifications of the concept to turn the tables on former proprietors/appropriators and, in doing so, to help Henson "ge[t] even" ("An Interview" 186). We know that Stowe actually owned in a 1876 letter that a "sketch of [Henson's] life . . . furnished me many of the finest conceptions and incidents of 'Uncle Tom's character," yet six years after she would deny that Uncle Tom's was "the biography of any one man."[4] But the historical truth of Henson's meeting with, and influence on, Stowe concerns Reed less. What Reed does care about is Stowe's use of a tragic life—Henson's, Bibb's, Douglass's, or any other runaway slave's for that matter—and her turning such a communal destiny into a sentimental tale whose protagonist became "the most frequently sold slave in American history."[5]

PURLOINING POE

> Poe, . . . that scream from the smiling face of America. (Doctorow, *The Book of Daniel* 177)
>
> No early American writer is more important to the concept of African Americanism than Poe. (Morrison 32)

Reed's reference to Stowe's attack on Byron and to the "haunting" story coming back to "get" her segues us into Poe's world and cultural imaginary. To Reed, Poe's work is a vehicle for a message reaching beyond the past and the fictional. "Why," Reed asks,

> isn't Edgar Allan Poe recognized as the principal biographer of that strange [Civil] war? Fiction, you say? Where does fact begin and fiction leave off? Why does the perfectly rational, in its own time, often sound like mumbo-jumbo? Where did it leave off for Poe, prophet of a civilization buried alive, where, according to witnesses, people were often whipped for no reason. No reason? Will we ever know, since there are so few traces left of the civilization the planters called "the fairest civilization the sun ever shown upon," and the slaves called "Satan's Kingdom." Poe got it down. Poe says more in a few stories than all the volumes by historians. (10)

This passage sets off the paramount role the Poe corpus holds in the rewriting apparatus of the novel. The *Flight* literally feeds on this literary body. It relentlessly purloins, pilfers, displaces, puts away,[6] and redoes the absolute master of cultural purloining, Poe. The novel abounds with references to, and rewritings of, "Annabel Lee," "Berenice," "Ligeia," "The Fall of the House of Usher," "Premature Burial," "The Masque of the Red Death," "The Raven," and other Poe texts. Reed revisits such works to draw out meanings that have allegedly eluded professional historians. "Interpolated" by Reed, Poe's stories prove to be somehow superior to history and scientific accounts. Fiction gains access to facts that evade science's grasp. It crayons the psychological portrait of an epoch by laying bare morbid, Sadistic,[7] or necrophilic drives as core components of a definition of slavery and "Nobility" simultaneously. The careful reader cannot miss, for instance, Reed's frequent puns on flagellation, which indicts slavery as a socially sadistic system at the same time that it seizes upon Sadism as the defining "enslaving" practice of the "new feudalism" (*Flight* 96) and Poe's work as its insightful yet unacknowledged chronicle. Massa Swille, who secretly longs for the title of "Marquis d'Swille" (109), "loved the sound of the screamings coming from the various parts of the plantation, day and night." What is more, the narrator notes that "Eddie Poe had gone bonkers over [Swille's fettering] equipment and used some of it in his short stories" (108).

Robert Elliot Fox observes that Swille's name suggests devouring greed and debasing will—the will to possess and annihilate the other in the deadly, equivocal act of possession. In brief, the character embodies the age's "disease of mastership" (69). In terms of my reading, the sadistic master foregrounds a crucial moment in the midnineteenth-century pathology of appropriation, a sociocultural "disorder" that the *Flight* sets out to battle by reappropriating (rewriting) the very agents and instances of enslaving desire. Reed discerns and insistently plays upon Poe's own understanding of a terrible and very complex truth: "[T]here is nothing more compelling than *possession*" (Dayan, "Romance" 95). It is this twisted and many-sided—erotic, economic, political—concept that knots together and complicates romance and race, desire and ownership. Reed shows how this notion infuses Poe's imagination. And he does not hesitate to employ this imagination to further illuminate a fact, again, not unknown to Poe, namely, that "the language of romanticism allowed the covert continuation of inequality" (Dayan, "Romance" 95).

Manipulating Poe's work, Reed carries out a political reinterpretation of the Poesque "Dark Night of Sense" (Allen Tate 192), rendering socially explicit what in Poe remains implicit or formulated vaguely. Reed's political analysis picks up where Poe's psychological explorations end, one might say. He further scrutinizes the nocturnal landscapes of Poesque desire to peel off the rational discourse that romances and disguises racism's violent irrationality, the true human relations lurking behind the chivalrous, lofty rhetoric of the South—or, in Kathryn Hume's words, the "Poe nightmare" underneath the "Poe midsummer day's dream" (508–9). It is noteworthy that the *Flight* teems with references and flippant allusions to King Arthur (*Arthur* is also Swille's first name), Dracula, Camelot—which the South cannot but simulate (96)—T. S. Eliot isolating himself in the feudal tower of aestheticism and therefore unable to "understand" America (104), Sir Walter Scott,[8] Tennyson, Walt Whitman, Dickens, Oscar Wilde, and so on.

What may appear to make up a sundry list of medieval figures, romantics, Victorians, modernists, decadents, and "avant-garde rackets" (105) traces in fact, Reed avers, a consistent, ethically and culturally insightful profile of the South:

> Raised by mammies, the South is dandyish, foppish, pimpish; its writers are Scott, Poe, Wilde, Tennyson . . . Davis, who was accused by *The Charleston Mercury* of treating Southerners like "white Negroes," misread his people. It wasn't the idea of winning that appealed to them. It was the idea of being ravished. Decadent and Victorian writing both use the romantic theme of fair youth slumbering. Fair youth daydreaming. Fair youth struck down. (141–42)

Haughty manners, aristocratic pose, symbolist perfumes, noble imagery, stylistic refinement, but also gloomy realism, narcissism, melancholia, self-destructive impulse, masochism, sepulchral obsessions, fetishism, crepuscular sexuality, violence: all represent, according to Reed, southern features on which Poe's work sheds revealing light. Indeed, Poe is the emblem of "the land of the hunted and the haunted" (173). And, Reed argues, slavery's specters of violence, exploitation, and injustice are haunting us even after slaves' "emancipation." They "visitate" our time in emancipation's failures, aborted promises and projects, or even "demise." This might help us understand Reed's *calembour* that makes, oddly enough, the notion of "emancipation" recall the "emaciation" of Poe's characters.[9] Slavery is officially dead; but somehow its emaciated ghosts keep roaming our world—and this is where Reed's "spectral analysis" comes in. Slavery's "system" lingers on in a state of mind much harder to abolish. Yet, as we shall see, if "Canada is a state of mind," so might the lack of freedom prove to be. Reed's original perusal and subsequent "retextualizing" of Poe draw our attention to this possibility.

Reed interprets Poe. He reads, into Poe's works, the "death drive" of a whole society "founded upon *thanatos*" (Weixlmann, "Politics" 48) and then ridicules that society by parodying Poe's motifs and language. *Flight*, though, is neither plain satire nor reverent imitation of Poe. The novel may caricaturize Poe but at the same time seems to value his vision and sharpen this vision's critical edge. The criticism of Poe's world entails no wholesale rejection of Poe's work. Reed does not overlook the critical potential of the text of "the master subversive Poe" (Doctorow, *The Book of Daniel* 177), as much as he whimsically draws upon its "blind spots," upon both its latent and manifest racial prejudices.[10] Consequently, the novel spins off a sort of a "two-toned" dialogue (Gates, *Black Literature* 6) where the voices of the performer and the performed, of the rewriter and the rewritten mix but can still be sorted out.

To be sure, this is no easy task as Reed's treatment of Poe throughout the novel wavers considerably. Rewriting in the *Flight* may, for instance, yield a parody that preserves the specific style and format of the original. After Raven escapes through the back window while his followers, the "human being-burglars" of *Nebraska Tracers, Inc.*, are looking at a first edition of *Uncle Tom's Cabin*, he suddenly thinks of finally "understanding Elymas Payson Rogers'[11] poem" on "invaded human rights" (64–65). Through this poem, Reed mimics the lyric tone, images, formal pattern, and even specific rhymes of "Annabel Lee." Interestingly, not only do we distinguish in this fragment Poe's style and Reed's mocking his romantic, solemn tone; the rewrite also incorporates the language of contemporary politics, seeming to deliberately conflate abolitionist phraseology and the more recent human rights pathos. It "overacts" the latter's "emancipatory" rhetoric, rejecting it as a new and shallow romantic pose—it is perhaps worth remembering that Raven's new residence, which he flees when the Nebraskaites attempt to "repossess" him (61), is the ironically named Emancipation City. To sum up, in parroting Poe's poetic patterns and parodying certain lines of "Annabel Lee," Reed undertakes a double critique: of the model itself and of the contemporary discourse of liberation. The parody's language also throws light on Reed's targets: the past and the present, literary history and history in general, the former serving as a medium through which the reader deciphers the latter. "Scratching" Poe's palimpsest, Reed's rewriting exposes an enciphered "disgrace" of slavery.

The novelist stops short of abusing or allegorizing Poe. He modulates the poem's thanatic tropes in such a way as to make them issue forth meanings valid only within the revisionist framework the *Flight* sets up. We are not confronted here, I would contend, with a vulgar reading or misreading of "Annabel Lee," but with a defiant, critical reply that approaches its object from a political and aesthetic angle falling in line with the novel's nimble-witted strategy. In this regard, Raven's recalling the poem while fleeing his pursuers is highly significant. The "manhandlers" apparently share Annabel Lee's somber destiny. But in fact, in contrast to the famous character, their memory "shall rot," prey to the "Conqueror Worm" Ligeia invokes in her "terminal" poem. Reed appropriates "Annabel Lee" to sanction Raven's resistance to be "appropriated" or "repossessed," as Reed says. Moreover, Elymas Payson Rogers's poem performs a "funeral dirge" at slavery's "premature burial" (a phrase that recalls Poe) by pirating Poe's rhetoric. Thus, Reed's waggish imitation of Poe's poem once again situates Raven culturally and politically within the narrative. A fugitive and a writer, he masters what Henry Bibb has called "the art of running away" (15). Raven Quickskill uses this art and related quick skills to "get to our aesthetic Canada, no matter how many dogs they send after us," as Reed explains (*Conversations* 21).

DANCING TO THE TYPEWRITER

Raven's "fugitive" poetics has another model in the novel, Carpenter. A "freedom writer," Carpenter evokes Henry Bibb's and especially William Wells Brown's biography and composite style. Carpenter is the author who, following in Douglass's and Bibb's footsteps, authors his own freedom:

> While others had their tarot cards, their ouija boards, their I-Ching, their cowrie shells, he [Carpenter] had his "writings." They were his bows and arrows. He was so much against slavery that he had begun to include prose and poetry in the same book, so that there would be no arbitrary boundaries between them . . . it was his writing that got him [Raven] to Canada. "Flight to Canada" was responsible for getting him to Canada. And so for him, freedom was his writing. His writing was his HooDoo. Others had their way of HooDoo, but his was his writing. It fascinated him, it possessed him; his typewriter was his drum he danced to. (88–89)

This passage spells out a core component of Reed's aesthetics: the political bearings of textual—and intertextual—practice. The whole fragment revolves around the perceptive analogy between race and genre, more to the point, between racial segregation and miscegenation anxieties, on the one hand, and cultural conservatism, on the other hand. Insightfully, Reed disallows the latter as an aesthetic apartheid of sorts: it arbitrarily keeps different genres apart. Conversely, he pins down racism as a prescriptive "poetics" that rules out what might be called "social intertextuality": the intermingling of racially different subjects. The counterpart of the exclusionary logic undergirding both racism and aesthetic "purism" is the heterogeneous, hybrid "Neo-Hoodoo" Reed has advocated throughout his career.

Neo-Hoodoo is, in an important sense, a theory and practice of writing—and rewriting, I might add. Indeed, it explains why Reed has "included prose and poetry in the same book [the *Flight*]." It cuts across discursive boundaries in a way that programmatically allows its author to ward off cultural bondage. Reed wants to "be himself" and not a "slave of tradition," be that even *his* tradition. As Richard Walsh maintains, "the most important quality of Reed's Voodoo aesthetic is its syncretism, because it is at this point that aesthetics and politics meet" ("'A Man's Story'" 60). It is by virtue of this syncretism that poetry and prose, as well as the "macrodiscourses" of races and cultures, blend in one of the most powerful "critique[s] of monoculturalism" (61). Since Beethoven, Japanese art, or French cubists show, according to Reed, how "everybody's mixed" ("Interview" 130), asking that writers cultivate only "pure," "original" molds of culturally specific discourses is an absurd request. Of course, this does not superannuate the notions of "difference" and "ancestry"; it is through these concepts that Reed's HooDoo (VooDoo) theory of rewriting works. What the author puts forward here is a dialectic conception. A dogmatic understanding of "origins," he implies, would go against the grain of the spirit of spectacular rewriting at play in various cultural lines, which inevitably combines themes, tropes, and styles. Furthermore, neither Western nor African American traditions rest solely on such "pure roots," which allows Reed to rewrite both black and white authors, to play out both the difference and the profound "hybridity" of the performed texts.

The *Flight*'s cultural repertoire is extremely telling in this respect. The novel's raven motif, for instance, as Reed suggests, does not come from one single source, Poe's poem. No doubt, Reed does have in mind the "ebony bird," which, ironically "perched upon a bust of Pallas," torments the poet with his ominous "nevermore," much as the *Flight*'s Raven, himself a poet, haunts Swille with his refusal to ever submit. But the interplay of Poe's famous poem, slave poetry, and Native American mythology (Weixlmann, "Ishmael Reed's Raven" 205) renders the very notion of "source" highly problematic. What is more, Reed compounds the complexity of this intertext through his own rewriting. On the one hand, texts and people, aesthetic objects and social subjects, he implies, are palimpsests, mixtures of various lineages and linkages that complicate the notions of origin, purity, absolute difference. On the other, it is precisely such a cultural and ethnic difference that alerts us to this "palimpsestic condition."

NECROMANTIC REWRITING: BONDS OF DESIRE

> Ishmael Reed's fiction rests upon the assumptions that before a true black aesthetic can emerge, before black consciousness can overcome the repression of white American society, American history—western history—must be dismantled and rewritten using the racial focus of Afro-Americans. (Richard Martin 499)

Evoking explicitly "Annabel Lee," Swille's relationship with his dead sister Vivian is a good example of the displacement rewriting sets in motion. Tying into the social pathology of possession and enslavement, incest is another "unnatural act," adding to the oddity of Swille's figure.

Liable to take psychological or social forms, enslaving and incestuous ties are underlaid, Reed suggests, by essentially identical desire. In Swille, this brings out opposite forms of *excessive* desire: either abysmal submission or absolute dominance; either irresistible drive to "be one" with the ("forbidden") other, that is, incest, or the impulse to enslave him or her. In either case, Swille comes off as a lustful, "macabre fiend" (*Flight* 126). "No wonder he has Poe down here all the time," his son comments. When his wife charges him with being a "Moloch [, . . . a] Mammon [, . . . a] Beelzebub," Swille takes her outburst as a "melancholic" effect "induced by the miasma in our atmosphere" (133), alluding to Poe's fictional settings of "The Fall of the House of Usher." But his own will (desire)—himself and *his self*, after all (*Swille*'s *will*)—is another important text-in-the-text that gives the lie to this argument.

Swille's testament is the most remarkable moment in the novel's figuration of the links among possession, ambiguously Poesque desire, and slavery, whimsically underscoring Reed's interplay of rewriting and symbolic appropriation of writing subjects. His "final request," Swille admits by hinting at "Annabel Lee," "may sound a little odd to the Yankees who've invaded our bucolic haven, but I wish to be buried in my sister's sepulcher by the sea, joined in the Kama Sutra position below" (168–69). I propose to read this and other "sepulchral," mock-Poesque passages against the backdrop of Reed's theory of writing as necromantic rereading and rewriting. Kindling the "root meaning of the word" (Allan Tate 193), Poe's own necromancy and his "heroes become necromancers" (193) may have also played a role, along with African magic, in the genesis of Reed's own notion. This notion sets off the word's original sense. The etymology is important here because Reed manipulates it to reinvent the meaning of Poe's necromancy. While the latter acts out a destructive drive, Reed's is charged with a positive, culturally significant sense. The novelist juggles both scientific and folk etymology, which has redefined the ancient Greek *nekrós* ("dead") as the Latin form, *nigro* (derived from *niger*, "black"), to show how necromancy as "communication with the dead" (*nekrói*) through *manteía* ("divination," also in ancient Greek) is *nigro*-mantic, that is, specific to *black* culture. Trading upon this semantic contamination, Reed seizes necromantic practice as an empowering form of black writing, which integrates the "manipulation of nature" and the "manipulation of the word." "The Afro-American artist," he tells us in the introduction to *Nineteen Necromancers from Now*, "is similar to the Necromancer (a word whose etymology itself is revealing!). He is a conjuror who works JuJu upon his oppressors" (xvii). "Necromancers," he says elsewhere, "used to lie in the guts of the dead or in tombs to receive visions of the future. That is prophecy. The black writer lies in the guts of Old America, making readings about the future" ("Ishmael Reed" 133). And this is precisely what the *Flight*'s writer does while "practis[ing] his [own] necromancy" (Walsh, "'A Man's Story'" 63): he explores the literary "guts" of America, its cultural archive, to dig out the unspeakable, moreover, to "read" the latter's anachronistic presence underneath contemporary disguises.

What we discern through Swille's morbid will is the twilight of Swille's world. Slavery is macabre and inhuman, a "thanatic" impulse translated socially. A trope of death and form of "death drive" at the same time, it is bound to slope off, frantically relinquishing its exit. One should bear in mind, though, that Swille's testament is a fabrication. Robin literally rewrites, "correct[s]" Swille's original will to his own advantage by mimicking the slaveholder's "dyslexia," which "scramble[s] and jumble[s]" Swille's words. "Helping" his master to overcome his speech and reading impediments, Uncle Robin "bec[omes] his reading and writing," his human word processor and, as such, ironic adaptation of the ancient figure of the amanuensis. The "enslaved computer," however, has its own "program": to become its own owner, moreover, to "le[ave] itself Swille's whole estate. Property joining forces with property. I left me his whole estate. I'm it, too. Me and it got more it" (*Flight* 171). Robin also does a take-off on Swille's pathological obsessions. He copies yet also mocks the *master('s) style*, habits or fixations to make up a verisimilar imitation of the "original." He fakes Swille's writing, dis-locates it, much as the *Flight*'s author "purloins" Poe's works and makes their style, obsessions, and plots serve a new purpose in a new textual "locale." Again, rewriting does not dump the initial code—it is *a forging recodification that "outwrites" that code.* Reed and his (re)writers turn the writing meant to write them off as subjects *against* the initial author. Uncle Robin "edits" Swille's manuscript, seemingly "healing" the "bad-worded" ("*dys-lexic*") text. In actual fact, he redoes it, rewriting it against its very grain and generally doing as a character what his author accomplishes throughout the novel. Rewriting here signifies, as Robert Elliot Fox has argued, a "double refusal: to be silent as well as to (slavishly) imitate" (71). Robin declines to copy—comply with—Swille's will as much as his author and others like him resist copying extant narrative models whatever their nature. Further, if Reed "expropriates [Stowe,] the expropriato[r]" (McGee 37) by recasting Uncle Tom (Henson) as Uncle Robin, the latter's rewriting expropriates Swille, the proprietor and writer of the testament. Worth recalling here is the tradition in whose footsteps Reed's discourse of reappropriation follows. Henson and Bibb often point out that they were considered "property," not men; it is the "laws of property, not humanity," as Henson writes (56), that were governing their lives. Understandably, the former slaves dream of "becoming independent proprietors themselves" (76). "I was no longer property," Henson tells us proudly. In Canada, Bibb writes in his turn, "I was regarded as a man, and not as a thing" (16), whereas in the slaveholding States, he "could possess nothing, nor acquire anything" (17) because "[he] was regarded as property" (122).

Rewriting the master('s) desire (will) against the master's intention, Robin *de-authorizes* the document's author in a fashion that certain critics and legal scholars have called "postmodern" (Rosenau 32). He allows property to appropriate *itself* and become *himself*, free and therefore human. The "Thing" is humanized in the process of rewriting-as-reappropriation. "It" turns into an "I (Am)" (*Flight* 82) and regains the identity denied by both the fictional story as told by Stowe and real history (the history of slavery). Textual history has now completed both the genealogy and the reconstruction of the textual subject: Robin's I Am actually *writes*—and therefore *is*—the culmination of a whole process of cultural and political liberation. He figures both black history, that is, the former slaves' ("things"') growth into "subjectivity," and literary history as a *history of rewriting*.

CHAPTER 2

Middle Passages: "(Re)Writing Furiously"

The middle passage is writing. (Scott III 653)

"REWORDING": BLACKNESS AND LITERARY AGON

Blackness exists, but "only" as a function of its signifiers. (Gates, *Signifying Monkey* 237)

Drawing from Maurice Merleau-Ponty's phenomenological interpretation of language as a pathway to the "Other," Charles Johnson argues in *Being and Race* that "to read is to inhabit the role and real place of others." "To write," he insists, "is a stranger experience yet." For writing involves "a corresponding act of self-surrender such that my perceptions and experiences are allowed to coincide with those who came before me and despoiled words, shaped their sense and use" (39). It follows that insofar as it deals with language, writing cannot but confront those who have used and misused linguistic materials and structures and by the same token have left their imprints—their values, meanings, and viewpoints—on words and "cities of words," to quote the title of Tony Tanner's book. As Johnson puts it in a sentence recalling not only Husserl and Merleau-Ponty but also Bakhtin, "like a palimpsest, the word is a tissue of interpretations, . . . the experience, the sight (broad or blind) of others formed into word" (*Being and Race* 39). As a result, the word has since long lost its innocence. In fact, many words may be "male-chauvinist," "bigoted," or simply "blind" (39)—and it is precisely the struggle to displace words' "blindness" and the spell this casts on people that moves Johnson's rewriting project.

To prevent this project from slipping "toward dogma that ends the process of literary discovery, . . . toward Kitsch" (29), the "counteracting of cultural lies" likely to give birth to new images and allow people to control their own representations must recognize first that no experience is "raw" (31), "[un]*interpreted* by others" (4). Thus, the new story and its novel ways of "wording" experience pick up the gauntlet thrown down by the "others" and take on their interpretations—on their insights or blindness. Here is, of course, where Johnson's notion of alterity parts company with Bakhtin's. The others and their perceptions do bear on us, but the new story seeks to aggressively transform them through intensive rewriting. An act of creative resistance rather than of "surrendering" or "uncritical mimesis" (5), it even "tri[es] to subdue the disquieting existence of others" (Merleau-Ponty, *Sense and Non-Sense* 29), their disquieting stories and storied worlds.

This agonal, "palimpsestic" view of language and culture shapes Johnson's entire fiction. Grounded in an intersubjective view of literature, his novels and tales set up a vivid, transforming dialogue with literary history and forms, with the countless "dead artists" whose names are inscribed in the "graveyard" of the writer's own prose. Lifted by Johnson from André Malraux's *Voices of Silence* (*Being and Race* 52), this spectral trope of cultural dialogics captures the essence of the black author's programmatic rewording and reordering of inherited words. Like other writers discussed in this book, he sees literature as a medium *and* outcome of ceaseless exchange, a steady revisiting of the past. New writing refashions this past, endowing it with novel meanings in an attempt, as literary as political, to write off, as it were, the negativity embedded in texts and in the words constituting them. Which means that the writer cannot avoid dealing with the historical mediation of this experience, unwrapping as he does the various cultural packages in which the "facts" come. Specifically, in Johnson's own work this involves both serious and playful flaunting of a twofold conversation across genres, ages, races, and cultures: a conversation, that is, with the African American spiritual heritage, namely, the folktale, the slave narrative, "pivotal books" (7) like William Wells Brown's *Clotelle*, and with such modernists as Baldwin, Wright, or Ellison; but, like in Reed, also a rereading of white, literary and philosophical tradition. An outcome of this double and deep-running dialogue, "cross-cultural fertilization," Johnson assures us, "keeps the form alive" (*Being and Race* 47). And the form of his own narratives is no exception.

His 1974 novel, *Faith and the Good Thing*, already hints at how rewriting as crosscultural fertilizations works. One could identify at least three cultural layers in the book's structure. The deepest weaves together black mythology and humor, witchcraft and necromantic practices, folk tales and storytelling registers. The second, which also knits African American materials together, marks off an exclusively literary zone: Johnson's ironic response to Wright (*The Outsider*) and, more precisely, Ellison (*Invisible Man*). The third carries out through Faith, the woman protagonist, and her quest for the mythic "Good Thing" lost in "the winter of the Age of Reason" (*Faith* 192), the author's intervention both in the "Great Migration" and picaro traditions, genres fueling the plot of virtually all of Johnson's narratives. It is here, too, that Johnson takes, if in a fairly roundabout way, on mainstream literary figures such as Dreiser and Melville, announcing his more complex, later plays upon Defoe and Mary Shelley in the "tales and conjurations" of *The Sorcerer's Apprentice.*

Adopting as a motto the Kafkian hypothesis of "the existence of different subjects in the same human being," the 1982 novel *Oxherding Tale* upgrades the political and existential stakes of rewriting, especially of "black-on-white" rewriting. The plot keeps tapping the resources of the picaresque; but the dominant genre this time around is an autobiographic narrative blending nineteenth-century African American sources, especially Frederick Douglass, and jestingly fictionalized autobiography in the Laurence Sterne tradition (Coleman 634). Like *Tristram Shandy*, for instance, the novel begins with the story of the protagonist's conception. The narration of Andrew Hawkins's "origins" is characteristic of Johnson's crosscultural strategy as the writer employs a prestigious intertext to play out—and replay—the old topos of miscegenation fears. Conceived through a "trick" as the son of a white woman and her slave, Hawkins is symbolically "crossfertilized" by two cultural lines: the picaro and the trickster. He lives under different names, goes places, and proves able to body forth strikingly diverse facets of "Being." He is successively a servant at Cripplegate, a South Carolina cotton plantation where Ezekiel tutors him in the liberal arts; "in the service of the senses," Flo Hatfield's senses, that is, at her "Leviathan" estate—as it turns out, a verily most sensuous empire; a runaway hunted by Soulcatcher, and, finally, a husband of Peggy Undercliff. Palimpsestlike (Little 143), his "identity" is dazzlingly multifarious and dynamic, hard to pin down, as he can also pass for a white man into whose "World" he works an apparently "unmarked" passage (Johnson, *Oxherding Tale* 128). Thus, his story mounts a radical challenge to "the belief in personal identity," as Vet, another character, tells him (58). On the other hand, even though there are no "'Negroes,' . . . [no] *essences*" (146), Hawkins's identity emerges only through its "differential" impact, as Soulcatcher's relentlessness painfully proves. Stressing this paradox, Johnson suggests that even though we remain inescapably different, we stay deeply engaged in an unremitting production of our difference. Further, we can be different in terms of race, nationality, gender, class, belief, upbringing style, and so on; we embody, nonetheless, distinct possibilities within, across, and outside these categories. Finally, these possibilities—as many abilities to become and be identified as what we are or want to be—are not completely in our hands. They also depend, as race theorists such as Stuart Hall, Anthony Kwame Appiah, and Homi Bhabha have argued lately, on others, on how they feel about us but also on how they feel about themselves, about their own identities.

Whatever portions or procedures have been pinned down as "metafictional" in *Oxherding Tale*, they problematize precisely such a polemically intracategorial and transcategorial mapping of identity, Johnson's longstanding theme. Thus, much like Ishmael Reed's fiction, *Oxherding Tale* employs text and "genre crossing" (*Being and Race* 48) to foreground the "genetic mongrelization" (52) that projects the "Self" as "a palimpsest, interwoven with everything" (*Oxherding Tale* 152). To do this, the novel trades upon Western (Schopenhauerian, Marxist, Transcendentalist) and African American philosophical metanarratives and rhetorical modes alike. Chapters VIII ("On the Nature of Slave Narratives") and XI ("The Manumission of the First-Person Viewpoint") open up brief yet dense "intermissions" persuasively theorizing the fundamental link between the bondage of slavery and the obedience to traditional—and traditionally separated—literary forms. Through mobile narrative viewpoint and lack of stylistic inhibition, the novel envisages a radical "liberation" (153) from the canonical model of the slave narrative, which, according to the author/narrator, ties in with the protagonist's impending emancipation.

RUTHERFORD, THE SCRIVENER: REWRITING AS MANUMISSION

Middle Passage stands out as Johnson's full-dress, most intensive and extensive rewrite to date. While previous narratives feature primarily episodic and allusive rewriting, and recover genres, styles, and motifs rather than individual texts, the 1990 novel undertakes a thorough reworking of particular pieces by Melville: *Billy Budd*, *Benito Cereno*, and, above all, *Moby-Dick*. In fact, *Middle Passage* has struck critics as a carefully erected analogy to the latter. Indeed, "haunted" by *Moby-Dick*'s white text, Johnson's black "textual universe" purposefully "parallels"[12] it to lay out another "anti-essentialist space in which the individual character is a shape-shifting construct" (Nielsen 167). Personally, I take *Middle Passage* to be more than a parallel—or duplicate, echo, intertextual play, imitation, or parodic reply—to Melville. In short, we are dealing here, I believe, with a narratively and ideologically complex revisiting of Melville's 1851 novel, a rewrite so far reaching that we can no longer re-read Melville's book as we did prior to its re-writing. The "palimpsestic Black tex[t]"[13] winds up "interpolating," methodically adulterating and playing with—while "playing back"—the "master text" so that the latter's "spirit" will never be the same much though its letter does not change.

The Johnsonian theme of the African American picaro retains its importance in this context. But other literary and historical/testimonial genres become structurally determinant: slave trade records and Middle Passage memoirs like the 1789 *Interesting Narrative of the Life of Olaudah Equiano, or Gustavus Vassa, the African*; accounts of black revolts such as the famous 1839 *Amistad* mutiny; the diary, the logbook, and first and foremost, I would argue, Melvillelike travel romance[14] whose first-person storyteller and main hero is Rutherford Calhoon, a fictional heir of Andrew Hawkins. A black "petty thief" and manumitted bondsman from Illinois, Calhoon is drawn to New Orleans's "exotic fringes of life." He stows away, though, on an Africa-bound slave clipper, the *Republic*, on 14 April 1830 to evade Isadora Bailey, whom Philippe "Papa" Zeringue, the local "Ur-Type of Gangster" (Johnson, *Middle Passage* 13), has decided that Calhoon must join in holy matrimony. On the way back, the captives—Johnson's mysterious tribe, Allmuseri—take over the ship, like in *Benito Cereno*. And, also like the mutineers of *San Dominick*, they cannot "govern" the vessel. The *Republic* is slowly falling apart and drifts off its course. Cannibalistic acts testing the "limit of bein' human" (174) and similar ordeals follow suit before the ship, like its transparently Melvillean "prototype," the *Pequod*, goes down only to become what it has actually been all along: a "wooden sepulcher" (21). If Ishmael survives on Queequeg's coffin, Calhoon stays afloat on a hammock and is eventually taken aboard the *Juno*. Here, *deus ex machina*, he bumps into "Papa," who has set his mind on marrying Isadora himself. But Calhoon pulls out his logbook, which shows that Papa was among the *Republic*'s shareholders, stops the wedding and regains his faithful, pet-sweater-knitting Penelope.

The logbook is a fairly complex genre and textual figure in *Middle Passage*. In a quite literal way, it constitutes the "biography" of Johnson's novel, the *log* of the *book* itself—the diary of its progress. It records, in other words, the process by which *Middle Passage* comes to be what it is, by the same token showing how intensive-extensive rewriting works. *Mise en abyme*-fashion, logbook writing dramatizes the *inter*textual, literary-historical relationship between Johnson and Melville—the rewriter and the rewritten—as *intra*textual (fictional) writing contest between Calhoon and Ebenezer Falcon. If Melville's book tells one of the most canonical stories in American culture, Johnson's retelling of Melville's tale turns out a *counterhistory*, to quote Falcon's own ironically anachronistic term (100). Rutherford's journal entries and implicitly *Middle Passage* compose an "alternate" story in whose "parallel world" (100) Ahab alias Falcon—and vice versa—is violently dethroned. Falcon perceives this story as a dangerous possibility, yet nonetheless a hypothesis postulated on the Allmuseri ontology; reenacting *Benito Cereno*'s counternarrative as well as the mates' foresights of doom in *Moby-Dick*, Rutherford's journal chronicles this hypothesis's becoming reality and "disaster" (40). But it is important to remember, again, that Rutherford is not the original "owner" of the journal, much as Johnson does not "own"—has not invented *ex nihilo*—*Middle Passage*'s story. The logbook becomes his as he wrests it from its initial keeper and *writes on, across, and against* it—as he rewrites Falcon's writing and the whole ideology of domination and ownership ingrained in the skipper's diary. "Possessing a few of the solitary virtues and the entire twisted will of Puritanism" (51), Ebenezer Falcon is recognizably modeled on Ahab through a series of striking parallelisms of similitude and contrast. In Falcon's figure, Johnson sets in motion a half-serious, half-ironic critique of Ahab's and the value systems underlying it. More to the point, the author spells out, renders explicit, and jestingly extrapolates an entire philosophy and politics that in Melville's hero remain toned down, disguised, and strewn in misty symbols that are not so much political as religious, moral, and aesthetic. Rewriting in *Middle-Passage* thus takes place through a valiant, decidedly political literalizing of *Moby-Dick*'s amphibological architecture.

The only child of "a close-mouthed Nantucket minister," Falcon is a sturdy, short-legged dwarf who will later on lose his legs altogether before losing his life. His eye sockets, Rutherford tells us, seemed "anthracite furnaces," while his "great bulging forehead . . . looked harder than whalebone" (29). Having the "air of a man who desperately wanted to die" (52)—"he doesn't *want* to return," a mate suspects (62)—the captain is, as the newspapers report, equally a "patriot," a Franklinian-Emersonian monument of "self-reliance" (144). But Johnson constructs Falcon's self-reliance, along with his Puritan rigorism and transcendentalist vision of the all-embracing, aggressively integrating ego, as an imperialist drive of "Americanizing" the planet (30) and "plundering" its cultural shrines (48). In so doing, he ironically recasts Ahab's obsession. Falcon's hunting the *black(s)*—not the *white*—conflict and hegemony rest, according to him, on a sort of a priori makeup of human mind, that is, on the split between subject and object, self and other, which are ever at war. Falcon calls this split a "dee[p], ontic wound" (98) and argues that slavery is just the unavoidable social "correlate" of a profound, ontic rift. The captain's journal accurately bears out the author's ideas and, by extension, the philosophies and politics of Puritan America and the West generally. "The man who emerged in th[e] journal entries," Rutherford keenly observes, "possessed a few of the solitary virtues and the entire twisted will of Puritanism: a desire to achieve perfection; the loneliness, self punishment, and bouts of suicide this brings; and a profound disdain for anyone who failed to meet his nearly superhuman standards" (51). Furthermore, "the master of the *Republic*" (51) manages to survive "in uncertain times" through "a series of exercises he'd developed, written in Latin, French, and Greek—for he thought simultaneously in all three languages—under the heading 'Self-Reliance'" (51). Both in substance and style, the journal's "cramped yet even script we associate with scriveners" (49) is Falcon *lui-même*, the dramatic "script" of his most intimate "nightmare" (54): the author's "heart" (48), which Rutherford sets out to "know" (48). But it also is a core *pars pro toto*, an emblematic chapter in the Western discourse of domination. Initially agreeing to complete the story in the log according to the moribund Falcon's last wish, Rutherford takes over the logbook and promises himself that "even though I'd tell the story (I knew he wanted to be remembered), it would be, first and foremost, as I saw it" (146). Rutherford the scrivener thus accedes to authorship, determined as he is to write down his (counter)history along, and against, Falcon's—against what he has just read about in the latter (51). He starts out by subverting, de-authorizing the original author and winds up "re-vitalizing textual authority" (Scott III)—his own authority as storyteller. Notably, the logbook is the only item Rutherford "salvages after the shipwreck." In it, he "write[s] furiously," recounting, once again symbolically, the "loss of the *Republic*" (201), to wit, the falling apart of an entire narrative of oppression and displacement. Spaced out throughout the summer of 1830, only two years after the events described in "Narrative of the *Globe* Mutiny" (from which Melville lifts a motto in *Moby-Dick*'s opening), Rutherford's logbook entries make up, after all, *Middle Passage*'s chapters. They supersede the master('s) writing, dislodging and controlling it and its author as the latter becomes "subject" to Rutherford's storytelling mastery. Thus, he carries his "counterstory" through by alternating realistic "transcription" and political-philosophical "transfiguration," to use Rutherford's own self-conscious terminology (190). At the end of this process, Falcon's worst cultural nightmare becomes reality: at Johnson's hands, *Moby-Dick* ends like *Benito Cereno*, whose intertextual presence Johnson does his best to flaunt—*Middle Passage* includes, for example, slave rebels such as Babo and Atufal, named after the mutineers on the *San Dominick*; also, Cringle, an officer of the *Republic*, is a telltale replica of Benito Cereno and directly refers to "writers such as Amasa Delano," who "have slandered black rebels in their tales" (173).

This is another indication that Rutherford's relation to Falcon refigures—or, as above, "transfigures"—at the plot level Johnson's "feeding" on the Melvillean imagination both as necessary indebtedness and critique. Along these lines, it is worth recalling that Rutherford calls himself a "parasite" (2) and dexterous "thief" (1, 20, 23); a "stowaway" who steals a mate's papers—his "identity," ultimately—to sneak aboard the *Republic*; a "liar" (3) and a trickster, an impersonator aware of the stakes of his performance. "Theft," Rutherford says, "was the closest thing I knew to transcendence" (46). Doubtlessly, this admission responds to Falcon's transcendental argument about slavery as "legitimate" appropriation, both turning on the fundamental issue of property, possession, and de-propriation, problems also fascinating Ishmael Reed, as we saw above. Falcon is a former pirate and plunderer (48) of subdued cultures; Rutherford does some pirating and "poaching" of his own, yet the justification and outcome are strikingly different. "Believe me," he addresses his journal's narratee, "I was a parasite to the core. I poached watches from Chandler's bureau and biscuits from the kitchen; I pirated from Jackson's trousers the change he made selling vegetables from his own garden; I listened to everyone and took notes: I was open, like a hingeless door, to everything" (162). Other people's scattered memories, experiences, words—"scraps and rags of language"—come to *be* Rutherford and define the "poacher"'s selfhood and, by extension, the complexity of African American identity.[15] "In myself," Rutherford discloses in a confession that paraphrases Johnson's own analogy[16] between intersubjectivity and intertextuality,[17] "I found nothing I could rightly call Rutherford Calhoon, only pieces and fragments of all the people who had touched me, all the places I had seen, all the houses I had broken into. The 'I' that I was, was a mosaic of many countries, a patchwork of others and objects stretching backward to perhaps the beginning of time" (162–63). Importantly, Rutherford's heterogenous self pulls itself together and recuperates its own agency and ethos as it discovers the bonds between the enslaved blacks and itself. "Furious writing"—the rewriting of the master's book—is the intertextual operation by which, paradoxically enough, Rutherford overcomes the powerless fragmentation, the "negative" intertextuality of his self. It is true, the latter remains a mosaic, a self-conscious plurality "fertilized" by "crosscurrents of culture" (176). Yet this multiplicity no longer acts as a passive receptacle. It actively reaches out and intervenes in the outside world, in the possessions, books, and lives of the others, taking them up and apart, redoing them. Rutherford's intertextual struggle instantiates his author's phenomenological view of collective and individual selves where interconnectedness and mutual transformation are key. According to this phenomenology of writing-as-rewriting, Rutherford—and his author—"situates his text in a system of intertexts that mediate and change that text, as his text mediates and changes the intertext." True, the black text is "influenced by white perspectives, and by all the perspectives inscribed among the intertexts." But, at the same time, it "provides counter-influences to the portrayals of blackness set forth by whites and others" (Coleman 632).

Appropriated by Rutherford, Falcon's (log)book turns, defeating its original purposes, into a testimony of slavery's horrors—an "antislavery narrative" (Sarah Robbins 531). Simultaneously, the diary is the locus where Rutherford organizes and conceptualizes his selfhood without freezing it. He writes it down without nailing it down, so to speak. And it is his work that proves he is more than a "wreck of the *Republic*," an offal of America. ("A ship is a society . . . a commonwealth" [175], Falcon himself explicates Johnson's allegory.[18]) A fictional *corpus*, this work endows with a body, shape, and miraculous force "the (black) self . . . the greatest of all fictions" (171). Notably, fiction impacts reality as Rutherford uses his testimonial narrative against slave traders, including those disguised as "patrons of the race" (198) such as Papa Zeringue. In doing this, the rewriter discovers the power of his work, fighting slavery—the power of "property" (199)—with his ownership of, and literary mastery over, the incriminating (log)book and himself ultimately. In effect, as a character in his story, he is "manumitting" himself, as it were, all over again. For, if we remember that Rutherford had been owned by a Reverend Peleg Chandler and that a Captain Peleg is among the *Pequod*'s owners (Nielsen 160), the question of ownership—of people and texts alike[19]—appears all the more urgent. Conspicuously, Johnson redoes Melville *as* Rutherford's writing rewrites Falcon's; Johnson retells Melville, tells us what in *Moby-Dick* and *Benito Cereno* remains untold or utterly silenced, or, finally, merely transposes in allusively contemporary terms what Melville found the strength to tell *his* contemporaries. While doing so, Johnson joins, originally and polemically, in a current conversation around race issues that often falls prey to worn-out clichés and unscrutinized "essences." Rutherford's playfully anachronistic references and Falcon's affirmative action tirade are among countless instances where *Middle Passage* signals that it is about midnineteenth-century events and texts as much as about late twentieth-century identity anxieties and prejudices.

CHAPTER 3

Hip-Hop Rewriting: Toward a "Postliberated" Aesthetic

> [T]he so-called New Black Aesthetic . . . a Harlem Renaissance on floppy disk. (Lott, "Hip-Hop Fiction" 691)

> [We] have inherited an open-ended New Black Aesthetic from the 70s pioneers that shamelessly borrows and reassembles across both race and class lines. (Ellis, "The New Black Aesthetic" 234)

BLACK *GLASNOST* AND "CROSS-POLLINATING" REASSEMBLAGES

In the opening of his "urban parable" *Negrophobia*, Darius James reproduces from one Doctor Snakeskin's *Blackman's Guide to Seducing White Women with the Amazing Power of Voodoo* the following definition: "Voodoo is a religion, but not a centralized one. Its acts are personalized—mutating, changing shape, adapting to their particular time and locale. As a result," the *Guide*'s author concludes, "present-day urban America has spawned a new generation of loa out of concrete and steel, out of radio and TV, out of comics and film. The new loa are invoked by beat-box rhythm, Burroughsian cutup, industrial music, and the extreme edges of performance art" (James 2). According to James's Snakeskin, the Voodoo spiritual patrons and ferments of African American creativity, as well as their themes and stylistic patterns, change in time. Not only does Voodoo produce discourse, namely, a specifically black discourse that, as we have noticed, writers such as Reed have abundantly rehearsed. It is in its turn inflected by novel sociocultural moments and situations. Far from providing an ahistorical mechanism of cultural incorporations, the West African–originated, Haitian-adapted spiritual and cultural practice is entangled with history. Bending and blending the historical materials and styles it comes to bear upon according to its crosscultural logic, Voodoo "mutates" them; yet at the same time, it is mutated by history.

Through the programmatic Voodoo epigraph but primarily

through its text itself, James's 1992 bric-à-brac novel *Negrophobia* purveys a perfect example for such a twofold "mutation." Raiding both mainstream and popular archives, the book riotously rounds up an incredibly wide range of bits and pieces, actual and made up, black and white, from Louis Farrakhan's thoughts on racial violence made public on *Donahue* to Paulo Freire's *Pedagogy of the Oppressed* to an Uncle H. Rap Remus's praise of Dada. Sprawling collage of cartoonish episodes, vaudeville-shaped and oversaturated with pseudo-blackface scenes, *Negrophobia* brims over with the combinatory energy of Reed's "Neo-HooDoo Manifesto" and emulates *Yellow Back Radio Broke Down*'s "heteroglossia," its popular infestation of the high-brow and deep suspicion of aesthetic taxonomies. Although it recommends itself as "a novel," James's dramatic potpourri is as hard to classify as Reed's. In both, Voodoo aesthetics comes down to a fast-paced *ars combinatoria* and deep-rooted reluctance to take the usual roads. No doubt, these two elements keep making Reed a powerful and enduring influence on young African American writers. His fiction and criticism lay out the template on which they build and reinvent themselves. Such a reinvention entails refiguring their precursors in the tropological sense that renders African American narrative a matrix of themes, tropes, styles, structures, and strictures subjected to refiguration, mimicry, and rewriting.

The combinatory thrust of intertextual machines operated by newly recognized writers such as Darius James and Trey Ellis works, as in Reed, Charles Johnson, and others, on both sides of the racial-cultural divide. But the so-called "hip-hop" generation of the late 80s and early 90s tends to fudge the boundaries among races, cultures, social classes and genres more programmatically and aggressively than Reed and Johnson. James's and Ellis's works stand out as prime documents of the new, hip-hop transgressive dynamic, where "identity, far from being reducible to essentializing categories such as race, class, and gender, is in fact more of a patchwork of overlapping—and, in some cases, *conflicting*—identities" (Potter 13). As a matter of fact, without becoming completely debunked, the very notions of divide and boundary are getting increasingly challenged by hip-hop authors such as Ellis while they search for their own identities. It seems to me that this is precisely where Reed's Hoodoo-style, militant syncretism and the new African American writers' "eclectic inspirations" (Ellis, "New Black Aesthetic" 234) commence to drift apart. In Doctor Snakeskin's words, this would be the turning point where the latter "mutate" the former.

A spokesperson and in all likelihood the most representative writer of his generation, Ellis has propounded a theory of crosscultural exchanges whose tight argumentation warrants a closer look. While scrutinizing the important points he makes in his "New Black Aesthetic" ("NBA") "ideological manifesto" (Favor 694), I will also show how they might suggest the rise, during the late 80s, of a new model of cultural appropriation as a symbolic instrument of identity reconstruction in African American postmodernism. Finally, I propose to see how Ellis's theory actually works, that is, how the transgressive identity he envisages forms through rewriting in his first novel, *Platitudes*.

The recent eclecticism of African American writers such as Darius James, Terry McMillan, and Ellis himself, rappers, film directors and actors (Spike Lee, Eddie Murphy, Chris Rock) crosses, with unprecedented audacity, the "battle lines" Addison Gayle was talking about in the late 60s and early 70s. Synthesizing "the last two black art revivals, the Harlem Renaissance and the Black Arts Movement" (Ellis, "Response" 250) at the same time that it participates in the "mainstream" postmodern logic (Lott, "Response" 244), the NBA queries the vernacular and "black experience" notions. What comes out of this interrogation is a "Disturbatory Art," as Ellis calls it after Arthur Danto. This art "shakes you up" by subjecting its ancestry to a "sacrilegious" form of "revisionism" ("NBA" 239). The young revisionists and their untamed "loa" may still be a minority. But this group does cut a distinct and heatedly debated profile, owing to a style involving more rupture than continuity. The NBA may "stem," as Ellis would have it, "straight from [a] tradition" comprising "the Civil Rights and black Nationalist movement" (239). Yet it has been noted chiefly for bringing a vivid "revisionism" to the "understanding" of these important moments and movements. "Like any new movement of artists and like most people in their mid-twenties," Ellis contends, "part of the process of stamping out our own adult identities includes rebelling against our parents, cautioning ourselves against their pitfalls." Notably, this "ritual dismemberment of the elders" (Lott, "Hip-Hop Fiction" 691) aims at "either expand[ing] or explod[ing] the old definition of blackness" (237). To achieve this goal, it incorporates the criticist dimensions of the Harlem Renaissance's aestheticism and the black avant-garde of the mid-70s, which includes Ishmael Reed, Toni Morrison, Clarence Major, John Edgar Wideman, George Clinton, David Hammons, and Richard Pryor.

It goes without saying, the NBA artists who carry out this "subversive" project also run the risk—which writers such as Reed also confronted—of being "branded either counter-revolutionary, too artsy or just not too good propagandists" (237). Putting his argument in historical perspective, Ellis acknowledges that there has been a tremendous pressure of the black cultural and political "mainstream" on African American artists to deal with certain topics or types of conflict. All these have usually been coterminous with overt black militantism. It is this limitation, increasingly intimated by writers from Ellison to Baldwin to James Alan McPherson, Major, and, again, Reed, that makes young authors like Ellis uneasy. They do recognize the necessity to keep old ideas and ideals alive. But they eschew what they see as a "propagandistic positivism" (238) that has run its course. A "postnationalist generation" (Lott, "Hip-Hop Fiction" 691), they insist on defining themselves through a critical dialogue with the African American cultural-militant heritage. This dialogue uses tradition to "mutate" it and make this "recombinant historical irony" (Lott, "Response" 245) and the parodying of black nationalism[20] an NBA "telltale sign" (Ellis, "NBA" 236).

In fact, Ellis has gone as far as to declare that his generation is enjoying a *sui generis* black *Glasnost* (234). He manipulates the term to suggest the increasing stylistic autonomy within the black arts of the late 80s. Reflecting this autonomy is a "postliberated aesthetic," to recall *Village Voice* critic Greg Tate's formula (8). Young artists both effect and benefit from a "vernacular" *perestroika* of sorts where, as Tate maintains, the artists' "appropriation of their power of signification" creates not only literary discourse but also "democracy." Now more aggressively than ever, black artists "borro[w] and reassembl[e]," as Ellis observes in the epigraph above, "across both race and class lines." This viewpoint undercuts current critical accounts of the hip-hop as a "plagiaristic commerce between white and black culture," accounts that tend to focus exclusively on the role of white "appropriations" of black art. It is certainly "important to remember," as Andrew Ross urges us in his essay "Hip, and the Long Front of Color," "that this *overexchanged* and *overbartered* record of miscegenated cultural production everywhere bespeaks a racist history of exploitation exclusively weighted to dominant white interest" (*No Respect* 68). But it is exactly this traditionally one-way intake of "raw material . . . appropriated and reduced in cultural force and meaning" (70) that late African American postmodernism battles. Raised in an increasingly multicultural society and giving rise, in their turn, to "a mongrel mix of classes and types" (Ellis, "NBA" 234), hip-hop artists revert the unidirectional flow of cultural annexations. In doing so, they straddle what Ross appears to conceive of as a fixed "color front," and it is through this ambiguous, mobile self-positioning that their identity unfolds. Redrawing by ironic, erudite touches the "tragic mulatto" figure of the 30s, the "cultural mulattoes" (Ellis, "NBA" 235) of the late 80s and 90s are feverishly immersed in intertextual and transcultural exchanges. Setting forth black postmodernism's revision of Du Bois's "double-consciousness" (Judy 255) and of the discourse of "blackness" generally, this "cross-pollination" (Ellis, "NBA" 240) is the subject of the following reading of *Platitudes* as an extensive rewrite.

THE PLEASURE OF THE HYPERTEXT

> [R]aces are like witches: however unreal witches are, *belief* in witches, like belief in races, has had—and in many communities continues to have—profound consequences for human social life. (Kwame Anthony Appiah, Lentricchia and McLaughlin 277)

> The entire corpus of existing literature should be regarded as a limbo from which discerning authors could draw their characters as required, creating only when they failed to find a suitable existing puppet. *The modern novel should be largely a work of reference.* (Flann O'Brien qtd. in Ellis, *Platitudes* 2)

J. Martin Favor observes that "in his effort to discover what, if anything, constitutes authentic African American experience and expression, Trey Ellis sets up a narrative apparatus by which he can question the whole notion of 'race writing'" (694). Granted, the novelist cannot and would not ignore black life. In fact, fueled by a "postnationalist" aesthetic, *Platitudes*' revisionist machine processes fictions of "blackness" with unique force. Moreover, although the NBA defies class and race boundaries, Ellis goes farther than most head-on approaches to racial identity as he attempts "to describe the production of collective identity in terms of discursive effect" (Judy 267). Resulting is a typically hip-hop scrutiny of the "canonical" modes of telling the "collective narrative of shared historical experience" (270). *Platitudes*' "jazzy scatting around the traditional novel" (Austin 20) tackles race by revisiting narrative regimes under which race has been configured since Frederick Douglass. What comes out of this is a novel that dramatizes the cultural mediation of racial identity throughout African American history.

Doubtlessly, previous stories of race such as the slave narrative, Harlem Renaissance novels, and black fiction of the late 60s and 70s mark a necessary, archival detour in *Platitudes*. Ellis reads and writes, in Eavan Boland's inspired words, "in the shadow" of these stories, themselves memorable acts of race reading and writing. In short, *Platitudes* deals with race chiefly by overhauling—mimicking, parodying, signifyin(g)—traditional writing about race. In breaking "open the past by reordering its texts" (13), the novelist deploys a Bakhtinian "heteroglossic structure" (Favor 695) within which he pursues an interpellation of African American narrative and its languages, themes, and morphology. If something does happen in *Platitudes*, then it is a "positive," I might say, "reconstructive" displacement of inherited forms and images that actually takes place, through a fast-paced, self-conscious exchange between the characters/writers on the novel's scene of writing and rewriting. In this sense, the book instantiates postmodern self-consciousness and, I should add, recent African American postmodernism's political consciousness.

Platitudes teems with stereotypes and "packaged" problematics, which its rewriting apparatus purports to unwrap, take apart, and recombine. The characters scramble to break the mold of pigeonholing commonplaces. Their creator's most efficient way to help them out is to expose the racial commonplaces *as* commonplaces, to turn the "genealogy" of race writing into the novel's main objective. Thus, it is clear that by substituting the "adventure of writing" for the "writing of adventure," to use Kristeva's famed formula, Ellis does not simply bow to the fad of self-referentiality. Quite on the contrary. His narrative pursuit of the "witches" of race is culturally motivated. Like most NBA artists, he feels that self-definition cannot but *work through* extant definitions, representations, and cultural myths. He must retell other(s') stories to get to tell his own, and it is with this goal in mind that he chooses, as we shall note, his "format."

This retelling stages an entire comedy of contending styles, discourses, and their underlying value repertoires. Invited to this contest are established and not-so-established storytelling forms and signifying systems from pop culture to computer software to sentimental prose to talk shows, fashion, and metafiction. In NBA fashion (Greg Tate 8) "art produced by nonblacks" is also woven into *Platitudes*'s "mutant assemblage," the outcome of which is "something like crossing Spike Lee with Gilbert Sorrentino" (Lott, "Hip-Hop Fiction" 691). It is the celebration of this heterogeneity and the erosion of the oppositions between "high" and "low," aesthetic and nonaesthetic genres, representation and self-representation, fiction and theory, even "black" and "white" forms of expression that might justify Tate's defining the NBA as "popular black post-structuralism" (Judy 250).

A perfect illustration of this model of cultural hybridization, *Platitudes* can be seized as a *story of storywriting and rewriting*. Pointedly, the "decentered" nature, "multivocality" (Landow, *Hypertext 2.0* 36) and recursiveness of writing and rewriting acts in the novel allow for the latter's discussion in terms of hypertextuality. It is such a discussion that I intend to open up here. Specifically, I want to indicate how rewriting follows certain hypertextual protocols and how these protocols are entangled with notable sociocultural maneuvers. It would be only fair to add, though, that Ellis's narrative both exemplifies and toys with the notion of hypertextuality as defined by hypertext critics from Theodor H. Nelson to George Landow, Michael Joyce, and, recently, Silvio Gaggi. The genre staples are easily identifiable, but, especially toward the end, *Platitudes* starts effacing them to suggest, at least, a "closure" rather atypical of most hypertext narratives.

To begin with, the actual model—and frequent fictional scene—of writing in *Platitudes* is digital rather than textual. Tellingly, hypermedia, computers, PC-generated, edited and reedited materials pop up everywhere in the novel, from the front cover to the writing courses and multiple-choice tests various characters take. What is more important, the story itself heavily indulges an incurable addiction to nonlinearity, a foremost hypertextual symptom. Consequently, the novel looks like a nonsequential assemblage of "blocks" or "lexias," to recall Roland Barthes's *S/Z*. In *Platitudes*, causality and organicity tend to give way to a sort of "unfinished textuality" appropriately "described by terms like *link*, *node*, *network*, *web*, and *path*" (Landow, *Hypertext 2.0* 3). Thus, Ellis motions his readers into "a textual space available for exploration" (Gaggi 123) rather than mapping out this space for them.

Despite all these intricacies, the actual plot is remarkably simple. Writer Dewayne Wellington is trying to tell the story of black, New Yorker teenagers Earle and Dorothy. At some point, however, he confesses that he does not "know what more to write" (Ellis, *Platitutes* 14) and asks, half in earnest, half in jest, for public help. He also promises to "incorporate [the] suggestions and keep the ship sailing smoothly from here on in." Fortunately, his literary S.O.S. receives a prompt response from an established woman writer, Isshee Ayam, whose name arguably anagrams Ishmael Reed's and possibly Alice Walker's, ironically endowing the author of *Mumbo Jumbo* with a feminine identity and thus hinting at Reed's disputes with black women writers, Walker included. This is just one example of how the novel shows off its playfully postmodern determination to churn the fictionality regimens of traditional prose. For, in Ellis, the author no longer remains outside the fictional world. And, what is more notable, the reader also becomes a character, an "internal" reader as Ayam takes part in the book's writing. Certainly, Ellis's is not a "ready-only" (Landow, *Hyper/Text/Theory* 9) hypertext. Ayam adds "links," revises previous text blocks, "counterwrites" as much as she reads and judges Wellington's work. Thus, she illustrates the intriguing input of the typical "hypertext reader," who "in a very real sense writes (or rewrites) hypertexts" (Michael Joyce 20). It is basically through her that *Platitudes* integrates writing and reading so that the latter works as a constitutive part of the former. Thus, the text dramatizes its own hypertextual production, consumption, and reproduction, frequently in a jocose manner, playing with our expectations, trying out various plot alternatives, and so forth. In such a way, writing-as-process and writing *in* process draw our attention, somehow rendering the narrative "substance" less relevant in the texts's economy. Likewise, one could argue that *Platitudes*' language is "thicker," more "opaque," blocking out the "message"—a situation always problematic, "unethical" for authors coming from, or writing in, a tradition where an ideology of "transparency" and ideological priorities has often controlled literary production. But this simplistic distinction between form and content, which critics such as Gates and Barbara Christian have recently refuted, proves here particularly abusive as Ellis's novel adduces an example of structure treated as content. The interplay of different narrative forms and styles makes up the plot itself and, we will see, voices a powerful message.

The dialogue between Wellington and Ayam lies at the core of this complex hypertextual interface. The epistolary conversation, a genre that also informs Ellis's second novel, *Home Repairs*,[21] is not a mere exchange of literary opinions, but a contest of cultural codes, mentalities, aesthetics, modes of storytelling—and of telling and re-telling the same story. Wellington's literary manner is characteristically "disenchanted," ironic, and ludic, erratic and "excruciatingly nomadic," as Ayam holds it (*Platitudes* 109). "Are you so blindly enthralled with that postmodernist, semiological sophism (that incidentally *nobody* believes anymore) that the words 'narrative' and 'continuity' mean nothing to you? Have you never read Baldwin?" (79), Ayam asks. Through Wellington's writing, Ellis questions the traditional narrative, both "mainstream" and black, with a particular emphasis on the latter. Wellington's story of New York youngsters Earle, Andy, and Donald is fragmentary, heterogeneous, mirroring the existence of a couple of middle-class black characters caught up in a web of psychosocial conflicts typical to urban, computerized, postindustrial life. It is puzzling and even designed to look like a nonsequential puzzle, mock-Sorrentinian restaurant/computer menu, like a dictionary or acknowledged "less readable" list (52) of random events and objects.

But Wellington does dish out his own *Mulligan Stew*. His postmodern amalgam of intertexts, graffiti, TV commercials, computer games, edit software (*Platitudes* 30), radio talks, slang, photos, and fragments of textbooks is a "work of reference" (2) of sorts and source of "queer stuff" (2) outrageously aimless and utterly "unreadable" for Ayam:

> It's the Friday after Earle's embarrassing Monday. He hasn't been to school all week. Instead, he's watched shows like *The $25,000 Pyra-*

mid, where celebrity guests give contestants examples and the contestants must name the category described:

Casino Royale, *The Newlywed Game*, *The Dating Game*: films and game shows sporting themes both written and performed by sweaters, clocks, draft beer, tables, slot machines, all science-fiction robots, roads, caves, most formal organizations, potatoes, lettuce, corn: inanimate objects referred to anthropomorphically in everyday speech. *Bing*! [applause]. The trigger, the barrel, the sight, the butt, the infrared nightscope: parts of a high-powered, anti-terrorist rifle. *Bing*! [applause]. Tortilla Flats, The Mud and Soot, The Grime and the Weasel, The Grits and The Sweet [. . .] Prince Andrew, philosophers, prostitutes, wife-beaters, dogs that continually hump their master's leg or the legs of complete strangers, people who always hold the door open for others, [. . .] nurses, some doctors, den mothers, most blood donors, hypochondriacs, all Peace Corps volunteers, nerds," etc. (52–53).

Wellington's is a hardly "legible" story in the sense in which legibility implies both readability and, etymologically, conformity to law, in our case, the norm of traditional—especially black—narrative as understood by its more conservative practitioners like Ayam. She replies to Wellington's "postmodern," "Afro-Baroque," "mock Afro-Baroque" (75) "platitudes" (65) with a "true narrative." Wellington's "post-realistic," "piebald" "montage" (66) and "collage," which do not hesitate to insert into the text PSAT(EST) booklet sheets (another hypertextual metaphor) parodying civil rights news reports, ironically show off high self-awareness in the form of a tongue-in-cheek self-critique. Unlike his, Ayam's "simpering prose is a caricature of some of the mythologically oriented feminist writers" (Austin 20), a piece of "blind," sentimental (pseudo)realism. It rewrites Wellington's plot, borrows figures and facts from the New York story and relocates them in a legendary Georgia, substituting a narrowly defined racial conflict for the complex crisis affecting the "original" Earle and Dorothy.

It is fairly clear, I think, that, unless carefully defined, the terms of rewriting and originality may not accommodate each other within Ellis's "poststructuralist" (Judy 250) agenda. In this light, one should remember that it is Wellington, namely, Wellington-as-Ellis, the persona of the "postmodern" author, who first "rewrites" the traditional, racial plot, and then asks for "help," making Ayam "write back" and thereby redo his story. But it is the New York story that reveals itself as secondary, a modification of the slave narrative and later, mythical or sentimental fiction patterns whose reshaping infuriates Ayam. However, mocking this type of nostalgic rewriting, having Earle read in his English class *The Narrative of the Adventures of W. W. Ellis as a Former Captive in North America* (49), Ellis seems to imply that, if his own revisionism cannot totally dissolve the traditional form of black narrative, one cannot completely restore the latter's "genuine" coherence either. This is hardly possible simply because African American tradition, including W. W. Brown's 1847 *Narrative*, which Ellis ironically redoes, has been somehow Signifyin(g) and self-Signifyin(g) all along its history, as Gates reminds us, although in different ways. Consequently, Ayam's outburst seems pointless: "I must have been naive to have believed that after comparing my work with your own puerile, misogynistic, disjointed, and amateurish ejaculations (and I use the last word deliberately), you would have never again dared to defile the temple of black literature. The only consolation one can derive from your pathetic pornography is that it is so terribly bad that even the seamiest to vanity press would retch at the thought of ever publishing it" (39).

Ayam's attempt to restore through her own rewriting the "genuine" story aims at absolute "readability" within the canonical code of autobiographic and later, sentimental fiction portraying racial conflicts in an idealized, matriarchal Georgia. Her style, ostentatiously opposed to Wellington's, boasts absolute fluency, endless chains of modifiers, transparency, racially and culturally rigid divisions, and a "domino"-like linearity meant to polemically piece together the competitor's "puzzle." It is descriptive, mimetic, superfluously adjectival:

> The next morning's sun woke the heavens with a friendly warmth and glow that told all the earth's creatures that Sunday had finally and so gloriously arrived. . . . Six strong, big, and clean feet marched across the wood floor worn by generations of sharecropper births, deaths, pray meetings, and shindigs. . . . The family, like all the others around Lowndes County, all wearing proud, old clothes, pressed and starched and bleached respectable, walked down Route 49 toward the swelling hums and organ clouds of Sunday spirituals that surged from the clean white doors of Mt. Zion Baptist Church. . . . There, behind the shoulders of that bright, clean house of God, the three boys hid behind the tall, proud oak—God's oak, the simple, kind folk of Lowndes County called it. (40–43)

Ellis's stylistic pastiche and thematic parody merge the worn-out monody of the imitated "original" and the mocking imitation's voice-over into a Bakhtinian "double voice" of sorts. We feel of course Ellis's irony behind Ayam's earnest narrative, as we sense it in Wellington's "nomadic" and "pornographic" "platitudes."

In certain cases, this irony does not deploy, as above, an entire stylistic apparatus of rewriting but works through literary allusion. The stylistic palimpsest is thus interlarded with a tight allusive network. Scattered in the latter's fabric are direct and indirect references to the black narrative, which are "dragging [Wellington's] meager tale to its roots in Afro-American glory-stories" (19). *Platitudes* abounds especially with hints at black writers who have dealt with the opposition between the South and the North: Hurston, Wright, Ellison, and Toomer. We are not surprised to learn that Earle, Wellington's protagonist, does voluntary work at Jean Toomer Democratic Club, a culturally oversaturated, symbolic space. The "club" allegorizes the novel's "citational" method and its dream of becoming "largely a work of reference," as the Flann O'Brien epigraph (2) intimates. From the club's walls, Wellington writes, "stare collages of familiar faces: Malcolm X, Frederick Douglass, Sojourner Truth, Harriet Tubman, Martin Luther King, Jr., Stokely Carmichael, Amiri Baraka, Angela Davis, Huey Newton, Bobby Seale, John Carlos, Marcus Garvey, Sekou Touré, Jomo Kenyatta, Patrice Lumumba, Albert Luthuli, Nelson Mandela, Paul Robeson, Jean Toomer, Jesse Jackson, James Baldwin, Ralph Ellison, Richard Johnson, LeRoi Jones, Richard Wright, Toni Morrison, Alice Walker, Stevie Wonder, the Jacksons, and every major jazz artist ever" (131). An Ayam poster hangs there, too, informing us that her small Georgia town-based, "gem" of a novel, *Hog Jowl Junction*, "burns with the glow of righteousness, sparkles with the fire of a richly endowed imagination, and shimmers with the light of a brilliant and creative technique" (131). Ayam herself mentions James Baldwin reverently, as we saw, and one of her characters bears the name I. Corinthians (an allusion to Morrison's *Song of Solomon*).

CO-AUTHORING

Most significant, the famous "quotes"—names, works, passages, styles, themes, or structures—do not lead a passive life once incorporated into Ellis's "dictionary" or "menu," items obsessively reoccurring in the novel. These intertexts carry on a permanent, passionate conversation. They are being modified (rewritten, challenged) at the same time that they are modifying (writing back, disputing) Wellington's poetics and "philosophy." His story becomes surreptitiously more politically sensitive and less inclined to "erase the significance of race altogether" (Favor 698). While unknitting the thick weft of the racial text, this story is being interlaced with Ayam's. In its turn, the latter gets increasingly realistic, bold, unconventional. Finally, the two writers get together, and their previous literary exchange turns out the prologue of a more than literary affair, aroused (*stricto sensu*) by provoking, aphrodisiacal writing. In *Platitudes* texts—and their fictive authors—interact, intersect, mingle, mirror, rub up against—as they rewrite—each other. The hypertextual agon gradually yields, to paraphrase Ayam, to a new disposition to each other's works, even to textual co-operation. "Never a fan of you experimentalists," Ayam writes Wellington, "I must admit that I sometimes envy your stylistic liberty" (149). The competing stories sprouting up off the frame narrative's main "nodes" merge toward the end into a single, erotically charged story where Wellington and Ayam finally consume their textual/sexual affair. This consummation or rather "summation" of *Platitudes*' narrative possibilities brings about the suggestion of a closure clearer than in most "classical" hypertexts (Gaggi 123). Angry audience at first, Ayam turns into stylistic "contender" and finally into Wellington's "collaborator."[22] She co-authors his story, ultimately forcing Wellington to revise his assumptions and values. Not only does the hypertext rework, as intertextual play, several fictions of race and narrative forms. It also "rewrites the author" (Landow *Hypertext 2.0* 90), in fact, both authors and their apparently irreconcilable styles and politics.

To conclude, it seems to me that Ellis uses—and plays upon—the hypertext as a "hip-hop Signifyin(g)" apparatus of literary rewriting. He updates Gates's model in a narrative fashion evoking the "continuous linguistic slippage and play that drives the verbal engines of rap" (Potter 81). In doing so, Ellis proposes a literary modality of reinventing identity that doubtlessly recalls Reed's. Continuously cutting across race, class, and gender boundaries, narrative games in *Platitudes* issue forth, also in Potter's formulation, "a patchwork of overlapping—and in some cases, *conflicting*—identities" (13). Favor is certainly right to pinpoint the "liberating" perspective on race opened up by the "many types of blackness" (697) woven into Ellis's narrative texture. This is, again, NBA "cross-pollination," which defies essentialist categories as well as the transcendent view of a world—including the world of race—accessible to us directly, without narrative mediation. Ellis's novel is a moment in the more recent discourse on race increasingly reluctant to accept race as a natural object, a "fact" predating its description. Thus, Favor's comments on the absence of the real thing in the novel strike me as falling off the mark. In actuality, Ellis's novel persuasively reminds us that any take on "the real thing" of race must needs start with previous takes, talks, and stories. In other words, the "real thing"'s reality is always available as a cultural construction, as story. As such, it implies a narrative decision on one of the possible ways of telling the story of race or of an individual or class within the racial group.

Along these lines, the hypertext fulfills a double function. First, it analyzes the multiple narrative stratification and ramification of race.

Second, it acts this complexity out by inventing its characters, indeed, forming their races and identities "crosswise," at the intersection of stories, representations, and styles. Through various forms of rewriting, it plunges in the past to effect an archaeology—or, as I said above, a "genealogy"—of race at the same time that it launches into the future by pro-jecting, bodying forth fictions of race through Wellington, Ayam, Earle, and Dorothy. Ellis refuses to freeze the identity of his characters inside the iceboxes of extant paradigms and rubrics; nor can he completely place this identity outside those categories, in continuous, random flow. He locates it, or rather dramatizes its cultural and historical manifestation, its writing across and at the junctions of classes, races, genders, genres, and stories.

At the same time, it seems to me that Ellis's hypertextual cross-incorporation picks up where Reed's Hoodoo and skepticism regarding technology appear to leave off. Ellis's criticism and fiction align with hypertext theorists' efforts to legitimate hypertextual practices ethically and politically.[23] Needless to say, this has always been a daunting task as it cannot avoid postulating some sort of post-Enlightenment control over technology and, implicitly, over the discourse technology produces. I think, though, that in light of my analysis, one could argue that *Platitudes*' hypertext works like a rewriting machine allowing the rewriting subject to impact, restructure the structures—fables, fictions, narrative regimens, ideological constructs—constraining his or her representation. Ellis's book is anything but a narrative prison-house. It shows characters making choices, pursuing narrative paths, rejecting specific forms and formulations, suggesting alternatives, and considering alternatives to their own narrative versions, in short, participating in the writing of their stories. Identity is here a process of negotiations, of storytelling and retelling. Readers become writers and *re*writers. Not only do they resist narrative representation, but they also modify the stories through which others have defined and confined their lives.

PART IV

Writing Through: Rewriting, Plagiarism, Apocrypha

> [T]he best way to consider originality is to look not for first instances of a phenomenon, but rather to see duplication, parallelism, symmetry, parody, repetition, echoes of it. . . . The writer thinks less of writing originally, and more of rewriting. [T]he writer can be read as an individual whose impulse historically has been always to write through one or another given work. (Said 135–36)

> Imagination feeds on previous imagination. . . . This is an extreme but very instructive way of perceiving the whole process of imagination in terms of plagiarism. (Scholes, *Fabulation* 214–15)

THE METASTASES OF ORIGINALITY

David Foster Wallace's 1992 short story, "Tri-Stan: I Sold Sissee Nar to Ecko," features one Egon M. Nar, a TV network executive able to skillfully "shuffle & recombine proven entertainment formulas into configurations that allowed the muse of Familiarity to appear cross-dressed as Innovation" (McCaffery, *After Yesterday's Crash* 232). Thus, Nar's "programming *arche*" is "the metastasis of originality" (232). Wallace explains it as the redefinition of "creativity [as] manipulation of received themes" (237). "Transmogrification of 'timeless' myth" into contemporary camp-image" (238), the "metastatic" method brings about a mediatic "popularization" by means of which, for instance, Oprah reincarnates Isis and JFK reembodies Sigurd. The method both recuperates and "scraps," writes off, the original. On the one hand, TV and pop culture "metastasis" somehow helps the "original" survive in that classical authors, mythology, and tragedy become, through remakes, "accessible" and "popular." On the other, the classics "mutate," are actualized as fetishized reproductions saliently differing from the models. Further, a leveling, unifying, and thus metastatic process is triggered within culture's "body" by Nar's zooming back and forth between ages, authors, themes, elite and popular works. As a result, the distinction between the prototype and duplication, the classical piece and its pop replica—the Oedipus series and *Dynasty*, kabbala and Cable, Tristan and Tri-Star, to quote Wallace's witty puns—no longer holds water. All of these turn into cannon fodder for the "producer"'s transmogrifying apparatus, where reproduction and repetition suffuse the "aura" of "originality." Deprived of the latter, the "model" becomes metastatic in the rhetorical sense of the term: a trivial, derivative if not spurious object.

Let me summarize: fast-paced scuttling between works, codes, and cultural series, followed by their radical—hilarious, "sacrilegious"—transformation or "corruption"; Baudrillardian crisis of the "original"'s body in a world of voracious "camp" copies; transvaluation of the concept of originality as "popularizing," entertaining update of the "lofty" and the canonical—the new as ability to mass circulate the old under shocking forms: all are part and parcel of the rewriting model behind a whole strain of late twentieth-century culture, the avant-pop.

So far, we have scrutinized more closely "rewriterly mutations" in "metafiction" (Coover), in pop-postmodern "historiography" (Doctorow), in pseudo-"subgenres" such as "post-transcendentalist" private eye novels (Auster), and in contemporary African American narratives of cross-racial "mongrelization." Here, I want to attend to cultural and stylistic "transmogrification" in other zones of recent rewriting, beginning with the avant-pop as illustrated by writers such as Mark Leyner and, to a certain extent, Kathy Acker. Last, I turn to the transnational type of rewriting exemplified by Bharati Mukherjee. Bringing, like Acker, considerations of gender to bear upon rewriting, Mukherjee's fiction characteristically deploys postmodern and postcolonial-globalist strategies of narrative revisionism. All three authors take up related rewriting forms, engrafting, plagiarism and apocrypha, and target the same author, Hawthorne. Equally important, they renarrate Hawthorne "through" specific contemporary cultural forms or "through" the styles of certain authors. Finally, while the scope of critical rewriting varies, they engage with a similar problematic: language and the media; technology and the body; reality—virtual or otherwise—and the commodifying rule of the image; gender politics, masculinity, femininity, and their dramatic cultural-historical inscription in the text called "America," as well as in other texts this master text has intersected, borrowed from, or obliterated.

CHAPTER 1

Avant-Pop Graftings: Mark Leyner's Outrageous Body of Work

> JENNY JONES: And you were raising your daughter as a postmodernist?
>
> ALEX: Of course. That's what makes this particularly tragic. I mean, how do you explain to a 5-year old that self-consciously recycling cultural detritus is suddenly no longer a valid art form when, for her entire life, she's been taught that it is? (Leyner, "Geraldo" 11)

(RE)WORKING OUT

Leyner's texts reincorporate the "original"('s) *corpus* to reenact the writer's identity and the concept of originality—"original identity"—from an avant-pop standpoint. What I find of particular interest is his rewriting scenario for using the metastasis of the Hawthornian literary body as a means to lay open the "palimpsest condition," the cultural "texture" of bodies, "corporeality," and, generally, identity in our culture. In "reproducing" Hawthorne, Leyner sets up an intriguing model of *critically* producing and reproducing what has predominantly been seized as a natural given, "origin," and less as a cultural product: the body. Indeed, central to Leyner's project is the rich amphibology of the *body*, its revealing slippage into the textual semantics of *corpus* as playing out in phrases such as *body of knowledge*, *body of texts* (*literature*), or, to recall one of Acker's titles, *bodies of work*. Before seeing how Leyner taps this ambiguity by reembodying, giving a new identity to Hawthorne's textual body, a brief outline of avant-pop aesthetics is in order.

A former Fiction Collective member, Mark Leyner has published, since his more experimental, avant-garde 1983 book *I Smell Esther Williams and Other Stories*, four more volumes: *My Cousin, My Gastroenterologist* (1990), a series of high-density, often intensely poetic prose fragments, and the more narrative *Et Tu, Babe* (1992), *Tooth Imprints on a Corn Dog* (1995), and *The Tetherballs of Bougainville* (1997). Casting "Mark Leyner," his own fictional alter-ego, in the lead role of his fake-autobiographic books, Leyner has almost over night become a cult figure. His central place in current debates around the avant-pop seems to be a matter of course even though the author himself does not take the new label seriously. "Clever" as it may sound, the term itself, like "postmodernism," whose "fundamentalist offshoot" it represents ("Geraldo" 11), has lately become a target of Leyner's irony. But it is precisely this "irony enveloped in more irony" in jest thrashing itself for "indiscriminatingly incorporating any and all kinds of pop kitsch and schlock" (11) that exemplifies avant-pop cultural self-awareness. Thus, Larry McCaffery anthologizes Leyner's work in the standard collection *After Yesterday's Crash: The Avant-Pop Anthology*. And, distinguishing Acker's more postmodern rewrites such as *Great Expectations* and *Don Quixote* from typically avant-pop works, the critic lists under the same postmodern rubric "cover versions" of myths, biblical stories and fairy tales, by Barthelme, Coover, Barth, and Steve Katz as precursors of the avant-pop. His selection contains, in addition, pieces by Coover and Katz along with earlier metafictionists such as Sukenick and Federman, later authors such as DeLillo and Auster, as well as more recent, cyberpunk writers and hard-to-classify visionaries including William T. Vollmann, Bruce Sterling, William Gibson, Steve Erickson, Stephen Wright, Mark Amerika, Harold Jaffe, and Gerald Vizenor. McCaffery's roll call indicates, as we shall see momentarily, that the border between postmodern intertextuality and avant-pop bricolage is shifty. One can seize, at times, the latter as a particular spin-off of more mainstream rewriting initiated by Barth and Barthelme. Alternatively, authors and critics associated with the avant-pop have called it a "Post-Post-Modernist Aesthetic Phenomenon" (McCaffery, "13 Introductory Ways" 32). Putatively sanctioning the "death" of postmodernism, the avant-pop parodies postmodern forms, resulting in parodies of parodies, meta-metafictions. By the same token, the logic of both "mainstream" postmodernism and the avant-pop remains unchanged: "appropriation of other texts and characters" (Amerika and Olsen, "Smells" 15).

Acknowledging his debt to Lester Bowie, McCaffery points out that avant-pop authors turn pop culture into subject, fictive setting, and expressive medium of their work, trading upon their audience's familiarity with pop repertoires. In doing so, I might add, they strive to defamiliarize the all-too-familiar and thereby, as McCaffery insists, to "examin[e] the status of life and writing in contemporary America" ("Avant-Pop" xvii). But I should also stress that some avant-pop writers take for granted certain knowledge of "elite" culture, too. This assumption is, in fact, a prerequisite for avant-pop "transmogrifications" of revered "literary bodies." Leyner clearly counts on this twofold reading competence. To recall John Cage's method of "Writing through the Cantos,"[1] I would suggest that Leyner writes, indeed *rewrites through* an "original," a precursor work, as much as he writes through the roller-coastering world of pop simulacra: the media, new communication technologies, the icons of consumer culture, and its array of prevailingly visual forms from graffiti and comic strips to MTV, film, cyberpunk, hypertext—our "culture's dreck-machine" (Amerika and Olsen, "Smells" 11).

In the following, I show how avant-pop rewriting reinvents the metafictional postmodern for the mass culture, media-saturated era. In view of this objective, I would submit from the outset that Leyner's work stakes out an ambiguous area where recognized intertextual-metafictional procedures are articulated with massive intake of popular styles and materials. However, while most avant-pop criticism has privileged the latter on the assumption that literature's place in the avant-pop *ars combinatoria*'s storehouse has shrunk, I want to insist on the former, on its modalities and significance within the avant-pop project. In other words, I deal with Leyner's texts as avant-pop-adapted rewrites. These rewrites take certain shapes and hold precise roles for they "write through," or, as Leyner says, "slas[h] a path through the rank vegetation of American popular culture" (*Tooth Imprints* 145).

"MY BOOKS AND MY BODY": INSET, INSERT, TEXTUAL SURGERY

> I'd really love to be some sort of surgeon. . . . When I started writing *Et Tu, Babe*, which was about self-promotion and marketing and self-transformation in the most mercantile way, I started going to the gym a lot and the two just sort of seemed to dovetail. (Leyner, "An Interview" by Laurence 4)

> Writing means grafting. It is the same word. It is by becoming engrafted that something comes to be expressed. The graft does not engraft that initial thing proper. There is no such thing as an original text. (Derrida, *La Dissémination* 395; trans. mine)

Leyner hilariously dramatizes the interaction of the writer and his or her audience or "market"—in a way, the utmost tropes of the private and the public. This dramatization brings out the very performative sense of the term: especially in *Et Tu, Babe*, *Tooth Imprints*, and *The Tetherballs*, Leyner *performs* the social image of the author. His protagonist is a writer named Mark Leyner, who proves anxious to *produce* himself.

This production means, first and foremost, Leyner-the-character's "acting" on the stage of publicity, turning his image into the ultimate icon. Oddly enough, such comic modification in *Et Tu, Babe* requires the (com)modification of the author-hero's physicality. The author-in-the-novel manufactures his body, refashions it to better fit into the pattern of marketable icons the stardom culture feeds off. Intensely allusive and ironically bookish, *Et Tu, Babe* provides critical, half-satirical, half-autoironic insights into the contemporary mechanisms of success. Leyner takes on the author's myth, enormously inflates just to deflate it and thus obtain a comic effect through rewriting as renarrativization, restyling, and language games. Authors such as DeLillo—*Mao II* is a prime example here—also play out the whole "iconology" of the celebrated author. Yet DeLillo's character explicitly toils to protect his privacy, finally his identity, by refusing to *produce* texts and thus "produce" himself on the public stage. Quite the contrary, everything Leyner's author-hero does is subsumed to enhancing his public persona. He is obsessed with his body as his actual work, repeatedly writes and rewrites, "edits" and advertises it as such. He strives to turn it into his real masterpiece, a famed *corpus*, an exhilarating "body of writings." What Leyner's caricature of the "Überauthor"—"Überwriter," a critic calls him[2]—achieves is turn the usual "logic of the market" comically upside down: it is not the author who promotes his work; it is this work that must "peddle" its author. In his turn, "Leyner" uses his fame to endorse for outrageous fees products such as Diet Pepsi. He does it either through commercials or, à la Italo Calvino's character Flannery and his ghostwriters in *If on a winter's night a traveler*, by inserting various brand names into his books. In Leyner's oversaturated, "hypertextual world," books count less as aesthetic objects and increasingly as means to upgrade the author's marketability. But then, the writer has to live up to his social reflexion as a famed author. To achieve this, he needs to come up with a convenient image, that is, he must build, rebuild, and hyper up his body, through which he becomes a *hyper artist* in all senses: a very "pumped-up" author and a (self)promoter, a pro of (self-)advertising. Textual production through "inserts," intertextual "graftings," and retellings ironically serves as a kind of model and warm-up of the real production, the production of the author's body. Both activate identical mechanisms of cultural appropriation and reincorporation. "Leyner" (re)constructs himself as a hypermale *and* author by the same "procedure" of "hypertextual engrafting."[3]

Speaking to, and critiquing, "that strain of the American male psyche which yearns to grossly transform one's own body" (9), his obsession with vasectomy, dermatological "fixes," excision, "self-surgery," and "visceral tattoo[ing]" as writing and rewriting runs through all of his books. Looking at "Leyner"'s X-rays, we learn, "female medical technicians and nurses . . . go nuts" over the sexy tattoos engraved on his heart. Moreover, he rewrites, "interpolates," his body by grafting artificial muscles onto it. Writing and working out, text building and bodybuilding, artistic geniality and unbridled genitality are inseparable. If *My Cousin* purports to be "an autobiography written wearing wrist weighs" (5), *Et Tu, Babe* further strengthens this bizarre tie: "My books and my body," "Mark" declares, "my status as a reckless writer and a gorgeous male . . . are my iridescent plumage; they're the equivalent of the male" (127). "Leyner"'s comic, self-enhanced hypermaleness is, in brief, entirely an intertextual/hypertextual matter. His bodily practice of "grafting" spectacularly actualizes the illuminating etymology of the graft and the *greffe*: originally, grafting literally meant writing as it was derived from *graphein*, "to write." "I often feel like a surgeon trapped in a writer's body" (*Tooth Imprints* 2), Leyner tellingly owns, an "amateur dermatologist" (210) and tattooist exerting his art on himself as much as on others and their literary bodies, "a writer and aesthetician by trade, but an internist and surgeon by avocation" (113). His favorite place is "The Hyatt Self-Surgery Clinic," where he can be his own surgeon-tattooist and literally write (on) his body. But Leyner-the-character, the fictional "self-surgery" aficionado, shares his procedure with Leyner-the-author. Let us now watch the real self-surgeon at work giving himself various transplants meant, this time around, to "inset" writing and textuality not into the hero's "body" but into the Leyner *corpus*.

THRICE-TOLD TALES: HAWTHORNE, INC.

> inc., 1. engraved. [L *incisus*] 2. inclosure. 3. included. 4. including. 5. inclusive. 6. income. 7. incorporated. 8. increase. 9. incumbent. (*Webster's New Universal Unabridged Dictionary*)
>
> The process [of grafting] is much more direct than the distortion involved in most intertextual borrowings, or, in fact, than a simple act of quotation, for the reference to the other artist becomes the central focus of the argument, the point of departure for a meditation which involves a process of reception, revealing how one artist perceives the work of another, a process of mediation, how the significance of the work is emphasized in accordance with the preoccupations of the commentator-beholder, and an act of appropriation through which the complexity of another's thought is annexed to one's own work. (Russo 79)

The grafting of Hawthorne's 1835 tale "Young Goodman Brown" onto the "Young Bergdorf Goodman Brown" piece from *Tooth Imprints*

(13–95) is an exemplary avant-pop rewrite. Before discussing it in detail, I should note the author's frequent intertextual "operations" on the Hawthornian corpus. Chapter 5 of *Et Tu, Babe*, for example, features a restaging of *West Side Story* where the female hero lives for a while in a *Blithedale Romance*-like "socialistic community" (108). Even more intriguing is, in *Tetherballs*, what "Mark," a teenage "writer," describes as a "remake" (141) of Hawthorne's 1844 text, "The Artist of the Beautiful," during his sexual encounter with the warden of the prison where his father undergoes a botched execution. "Mark"'s outline of his Hawthornian source seems to me relevant to what he is up to. The story, he says,

> takes place in New England in, like, the 1830s, and it's about this guy Owen Warland who's this wimpy genius who's supposed to be a watchmaker but spends all his time working on this beautiful, intricate mechanical butterfly, and he's in love with a woman by the name of Annie Hovenden who's not really in love with him because I think she figures he's too wimpy and quixotic and he'll never amount to much career-wise, and she ends up marrying this stupid albeit totally buff blacksmith named Robert Danforth and they have a kid, and at the end of the story the kid accidentally crushes the mechanical butterfly. (140–41)

Aside from Leyner's "buff" body obsession, "Mark"'s summary is quite accurate. Embedded in this outline is a "reading" of the tale, which does not fall wide off the mark either. "The Artist of the Beautiful," "Mark" patiently clues in the warden, is "basically about how artists are too delicate to exist in a world where the ability to earn a living and having a good body are considered, like, the most important things" (141).

As the reader may recall, Hawthorne's story allegorizes the philosophical struggle between utilitarianism, which "restrains," as its narrator explains, creativity within materially limited purposes, and the genius's attempt to capture the "Beautiful Idea" and thereby "put the very spirit of Beauty into form" (*Tales* 916, 911) by stepping outside the realm of material incorporation. This attempt is bound to fail, as Hawthorne intimates here and in other stories written in the early 1840s, where his dialogue with transcendentalism is more vivid than anywhere. Taking up Emerson's neoplatonic argument on "oneness" laid out in the 1836 essay *Nature*, Hawthorne goes farther than Emerson and transcendentalists generally (Rucker 454) in his critique of Owen's "radical idealism" (447). Importantly, he queries the notion of "disembodied" creativity, refusing to accept the divorce between the "pure" vision of the Beautiful and its material, "visible shape" (Hawthorne, *Tales* 921). Personifying a "straw-man" radical dualism, Owen finds the concept of "the spiritualization of the matter" rather strange (917). His mechanical butterfly "incarnat[es] an idea" (928), but the materiality of the "incarnation" appears as a symbolically frail "trifle," a mere—and lost—opportunity for his spirit to "posses[s] itself" in the realm of Platonic "Reality" (931).

Rewriting "The Artist of the Beautiful," "Mark" takes up its plot while blowing out of proportions Hawthorne's resistance to Owen's idealism. "I had," "Mark" says,

> this idea to do a remake of "The Artist of the Beautiful" where, instead of just making this exquisite mechanical butterfly, Owen Warland makes one of these PFM-1 butterfly mines, and at the end when the kid starts playing with it, his father takes it away from him and, not being the brightest guy in the world, he starts pulling on its wings and it explodes and blows his hands off, and Annie, who's nothing if not pragmatic, realizes that Danforth's blacksmithing days are over and she finally acknowledges that maybe Owen has a future after all—apparently as a munitions expert—and leaves her maimed husband for the Artist of the Beautiful, and they live, like, happily ever after. (141)

In his "version," "Mark" assures the warden, "at least the reader would get some satisfaction" (142). But what kind of satisfaction might one derive from such a purposefully silly rewrite, we may ask. In what sense could one say to "enjoy" it? To answer these questions, I would begin by pointing out that "Mark"'s earnest claim is in fact Leyner's irony—another ironic layer on top of a text already tightly packed with "ironies within ironies." The Hawthorne "prototype" is lodged inside "Mark"'s rewrite, which is in its turn bracketed by the warden episode, which—finally—is encased Chinese boxlike[4] by the narrator's pseudomemoir. What results from this is not only a multilayered, self-mirroring narrative that parodies postmodern self-reflexiveness, but also a four-story, phony autobiographic edifice that sets up a multiply ironic distance between author, his teenage "rewriter," and Hawthorne. Granted, Leyner targets Hawthorne's romantic problematics and rhetoric. One might say he "de-romanticizes," de-idealizes them through "Mark"'s rewrite at the same time that he ironizes the latter by implying that the reader would enjoy the kitschy "highjacking" of the Hawthornian plot, which has the idealistic aesthete go into a materialistic kind of business.

"YOUNG BERGDORF GOODMAN BROWN": A "HEINOUS REVISION"

> [W]riting becomes plagiarism. (Hassan, *The Right Promethean Fire* 56)

Let me return to "Mark"'s bizarre emphasis on the buff body of Hawthorne's character, Robert Danforth. We are witnessing here a favorite technique of Leyner's avant-pop rewriting: deliberate misreading through the literalizing of a "matrix" text's element, followed by a reconstruction of the original by privileging and amplifying that literalization. It may be worth recalling, in this view, that Hawthorne makes only three references to Danforth's physical strength. He tells us about the "Iron Laborer"'s "arm of might" (908–9), "terrible energy" (909), and "massive substance" (924) to symbolically contrast the blacksmith's matter-chained spirit, his physicality, and Owen Warland's transcendent aspirations. In line with his comic insistence on the intriguing relation between his fictional alter-ego's Schwartzeneggerian "iron-pumping," body building, writing, and intertextual transplants, Leyner has "Mark" zero in on, and exaggerating, Danforth's physicality in the original tale. In a similar fashion, he plays upon Warland's name: whereas Hawthorne may suggest that his hero is at war with his time's commonly held beliefs on art and creativity, Leyner reads Warland's name as predestining his bearer to a lucrative career in weaponry systems. Thus, the rewrite foregrounds Leyner's favorite twin themes, through which he litters the aesthetic-metaphysical purity of Hawthorne's text: enhanced, hypermale corporeality and the "transmogrifying" commodification of the artist's work. Again, it cannot be enough emphasized that the two ideas are interrelated in more than one way: the author's male body becomes the ultimate commodity and increases the writer's market value as the writer recirculates and incorporates recognized cultural values through symbolic "self-tattooing," "auto-surgery," and other intertextual inse(r)ts. "Leyner"'s and Leyner's procedures are homologous.

Now, Leyner/"Leyner" knows full well that these "procedures" are risky business. Before undertaking what he calls his "dramatization" of "Young Goodman Brown," "Mark" pays a visit to his "mentor," former Brandeis University professor Philip Edelstein, who is doing time for "aggravated plagiarism" (*Tooth Imprints* 20) and "heinous revision" (23). Also, he is the one who suggests "Mark" to use the *deus ex machina* Mossad secret agents to give "Mark"'s own fictional "Mark"—"Mark" as the avant-pop, hip, and mockingly macho reincarnation of Goodman Brown—a means to get out of the Bergdorf Goodman store. Off-the-wall as it may seem, the Mossad suggestion is significant, at least for Edelstein's modus operandi. "Early in his career," Leyner tells us, his teacher had "received tremendous acclaim for his adaptations of English and American classics, which were almost verbatim recapitulations of the original texts, except that at the very end of the books, he would insert the Mossad into the narratives as a means of sudden resolution" (22). Rewriting *Moby-Dick*, for instance, Edelstein has Israeli navy seals kill the whale before Ahab gets to try it himself; likewise, in his version of *Wuthering Heights*, Edelstein blows up Heathcliff's carriage in a way that has left no doubt "within the intelligence community that the explosion has the 'fingerprints' of a Mossad operation." Eventually, Edelstein's taking on Nicholas Baker's *Vox* and Robert James Waller's *Bridges of Madison County* gets him in trouble, resulting in a fifteen-year conviction.

"Young Bergdorf Goodman Brown" dramatizes the Hawthorne tale in a triple sense: as revisionary thematization of particular notions; as genre adaptation; and, we shall observe below, as "comedy of styles." To begin with, *Tooth Imprints* attempts, as Leyner's "Leyner" announces, to "adapt Nathaniel Hawthorne's classic tale 'Young Goodman Brown' for the stage and to transpose its physical and temporal settings from a forest on the outskirts of Salem, Massachusetts, in the early 19th century to Bergdorf Goodman, a department store on Fifth Avenue and 57th St. in Manhattan on the eve of the 21st century" (15). As we learn, during a trip to Los Angeles to buy "a chain of hernia clinics" (15), "Mark" gets bored by the purchase negotiations and goes out for a stroll. Walking by a beauty salon, he glances through the window and glimpses a woman getting a pedicure—another Leyner hallmark—while she peruses "Young Goodman Brown" from a "large-print edition of *The Portable Hawthorne*." Not only is the reader impervious, under the "epidural anesthetic," to the otherwise painful procedure; she also appears unaware of the "peeping Tom with whom she shared the pleasure of her text" (16). This is when "Mark" sets his mind to "remake Hawthorne's great parable of evil" (17).

It is important to note that the characterization of Hawthorne's text once again shows that "Mark," very much like Mark Leyner, does a good job not only of playfully *misreading* and abusing Hawthorne, but also of simply reading it. This does not stop him, though, from "producing" the parable of Puritan ethics as a comedy of the contemporary culture of hyperconsumption and hypermasculinity. "[M]y protagonist," the narrator-writer says about "Mark,"

> would descend not down the footpaths of an encroaching forest, but through the revolving doors of a posh department store. And I would be that bedeviled pilgrim. I would become Young Bergdorf Goodman Brown. And that pilgrim's wife, who, as "Faith" in Hawthorne's original, "thrust her pretty head into the street, letting the wind play with the pink ribbons of her cap" would be my own Merci Pinto, who would "thrust her pretty Ecuadorian head into the street, letting the bus exhaust play with the Blimpie's wrapper she tore from her sub.

> 'Mark,' she'd mumble amidst mouthfuls of turkey and provolone, 'where the hell are you going at this hour? Bergdorf's is closed. Prithee put off your journey until sunrise, you dumb pendejo.'" (17)

As we remember, Hawthorne's hero, Goodman Brown, discovers, with the devil's assistance, in the Salem woods that the most respectable of his fellow villagers, including Faith, his wife, worship the archenemy. Startlingly enough, Leyner makes Hawthorne's forests into a Manhattan department store, devils into extraterrestrials, and Salemite "fiend-worshippers" into Mossad agents. The latter presumably work with their outer-space allies to kidnap "gentiles" (in Hawthorne, God-fearing citizens) "who've defaulted on their charge accounts" (66) and turn them into Power Rangers. The writer redoes the "goodman"'s journey through the sylvan landscapes of the Puritan psyche as "Mark"'s heroic-comic wandering through the world of "goods" in quest for an Armani Haute Barbie doll backpack (!) as a present for his daughter.

In view of such far-fetched plagiarism, it may be worth bearing in mind that Hawthorne's work in general and particularly the tale Leyner chooses unearth the flip side of Puritan self-righteousness, that is, a rhetorically dissimulated hypocrisy that stoops to social scapegoating and outcasting. Also, while debunking this rhetoric and its ideology, Leyner uses Hawthorne's tale as a prism through which he looks, and jeers at, the contemporary culture of paranoia. Taking up Puritan mysogynism, religious intolerance, and fear of otherness reflected in the Goodman Brown's suspicion that "there might be a devilish Indian behind every tree" (*Tales and Sketches* 277), or in the whipping of the Quaker woman (278), Leyner plays upon the anxieties generated in our culture of suspicion by theories of conspiracy.

However, one might want to heed an argument such as Robert D. Royar's, which revolves around "Young Bergdorf Goodman Brown"'s take on "consumerism." According to Royar, "Mark"'s department store search for the preposterous gift mimics the Virgilian-Dantesque *descensus ad inferos* to carry us into the inferno of consumption. Down there, in the store's "underground" (*Tooth Imprints* 66), consumers are consumed themselves, punished for their "greed" and dehumanized by what they (over)consume. To show the torments of his characters, Royar suggests, Leyner seizes upon the Puritan treatment of excessive consumption as a sin to be castigated in hell (Royar 5). The critic's reading aligns with similar interpretations that have stressed the "satiric" dimension in Leyner, whether this satire is seen as targeting the "publishing industry's marketing of hot new writers" (Dodge 227), advertising discourse, or, generally, the mediatic takeover of the private. But Royar's reading is more appealing because it links up the ideological ("extensive") and the formal ("intensive"), namely, the critical thrust of Leyner's rewrites and the narrative and stylistic means carrying out this critique.

Leyner's rewriting politics, his response to consumerist, commodifying, and hypermasculinist mythologies, works through intertextual implants and crossgeneric transplants. These are shocking operations on "open" discourses, styles, languages, and vocabularies—operations that nonetheless prove political moves, as we shall see. *Tooth Imprints*, "Young Bergdorf," its largest piece, and, finally, the "play"'s paragraphs and sentences are structurally akin in that essentially identic "transgenic protocols" (*Tetherballs* 230) regulate all of them: the narrative "macroadulteration" and the epidermic, stylistic "microsurgeries" "operate" at different levels of the textual and linguistic bodies Leyner reincorporates, but the overall procedure is the same.

Reflecting the avant-pop's interest in the present and its mass culture languages, Leyner's own stylistic comedy surveys primarily current popular idiolects and mass communication forms. The Hawthorne rewrite and others like it do add, however, an important historical dimension to this immersion in contemporary culture so that Leyner's work erects a funhouse/supermarket of fake styles and psuedotexts where one could shop for strangely "mutated" classics as well as phony pop idioms, commercial jargons, and technical lingoes as diverse as the goods available in a Manhattan department store. With undissimulated pleasure, Leyner gets behind a wrapping-up desk and packs the "originals" in his parodic and ironic foils. Mocking the miniaturizing folly of the commodity goods industry, for example, he has Claire, the salesperson who attends to "Mark" in "Young Bergdorf Goodman Brown," "Act One," present the new "robotic medical micro-Barbie." These "extraordinarily tiny Barbies" are designed, we find out, "to actually enter the human body and perform surgical procedures." And "there's," the clerk tells Leyner, "the original Angioplasty Barbie, for scouring out clogged arteries. There's Transurethral Barbie, who travels up and down the urethra and does prostatic curettage, biopsies, radical prostatectomies," and so on.

Drawing upon Leyner's earlier experience in advertising, the copywriting/catalogue pastiche absorbs the original jargon or technical style through dead-pan stylistic mimicry, preposterous permutation, litotic exaggeration, as in the above presentation of the miniature Barbie, or hyperbolic amplification, Leyner's more usual figure. This model informs most of "Young Bergdorf Goodman Brown"'s "stylizations." Available for immediate delivery/reading are, for example, fake reviews of bogus books; pseudo-scientific reports like the one on entomologist Dr. Astrid Swain's research experiments on the "pubic lice" of an "itinerant laborer" (41); radio news broadcasts on North Carolina Senator Jesse Helms's attempt to punish NEA for funding a "morally repugnant" calendar featuring a sodomite Santa Claus; and the list could go on to include the comic enumeration of the literary styles, real and imaginary, Polo, the graphomaniac chimpanzee of *Tetherballs* can work in: "techno-suspense, New Age inspirational, Sadean transgression, high lyricism, faux-naif ebonic, slacker confessional, magic realism, cut-up, avant pop, trailer-park minimalism, neo-gothic southern" (222).

Leyner's "jazzy" criss-crossings of medical, scientific, anthropological, or military idioms in continuously "hyperkinetic" (*Et Tu, Babe* 4) mode stress language and the rhetorical control it exerts over us. Fun as it may make of the postmodern talk of our "language-constituted" universe, reality as "cultural construct" and related clichés, Leyner's own self-consciously postmodern cannibalization of styles and idioms "high" and "low" is driven by a quite serious interest in such issues. His works, he insists, "evolve through a constant process of accumulating information or language" ("Maximum, Flat-Out Drug Overkill" 230) to make up an encyclopedic[5] "synthesis of seemingly random, unrelated chunks of public discourse, media languages, private codes and raw data" (225), which blends a wide variety of genres and subgenres, styles and languages. A virtuoso of the fake, Leyner sets in motion a whole pageant of phony literary forms: pseudoautobiography, the pseudodiary, and mock *Bildungsroman*; false science fiction, drama, and surrealist poetry; mock journalism, critical essay, "PoMo," anti-"PoMo," and post-"PoMo" parlance, talk show dialogues, imitations of various scientific terminologies, and so on. In doing this, he aims, notably, at producing "a kind of fiction that the reader can't skip, because it's so dense with pleasure, so unrelentingly enjoyable, so packed with event" (64).

No doubt, this event is first and foremost stylistic. But its cultural, indeed political scope should not be discounted either. "Using that elevated, exotic jargon in an ostensibly intimate context," Leyner explicates one of his extensive pastiches of scientific terminology, "creates an interesting opportunity to analyze the way this rhetoric functions in our lives . . . to see how this technological jargon confers authority, how it sounds so tough and peremptory in this masculine, macho kind of way . . . it's this collision of different kinds of language—phallic language and the language of technology—that together produces an exponentially bogus sense of power and authority" (237). Illuminating Leyner's half-serious, half-ironic poetics of the masculine, this passage is particularly remarkable for the mutual entangling of power as a form of masculinity, and language. Through insistent pastiche of the latter in its myriad of shapes, Leyner foregrounds the rhetorical fabric, the cultural construction of authority, and thus denaturalizes its substance. For

Leyner, authority is not "original." It can be pastiched, parodied, faked, much like its hypermasculine rhetoric. It can be rewritten—and this is his revisionist engraftings' ultimate goal.

MUTANT NARRATIVES: A TYPOLOGY

In *Tetherballs*, "Leyner" introduces an interesting concept: the "neo-narrative." This could be, for instance, a workout video, "no longer disparaged as a marginal, 'specialty' category, but . . . now regarded as a valid genre" due to "introduction of narrative elements associated with the conventional film—e.g., plot and character development, measured pace, laboriously constructed scenes, the story arc with its conflict and resolution, etc." (176). One can imagine, on this model, "melodramatic" exercise videos or even more perplexing "restagings" (216) and "creolizing" mixes: "Jean-Paul Sartre meets Jean-Claude Van Damme" (19), a "*Jurassic Park/Terms of Endearment* with a Greek myth/Warhol Twist" (*Tooth Imprints* 31), "*Miss Saigon* with book by Martin Buber" (*Et Tu, Babe* 107), tattoos depicting minutely Frank Lloyd Wright buildings (20), and so on. Here, established aesthetic techniques, works, and authors act like "chemical mutagens, irradiation, viral agents" (*Tetherballs* 230) transforming the popular original's body and causing what a reviewer calls "mutant prose" (*My Cousin* 1).

Or, the warden replies, we could restore "pure, classical proportion," indeed "Aristotelian unity" to film by doing the opposite: instead of "injecting" narrativity into aerobic videos, we simply "graft exercise into the structure of traditional movies" such as "the Renny Harlin 'Beautiful Backs' version of *Jude the Obscure*, Thomas Hardy's late-Victorian masterpiece" (*Tetherballs* 177–78). She uncovers here a second "inserting" pattern, through which the mutation of classical originals actually takes place in Leyner: the rewriting of canonical materials through riotous popular/commercial interpolations and relocations. In *Et Tu, Babe*, for example, "Leyner" walks into a book, record, and video store and asks the clerk to "customize" his favorite texts and movies. Such "customizing" is reminiscent of Woody Allen's "Kugelmass Episode," which magically writes its protagonist in *Madame Bovary* (but Emma also gets to spend some quality time in Manhattan). In Leyner, the method involves "inserting" Arnold Schwartzenegger in all sorts of films and texts from *My Fair Lady* to *The Diary of Anne Frank*. This is just one instance where the character thematizes his author's own feverishly, mock-hypermale transgressive poetics of cultural crossbreeding and genre amalgamation. Leyner's texts abound with similar intertextual mutants: Kung Fu versions of *The Catcher in the Rye* (*Et Tu, Babe* 151); Beckett's "brochure copy for the Hyatt Regency on Maui" (162); a Reservoir Dog-like portrait (of Dorian Gray!) (*Tooth Imprints* 115). Still more disturbing, Leyner thinks of "interpolating" (*Tooth Imprints* 187) Cather's *My Antonia*, haikus, *Anthony and Cleopatra*, and other classics in school textbooks with "product names" so that "kids come across a sponsor's product as if it were part of the original work"(187).

This inserting technique might be called "parasitic," in the sense abhorred by Borges's Pierre Menard. The latter detests "those parasitic books which plac[e] Christ on a boulevard, Hamlet on the Cannebière and Don Quixote on Wall Street" (Borges, *Ficciones* 48). An avant-pop Borges for whom the Mall of America and the Babel Tower become essentially the same, that is, sources of information and intertextual storehouses, Leyner indulges the "plebeian delight" of the "anachronism[s]" (48) Menard rejects. Unlike Menard, Leyner ("Leyner") is more pragmatic. The protagonist of "Pierre Menard, Author of Don Quixote" does not alter the "original"'s text but its meaning by placing the text in a new context and reproducing it literally. Leyner, though, operates by "adulterations" and additions "scrawled in the ["original"'s] margins" (*Et Tu, Babe* 25). The resulting rewrite is an implant or "marginalia" that "mutates" ("metastatizes") the host body to which it is appended. Thus, Leyner's is a "tetherball" or "appended" literature of sorts that both depends on and critiques the language and cultural imaginary of the host.

CHAPTER 2

"Re-Lettering" Hawthorne: Kathy Acker and récriture féminine

> I never liked the idea of originality, and so my whole life I've always written by taking other texts, inhabiting them in some way so that I can do something with them. (Acker, "The Path" 27)
>
> I write by using other written texts, rather than by expressing "reality." (Acker, "In the Tradition of Cervantes, Sort Of" 10)

Women's rewriting has a saliently political and cultural agenda. Addressing "female authorship and the act of rewriting," Liedeke Plate insists that, "akin to modernist 'mythical method' and the postmodernist 'recycling,' . . . re-plotting characteristic of female-authored rewritings is one which is motivated by a desire to counter a tradition of silence and alleged misrepresentation. Marked by a dual orientation"—toward "the textual past" and "the present reality," as I have stressed myself more than once—women's rewrites "can be said to have a higher, even ontological, stake in revisiting the texts of the past" ("Visions" 8). Plate deals with "specular fictions" by Hélène Cixous and Angela Carter, and "parodial texts" such as Christa Wolf's *Kassandra*, Jean Rhys's *Wide Sargasso Sea*, and Valerie Martin's *Mary Reilly*. These texts do back up the critic's claim. And so would many others, from Margaret Atwood's *Handmaid's Tale*, which (re)writes *The Scarlet Letter* into a powerfully feminist reformulation of utopian/dystopian tradition (Walker 144–70), to Jewelle Gomez's *Gilda Stories*, which re-encodes the vampire story from a black lesbian standpoint. One could also mention many other works by North American (both U.S. and Canadian), Asian American (Maxine Hong Kingston's *Tripmaster Monkey*, which redoes Whitman, and *China Men*, which reworks, among other texts, *Robinson Crusoe*), African American (Toni Morrison, Alice Walker, Octavia Butler), Jewish American (Rebecca Goldstein's refined "reproduction" of texts by Poe, Hawthorne, Thomas Hardy, and Henry James in *The Dark Sister*), Native American authors (Louise Erdrich's *Love Medicine*), and so on.

If "postmodern rewriting" in general, Plate also argues, "dramatizes its incapacity to write originally, female-authored rewritings create out of the inability to believe the stories of old" ("Visions" 10). This holds true for postmoderns such as Abish, Barth, and Federman, and women rewriters such as Cixous, Wolf, and Carter, respectively. Carter's "lethal rewrite[s]," as Salman Rushdie inspiringly calls them (Carter xi), target fairy tales and legends, and their undergirding, largely patriarchal mythologies, which, indeed, arouse skepticism. Such "revisionist imagination," to quote Rushdie again (xiii), can be discerned even more clearly, I think, in a woman rewriter such as Kathy Acker. She is, like most postmoderns, clearly troubled by the concept of originality; also, like other women rewriters, she provocatively "disbelieves" the original. In her work one distinguishes, more easily than elsewhere, a large-scale, intensive sort of rewriting that puts forth, conspicuously and systematically, "a feminist"—postfeminist, some have said—"critique of heterosexual relations and patriarchal authority" (Walsh, *Novel Arguments* 135).

Critics have seized Acker's rewrites as the literary territory where, at its most belligerent and acutely self-reflective, postmodernism meets, and fuels, the avant-pop. Indeed, either as a highly esteemed precursor[6]—"post-pomo, pre-the avant-pop" (Amerika 4)—or regular member of the avant-pop movement, Acker has been singled out for her deliberate rewriting practices, primarily for her bold "plagiarisms." In her case more than in Leyner's, though, commentators have stressed a certain politics of "borrowing," and rightly so. Writing-as-borrowing, writing-as-rewriting of former texts is serious business to Acker: not a matter of choice but of necessity. As she confesses, "I have always used appropriation in my works because I simply can't write any other way" ("The Path" 27). But, she also tells us, she has "inhabited" other(s') texts with the intention of doing something to and with them. "Do" what? one might ask. Here is, again, Acker's answer: "[w]riting *will* change things magically. Magic operates metaphorically. So: I will take one text . . . and change this text by placing another text on top of it" (*Bodies* 8). To be sure, Acker's rewriting, her intertextual practices generally are about—or simply are—change. Since, she insists, society is discourse, writing can intervene socially as extensive or revisionist rewriting through retextualization of previous texts and, by the same token, of the cultural-political discourses in the production of which these texts have participated. And in battling discourse with discourse, Acker strives to instill the same politics of (re)writing into the act of oppositional reading and "lead the reader into a labyrinth from which the reader cannot emerge without destroying the world" (66).

RENAMING, LANGUAGE, PIRACY

> I cannot separate language body and identity. (Acker, *Bodies* 167)
>
> The mind is the body. . . . The body is the first ground of knowledge. (Acker, *Don Quixote* 10, 167)
>
> The exclusion of women from language and the authority it confers has become a common trope in women's writing itself. (Walker 2)

To carry out this program, Acker turns to Shakespeare, the Brontës, Wittgenstein (*My Death My Life by Pier Paolo Pasolini*), Mary Shelley, Melville, Sade, Colette, Proust, Lampedusa (*Great Expectations*), Rimbaud and Faulkner (*In Memorian to Identity*), and others. To baptize her creations—should I say, *re*creations?—she raids the onomastic repository of Western literature from Cervantes to Baudelaire, Jean Genet, and William Burroughs. To name her books themselves, she "invents" titles such as *Great Expectations* (1982), *Don Quixote* (1986), and *Empire of the Senseless*[7] (1988).

In *Bodies of Work*, Acker explains such "abuses" in an elaborate argument on "naming" and "renaming" as fundamental strategies of cultural appropriation and cardinal features of her rewriting-based politics of identity. She starts out by talking about her own childhood, when she first experienced her outcast status. Specifically, she views that position as an exclusion from the realm of the named and the world, ultimately. A powerless "girl" deprived of self-sufficient "essence" and "form," she had no name, no being, that is, since "[f]or me, language was being. There was," she goes on, "no entry for me into language. As a receptacle, as a womb, as [Judith] Butler argues, I could be entered, but I could not enter, and so I could neither have nor make meaning in the world" (*Bodies* 161). Nonetheless, she adds, "though I couldn't be named, everyone was naming me." Naming—her being named by "others"—we understand, "erase[d] her presence." As an individual, in the same sense that the fathers and brothers *were* individuals, presences, she was—and was continuously being made—absent. Her being named by others actually "unnamed" and thus annihilated her as "being." It made her, in other words, speechless and simultaneously unable to "possess" herself in a deep, ontological sense. Denial of a personal language as tool of self-naming rendered her "improper" and "propertyless." "I was unspeakable," Acker reminisces, "so I ran into the language of others, . . . [i]nto [their] books" (161). This is how she "ha[s] become interested in languages which I cannot make up, which I cannot *create* or even *create in*: I have become interested in languages which I can only come upon (as I disappear), a pirate upon buried treasure" (166). These are the languages, the stories, the plots, the characters Acker-as-pirate, Acker-as-"poacher" and intertextualist "kleptoparasite" (Sciolino 63) "steals." These are culture's fragments she "salvages" (Jacobs 50–51) to rewrite and subsequent dismantles to re-compose her work and herself. In the process, she reenacts the formation of postmodern authorial self and its constituting "plurality of selves, personae seeking rather than signifying identity" (Walsh, *Novel Arguments* 157).

All of these bits and pieces are "constructed," however, within the system of constraints and exclusions of patriarchy (166): "the world of Fathers," as Acker writes in *Empire of the Senseless* (1), and their texts, themes, and styles.[8] The only language that challenges if not completely breaks away from this world and its underlying "definitions" (*Bodies* 166) is, she contends, the language of the body: flesh, blood, sexuality, untamed desire. The body is, she repeatedly suggests, a "de-constructive" site wherein the inherited binaries shaping our thinking tend to collapse. If *l'écriture féminine* is, à la Hélène Cixous, "rooted in the experience of the body," as virtually no critic fails to remind us apropos of Acker (Ellen G. Friedman 39), *re*writing "upgrades" the "revolutionary" involvement of woman's body throughout the literary process. Acker employs the expressive medium of corporeality to appropriate and put a personal twist on available languages and, along with them, on whole sets of beliefs, hierarchies, and power structures, by injecting unbridled *sexuality*—the exuberant, throbbing language of the body—into their "bodies of work" and their *textuality*. She writes through these texts, as we shall discover, as much as this writing—or rewriting, rather—takes place, to paraphrase the title of one of Jean Gallop's books, *through the body*. Frequently explored in recent feminist theory, the "ethical"[9] exchanges between femininity, corporeality, and its sexuality, on the one hand, and textuality and its sociocultural "con-textuality," on the other, lie right at the core of Acker's writing/rewriting dynamic. As she suggests above by means of a provocatively sexual metaphor, she places the language of the body "on top" of the "stolen" texts and their own languages, styles, and representations to rewrite and modify, dis-figure and re-figure them completely. Yet, again, she does not take them on directly, but through the literature developing them. Analogously, nor does she let the "language of the body" speak, "infect" other languages without literary mediation. Resulting from all this is a plagiarizing of a "target" text, a detailed refiltering of the latter's substance (narrative, characters, issues) "through" certain styles and authors that have distinguished themselves by an iconoclastic imaginary of the body.

HESTER PRYNNE IN HIGH SCHOOL: IMPURIFYING PURITANISM

> The poet *writes* the crime. . . . The book, *corpus delicti*. [Trans. mine] (Sartre 449)

> [I]t is in honor of their crimes that I am writing my book. (Genet 61)

In Acker, we acquaint ourselves with the intensive-extensive rewriter par excellence: systematic, relentless, pugnacious, aware of what is at stake. She valiantly takes rewriting to a level of unprecedented energy, best described by the author herself through a vocabulary of brutal annexation, martial aggression, insurgence, "terrorist" and "obscene" attack on "literary properties" and the "proper" conduct in the "bourgeois" world of authorship as she makes "plagiarism," "poaching," "theft," "piracy," and "cannibalism" her methods. Acker's intertextual "war machines" (Dix 58) make up one big "Arab"—read "non-Western," nontraditional—text; and Acker herself does what "Arab" artists allegedly do: "They write," as we learn in *Don Quixote*, "new stories paint new pictures et cetera only by embellishing old stories pictures. . . . They write by cutting chunks out of all-ready written texts and in other ways defacing traditions" (25). *Don Quixote* itself, a "de-secrating" rewrite among so many others in Acker, does "deface"—graffitilike—several narrative traditions by dis-figuring, "tattooing," "scribbling" or "scrawling another text across the original, blurring its outlines, assumptions, themes" (Hulley 178). Thus, prestigious authors are plagiarized-and-subverted, or, conversely, plagiarized-and-emulated, depending on how they position themselves in Western culture's dynamic of tradition and insurgence. Here, Cervantes himself is, of course, Acker's number one whipping boy due to his "masculinist" construction of the institution of knighthood. But writers like Baudelaire and other "pornographers" (*Don Quixote* 16) such as Sade, Jean Genet, William Burroughs are praised for their disruptions of inherited languages and discourses—and so is, for that matter, Charlotte Lennox, author of the 1752 novel *The Female Quixote, or, The Adventures of Arabella*, even though Acker never mentions Lennox's reply to Cervantes and, closer to her time, to Samuel Richardson.

A few years before *Don Quixote*, *Great Expectations* developed, interspersed with its own re-fictionalization of Dickens, a whole theory of this sort of plagiarizing collage in the opening chapter, titled—how else?—"Plagiarism" (5–55). What Acker does at the beginning of her fake-Dickensian book is propose, by mimicking Burroughs's cut-up-splice-in style, a theory of textual subversion. Right in the middle of a rape scene, she explains that "that's why one text must subvert (the meaning of) another text until there's only background music like reggae" (15); until, once rewritten à la Burroughs, the Victorian taboos, glossed away problems, silences, and ambiguities nested in the story of Pip's *bildungsromanesque* "bringing up by hand" blow up as (re)told in a shocking story of unprecedented horror, violence, and pain—new effects of meaning that ooze out, as it were, "between the cracks in [Dickens's] authorized textuality" (Hulley 172). This is Acker's method of writing or, even better, *rewriting through*: if Leyner retells Hawthorne through the "low-brow," pop culture languages of talk shows, commercials, and action movies, Acker redoes Hawthorne chiefly "through"—or "with"—Arthur Rimbaud, Georges Bataille, Henry Miller, William Burroughs, and Jean Genet.

No doubt, the "point" of this "(re)writing through"—the above mentioned "stakes" of rewriting—is more obvious in some of her books than in others. For instance, "cop[ying] verbatim" passages and plot details from William Gibson's 1984 cyberpunk novel, *Neuromancer*, *Empire of the Senseless* has been called a "literally 'pointless' . . . rewrite," with no "discernible purpose apart from that of producing the 'sampling' effect itself" (McHale, *Constructing* 234). It seems to me, though, that Acker's reproduction of Gibson's revolutionary cyborg narrative allows her to intervene in current, politically charged debates around "posthumanism." Furthermore, Gibson is not the only author Acker "poaches," that is, from whom she reproduces whole chunks of text, more or less textually—and, generally speaking, she hardly "steals randomly," as some critics have noticed (Hulley 173). "The last section of *Empire*," Acker discloses, "begins with the text of *Huckleberry Finn*, one of the main texts about freedom in American culture." "Twain," she adds, "was obsessed with racism; me, with sexism" (*Bodies* 13). Another glance at Acker's novel as a rewriting of "Twain-cum-Gibson"—and "with" other plagiarized/poached authors for that matter—may prove that her rewrite is anything but purposeless. Acker does manipulate Twain to reinvent an entire body politics. Through Twain and other intertexts, Acker lays out an empowering corporeal imaginary: "After having traveled through innumerable texts, written texts, texts of stories which people had told or shown me, texts found in myself, *Empire* ended with the hints of a possibility of beginning: the body, the actual flesh, almost wordless, romance, the beginning of a movement from no to yes, from nihilism to myth" (13). Nevertheless, some of her works are more effective than others in spelling out this possibility—the polemical[10] possibility and formal workings of rewriting. Exemplarily showcasing this effectiveness, the 1978 "novel" *Blood and Guts in High School* is worth closer examination.

Blood and Guts takes up one of the most intensely retold stories in American literature. John Updike (*A Month of Sundays*, *Roger's Version*, *S*), Samuel R. Delany (*Neveryóna*), Toni Morrison (*Sula*, *Beloved*), Margaret Atwood (*The Handmaid's Tale*) are among the most striking rewritings of *The Scarlet Letter.* A "punk porn," aggressively antiromantic "purloining" (Phillips 173) of Hawthorne's *Letter*, *Blood and Guts* revisits the romance from a gender-oriented—"radical feminist" (Phillips 177) some have said—perspective. Coming out of this revisitation is a Hawthorne that "sounds like" Henry Miller, Burroughs, Erica Jong, and, first and foremost, Jean Genet. Acker's narrative of pain and rebellion makes Hawthorne's romance "howl" (112), with "help"[11] from such iconoclastic Genetian works as the 1943 "novel" *Notre-Dame des Fleurs* [Our Lady of the Flowers], the 1949 *Journal du voleur* [The Thief's Journal], and the 1961 play *Les Paravents* [The Screens]. Employing a whole spectrum of plagiarizing methods,[12] such as restyling, quoting, and tacit "downloading" of fragments from Hawthorne and Genet, *Blood and Guts* carries out a rereading and rewriting of Hawthorne "through" Jean Genet, the uninhibited champion of social transgression, "corpo-reality," and (homo)sexuality. Like *Empire of the Senses*, where Acker also turns to Genet, *Blood and Guts* draws from his teasing out "the nexes between power, sexuality, and politics" (*Bodies* 12). These are the elements that, through Genet, Acker purposefully works back into a narrative and worldview from which they were violently expelled by Puritanism. Analyzing the hybrid style of Derrida's commentary on Hegel and Genet in *Glas*, Geoffrey Hartman notes that the French philosopher's essay, "quite literally, is written and risked 'between' Hegel and Genet" (*Saving the Text* xxii). Derrida's deconstructive "bricolage" unfolds "between styles" (xxiii) and subjects, between Hegel's and Genet's clashing, interlarding themes, taxonomies, figures, and writing patterns. If Derrida's discourse "risks" between Hegel and Genet, Acker's rewrite, I would propose, undertakes a similar task. It lays out a territory of risk between Hawthorne and Genet, or opens up, rather, a space of risk, of high stakes—stylistic, political—*through* Genet and onto Hawthorne's problems and problematic cultural mythology.

Similar to most of Acker's texts, *Blood and Guts* offers a representative sample of postmodern "interdiscursivity." The "overt plagiarisms" (Sciolino 63) and "undisguised reworkings" making it up (Phillips 172) meld—and flaunt, like Leyner's collages—a "variety of textual modes," genres, media languages, idioms and themes of diverse subcultures, and typographic techniques (Bal 65). Nevertheless, one could follow two major narrative lines in the novel. The first features Janey Smith and Johnny, Janey's father and boyfriend, both in one.

Johnny is the embodiment of Janey's/Acker's "incestuous," successively reenacted and rejected dependence on the world and words (texts) of "Fathers." To this world, the character/author responds "antioedipally" by "stealing the Father's s(t)ex(ts)" (Hulley 186). I would contend, though, that, initiated by the former victim herself, "textual intercourse" (178) as plagiarizing "castration" of the incestuous Father "blocks" the "incest" retroactively and symbolically—and let me note that Mr. Smith is also attracted to Sally, the "twenty-one-year-old starlet" and a "minister's daughter from Vermont" (*Blood and Guts* 18), who, however, denies him sexual favors.

The second narrative line turns this allusiveness into explicit reference. Janey goes to a New York high school where she ends up captured by a Persian "slave trader," who is intent upon using her as a prostitute. Like *Jean* Genet's narrator in *Our Lady of the Flowers*—the main Genetian texts that Acker places "on top" of the *Letter*—*Janey*, Janey as Jean[/]Genet, "beg]ins] to write down her life." As Hartman observes apropos Derrida's reading of Genet, "writing is always a *Journal du voleur* (*Saving the Text* 93), commemorating, "admitting" ("in writing") to the "thefts"—intertextuality—constituting it. But in *Glas*, Derrida points out that Genet's own writing suggests how its "filiation" (intertextual nature) disappears. To be sure, *la filiation se pert* (10) in Genet whereas Janey's diary makes a show of this filiation, in the "luxury" of self-acknowledged stealing (36), as she puts it. If Janey is thrown in an Alexandria "gaol" for the theft of two copies of Genet's 1947 novel *Pompes funèbres* [Funeral Rites], her journal, too, is a theft, a "thief's journal," and for a specific reason. The diary is the place where Hawthorne's as well as Genet's appropriation—the theft of the thief, so to speak—primarily and visibly occurs. Oddly enough, Janey's diary includes a "book report" on Hawthorne's book, doubling "en abyme" the rewriting undertaken by *Blood and Guts*. The report intertwines—to the reader's confusion but certainly not without purpose[13]—the Puritan and contemporary time frames. Janey, student author of the English class assignment, comes to identify with her favorite character, Hester. As she writes about the latter, she writes herself into the position of Hawthorne's character while concurrently bringing Hester Prynne into our time, "modernizing" the *Letter* (Phillips 177). Nevertheless, Janey is aware of both the continuities and discontinuities between the two historical moments. Hawthorne, she argues in her paper, "set his story in the time of the first Puritans: the first people who came to the northern North American shore and created the society Hawthorne lived in, the society that created the one we live in today." A reason the writer, she continues, "set his story in the past (in lies) was 'cause he couldn't say directly all the wild things he wanted to say. He was living in a society to which ideas and writing still mattered," whereas "right now I can speak as directly as I want 'cause no one gives a shit about writing and ideas, all anyone cares about is money" (*Blood and Guts* 66). In other words, Hawthorne's age enforced a "hypocritical" discourse on writers, censoring what they could communicate in their "letters." Arguably more permissive, our time has nonetheless become, according to Janey-as-Acker, simply uninterested in whatever writers are saying. Derived from "capitalistic ownership" (*Bodies* 10), this crass materialism does, at the reception end of literary communication, the job of bygone forms of censorship.

If money, possessions, property are what ultimately matters in our culture, Acker's plagiarisms and thefts mount a writer's symbolic attack. This is an assault not only on literary property but also on property in general as keystone of modern society's institutional infrastructure, which, as she claims, we should hold accountable for our having become desensitized to writing and art in general. Thus, staving off its own turning into big business, resisting to fuel the above-mentioned materialism, literary rewriting as artistic theft and copyright infringement—real or simulated—is of the nature of other sorts of "terrorist" attacks. Like those, it seeks to shock, draw attention, make a political statement a "careless" age that has "marginalized" its writers might heed. As Acker asserts in *Bodies of Work*, "the literary industry depends upon *copyright*. But not literature. Euripides, for instance, wrote his version of Electra while Sophocles's 'copyright' was still active. *Not* to mention Shakespeare's, Marlowe's, and Ford's use of each other's texts." "My worries with *copyright*, however," Acker adds, "are not so academic. My worries concern the increasing marginalization of writers and of their writings in society. Whenever writers are considered marginal to a society, something is deeply wrong, wrong in that society and wrong with the relations between writing and the society." For, she insists, "*to write* should be *to write the world* and, simultaneously, *to engage in the world*. But the literary industry as it now exists seems to be obfuscating relations between this society's writers and this society" (103).

In the wake of the avant-garde, poststructuralism, and postmodernism, critics have begun to wonder if the "imagination [is not] pla(y)giarism" (Federman, *Critifiction* 51). In fact, we saw that a whole form of cultural discourse, the avant-pop, and postmodernism at large have sprung from this realization and even gained social recognition. Trading upon these theoretical and cultural reorientations, upon the overall increasingly obvious limitations of the romantic aesthetics of authorship in our time, cultural legal scholars from Martha Woodmansee to Rosemarie J. Coombe have gone so far as to argue that recent cultural and artistic forms bring us closer to considering the notion that "authorship is possible only when future authors have the ability to borrow" and that "if too much of each work is reserved as private property through copyright, future would-be authors will find it impossible to create" (Yen 159). This newly emerged—let us call it "postmodern"[14]—view of cultural property and copyright issues may render Acker's anti-authorial/anti-authoritarian stance on copyright less cutting-edge than it was twenty years ago. Still, Acker's programmatic "infringements" and "plagiarisms" strike me as more aggressive than Raymond Federman's (*Double or Nothing*, *Take It or Leave It*), for example, which are driven essentially by "freeplay" (Roberson 38). Her "games"—with and through Hawthorne, Genet, and others—hold a more specific and visibly political role. This makes hers a rewriting of a singularly oppositional type, which carries social relevance in a time the obsession with material possessions, accumulation, and protection throws writers' talk into sheer "immateriality."

Janey-as-Jean Genet goes through brutally depicted sexual encounters and other exploits repeatedly reenacting the intimate practices and the "physiological abjection" on display in *Our Lady of the Flowers* (177). At the same time, these adventures recapitulate Hester Prynne's; oddly enough, Genet emerges, in Acker's rewriting, as Hawthorne's flipside. In addition, the French writer himself becomes a character in *Blood and Guts*. Simultaneously, he is made to impersonate a Hawthornian character, Roger Chillingworth, and, as such, he, too, abuses Janey (135). Genet "as" Chillingworth visits Janey "as" Hester, who, locked up in the slave trader's room, spends her time reading the *Letter*. Based on this reading, she decides that Hawthorne creates as writers usually do, "out of their own frightful agony and blood and mushed-up guts and horrible mixed-up insides" (100). Further, characters from the Arab setting of Genet's *Screens* are also plagiarized in several dramatic fragments patched onto the narrative. "*Now*, the narrator announces, "*the specific details can begin in the terrible plagiarism of* The Screens. *The writing is terrible plagiarism because all culture stinks and there is no reason to make new culture-stink*" (*Blood and Guts* 137).

In the book's second half, Acker splices the two subnarratives together. She weaves their threads into one, actually doing, at the story level, what one of her other models, William Burroughs, does primarily at the level of phrase and sentence. Janey takes Hester's name, and Hester comes to live, anachronistically, in a world of hippies, abusive police, and organic delis. The stories have become one, "top" and "bottom" can no longer be told apart. Simply put, it is precisely this unification and con-fusion, the deliberate mix-up of situations, places, ages, languages, and styles within the general framework of Hawthorne's plot that Acker employs to indicate how intolerance and oppression carry over across times and take new shapes: granted, she "updates" the *Letter*'s "politics to show its relevance for her contemporaries" (Ellen G. Friedman 44). It is important to observe that not only does Janey rename herself "Hester"; she also calls herself "Pearl." In effect, she does become Pearl while, analogously, Pearl becomes in her turn "wild"—wilder than Hawthorne may have fancied her. Janey-as-Hester yields to the slave trader as much as, according to Harold Bloom, Hester Prynne ultimately yields to the society condemning her ("Introduction" xiv) and "fall[s] back into herself" (*Blood and Guts* 100). But Janey-as-Pearl carries on, and upgrades à la Genet, Hester's initial rebellion through her explosive, "antisocial" sexuality. Janey and her Hawthornian alter-ego reject both Chillingworth, also revivified in the book, and Reverend Arthur Dimmesdale, whom Acker ironically rebaptizes "Dimwit." This rejection does not entail, though, utter rejection of sex and, by implication, of the masculinity that makes heterosexuality possible. Quite the opposite. "At this point in *The Scarlet Letter* and in my life," Janey the character and reader of Hawthorne tells us, "life [and] politics don't disappear but take place inside my body" (97)—a clear reaction to the Puritan politics that sought, as Hawthorne's *Letter* shows, to "police" woman's body, chiefly its sexuality.

In this view, it is noteworthy that Janey-as-Pearl, victim of various enslaving attempts, refuses to distinguish between culture and nature, politics and physiology, "mind slavery" and "body slavery" (*Blood and Guts* 111). This refusal illuminates the body as a wild, undomesticated locus where these territories overlap only to render physicality a political instrument in the hands—in the (whole) body—of the feminine subject. In Janey-as-Pearl, Hester finally "becomes woman" (56) in that her newly revealed femininity no longer plays into the hands of "Fathers," including the "hands"/the texts of Genet. Tellingly, the French writer and persona "doesn't know how to be a woman" (130), keeps hitting Janey, and this is somehow related to his remaining a "great writer" (131). But Acker responds to Janey's bodily "correction" with her own "feminist correction" (Phillips 178) of Genet's text, much as she "corrects" the *Letter* itself, (re)writing it "right." Far from warranting the survival of feminine subjectivity, Genet's textual/(homo)sexual strategy, we understand, "put[s]" this subjectivity "to death" (Brennan 250). Thus, his is not a model to be blindly imitated, but one to be poached, plagiarized, and pastiched, too. Doubtless, his work's status is, among Acker's other sources, privileged, but by no means absolute. Acker does not follow it humbly, intimidated by Genet's violently sexual rhetoric. Instead, she manipulates it, reshaping and mimicking it to constitute a self of her own and further the goals of a politics of the body—physical, literary, societal—that overruns Genet's.

We should therefore not be surprised to see Janey decline the status of an annex or instrument—social, economic, sexual—of the male presence and the institutions revolving around it, whether this presence is the cynical Chillingworth, Dimwit, or Genet's characters. Stealing (from) Hawthorne's book and age—as Janey steals Genet's books and thus reenacts episodes from his biography and autobiographic writings (118)—*Blood and Guts* is Acker's memorable *Journal du voleur*: another *Thief's Journal*, indeed, to recall Genet's fictionalized diary. As we know, Genet himself was sentenced to various prison terms for all sorts of felonies, theft included. *Blood and Guts* takes Genet's life *ad litteram*, takes it to, and on, the *Letter* itself. The novel becomes Acker's own literary theft, an act of "terrible plagiarism" where "terrorist" commandeering, "tattooing," "littering" and "junking" (Hulley 187) of Hawthorne's *Letter* both signal and complete a culturally and politically unique project.

CHAPTER 3

Hester Prynne in India: Bharati Mukherjee's Postcolonial Letter(s)

> [A]bove all it is necessary to read and reread those in whose wake I write, the "books" in whose margins and between whose lines I mark out and read a text simultaneously almost identical and entirely other. (Derrida, *Positions* 4)

> [T]he "American" literature I am talking about is no more than a vaguely apprehended "other," but a futural other, to which the actual literary texts we have and study are kinds of prefaces or notes toward; prologues written both after and before the fact, before the letter. They are necessarily written, then, in the old received letter, in the old words and forms, and are in a sense quotations of them. But they are no less, by a kind of ironic reinscription, quotations of the future, of their potential otherness. (Riddel 21)

POSTCOLONIALISM, POSTMODERNISM, REWRITING

Addressing "postcolonial intertextuality," Romita Choudhury observes that "no text is self-contained. Neither is it an obedient follower of its predecessors." "The conception of meaning as produced through repetition and difference," she specifies, "has become an important base for challenging hierarchical notions of the unity, authorship, authority and sanctity of the literary text" (315). Choudhury's argument on the "differential" politics of narrative "repetition" trades upon the tradition of poetics-based analysis of intertextuality and "second-degree literature," to quote Genette again. But, as we noted, critics from Bakhtin to Kristeva to John Frow have sought to overcome the formalism of this sort of analysis. Michael Worton and Judith Still, whom Choudhury also mentions, follow in the latter line of inquiry, interested as they are in the broader bearings of intertextuality. They stress that the phenomenon and, by implication, the debates around it are "inevitably political. . .

The practice of intertextual interpretation"—as much as literary intertextual practices at large—"is an attempt to struggle against both complicity and exclusion—perhaps something, some shifting of barriers, can thus be achieved even if, in general, none of our thinking can escape constructing identity against differences" (Worton and Still, "Introduction" 33). As one can notice, the two critics emphasize that intertextuality is unavoidably political. But they are less precise as to how writers and critics may achieve political goals while "doing" or "analyzing" intertexts, since we all are already enmeshed in a web of preexistent, sociocultural intertextuality, and hence our undertakings occur within preset norms, languages, structures, texts, and other "formations." Thus, as Worton and Still themselves point out à la Derrida, much though "the 'textual' and the 'extra-textual' inhabit each other"—which makes "the 'extra-textual'" "another kind of text"—"there is a need to draw out further the relations between social formations (one kind of text) and texts in the conventional sense" (33).

Throughout this book, I have striven to explain how and why literature that rewrites previous literature is a political act. To provide this explanation, we need to demonstrate, I have insisted, how reworking of extant texts redoes the sociocultural textuality, the con-textual formations surrounding and soaking through intertextual constructs. Merely postulating the ("progressive") politics of this process will not do. One must ascertain, again, how re-forming available literary forms would "extensively" impact "social formations" such as discourses and representations of gender, sexuality, class, race, ethnicity, nation, or belief, around which we usually organize our self. One has to spell out how, its own social "construction" notwithstanding, the *re-storying* of a former story resists the *restoring* of these categories and, by the same token, the reproduction of power configurations based on them; how, in other words, writing as *re*writing encroaches upon the "traditional" space of political agon.

The ever-expanding phenomenon of postcolonial rewriting perfectly illustrates this sort of resistance. For quite a while, former colonies have been "*re*writing back," aggressively taking on the "center"'s literary canon and disputing in the process the very notions of center and canon. South Africans such as J. M. Coetzee (*Foe*, *Life and Times of Michael K*), East Africans such as Ngugi wa Thiong'o (*A Grain of Wheat*), Caribbeans such as Jean Rhys (*Wide Sargasso Sea*) and Maryse Condé (*Windward Heights*), South Asians Salman Rushdie (*The Moor's Last Sigh*) and Hanif Kureishi (*The Buddha of Suburbia*), and New Zealanders like Witi Ihimera have responded to "metropolitan" texts by

Shakespeare, Dickens, the Brontës, Kipling, and many others. Resulting from this response is, John Thieme specifies, a cultural "cross-pollination" (5) that radically alters those texts.

Placed at the crossroads of postcolonial (postimperial) and American postmodern rewriting of Western narrative tradition, Bharati Mukherjee's 1993 novel *The Holder of the World* is a perfect example of this exchange. In a broad sense, Mukherjee's entire fictional work grows out of it, detailing the dramatic process of cultural adaptation, resituation, and reinvention of people and their selves, behavior codes, dress styles, languages, and favorite aesthetic objects such as books, movies, and music. In this view, novels such as *Wife* (1975) and *Jasmine* (1989), an "au pair narrative" that revisits *Jane Eyre* (Bruce Robbins 97–113), or short stories such as those included in *The Middleman and Other Stories* (1988), in which "A Wife's Story" reacts provocatively to David Mamet's 1984 play *Glengarry Glen Ross*, should be mentioned here. In the narrow sense that interests my book, though, the 1993 novel deserves particular scrutiny. Another reworking of Hawthorne's *Letter*, *The Holder* draws from—and, like Acker, redraws—a letter of our foundational cultural alphabet to spell out, too, an entire politics of gender. What is more, in doing so, the novel simultaneously en-genders an alternative history of empire, as well as of the canon—the "empire of letters" and its hierarchies. Compared to Leyner's and Acker's, Mukherjee's rewriting of Hawthorne bears upon a broader spectrum of identity categories and formations. By the same token, she enlarges and strengthens the cultural and political scope of rewriting. Retelling the celebrated romance, *The Holder* critically engages with a whole array of Western, British, and Puritan images, notions, and ideals, fancifully displacing them onto a "defamiliarizing," as the Russian Formalists might say, indeed, subversive context. This polemical renarrativization gives rise to a "postcolonial" or, even better, a "transnational" Hawthorne with a bold spin on feminine agency and history. In Mukherjee's "re-lettered" *Letter*, discourses of gender, race, religion, and ethnicity clash, intersect, and coalesce to decenter, multiply, and complicate the textual and ideological structure of the Hawthornian "matrix" and, through it, of a whole paradigm of power, cultural authority, and representation.

The Holder tells, like *Blood and Guts*, a double-layered story. Beigh Masters, the narrating protagonist, uncovers this structure from the outset when she points up "the past, the present, and the future" (5) in which she is simultaneously living. But this is not just the worn-out device allowing sci-fi heroes to shuttle back and forth between distinct time periods and places. It pinpoints, rather, a sort of informational time-space, a continuum whose prototype is the computer "grid" the narrator's boyfriend, an Indian immigrant named Venn, works on at

MIT. Yet technological verisimilitude and hi-tech details are, it seems to me, less consequential than what they hint at in Mukherjee's novel: a "model," metafictional as much as metapolitical, for the palimpsest structure, for the "interconnectedness" characteristic of the global age in general and *The Holder* as a cultural document of this age in particular. In this view, one has to grasp this interconnectedness in terms of the intertextual and crosscultural dynamic the novel itself acts out and thematizes. For, to emphasize this process, the book sets up a transformative dialogue between itself and previous texts, primarily the *Letter*. Mukherjee recirculates and remakes Hawthorne to foreground our time's unprecedented circulation and refashioning of cultural products, ideas, styles, symbols, and people. In fact, at the novel's very end, Beigh Masters, once again Bharati Mukherjee's mouthpiece, flaunts her intertextual/rewriterly *modus operandi*, specifically, the *Letter* as *The Holder*'s "source" along with other materials, such as the main characters' fictitious diaries, late seventeenth-century Mughal paintings, Puritan embroideries, and all sorts of other documents: "We have," she revealingly confesses, "the shipping and housing records, we have the letters and journals and the *Memoirs*, and of course we have *The Scarlet Letter*" (284). And, as the narrator goes on to ask rhetorically: "Who can blame Nathaniel Hawthorne for shying away from the real story of the brave Salem mother and her illegitimate daughter?" (284).

APOCRYPHAL (HI)STORIES

> Apcryphal history, creative anachronism, historical fantasy—these are the typical strategies of the postmodernist revisionist historical novel. The postmodernist historical novel is revisionist in two senses. First, it revises the *content* of the historical record, often demystifying or debunking the orthodox version of the past. Secondly, it revises, indeed transforms, the conventions and norms of historical fiction itself. The two meanings of revisionism converge especially in the postmodernist strategy of apocryphal and alternative history. (McHale, *Postmodernist Fiction* 90)

The Holder purports precisely to make up for this "lack" and recount the "real story" of Hester Prynne and her daughter, Pearl. Mukherjee's novel rewrites its "shy" "prototype" to counter the alleged Hawthornian "miswriting." To do this, it reinterprets, rereads Hawthorne's text and reads between its lines, even writes between those lines, wedging its own "parasite" narrative body in and between them. Mukherjee interpolates and develops the Hawthornian story, so much so that one could seize *The Holder* as an apocryphal refurbishing and "spin-off" of the

Hawthorne classic. It should be clear, though, that I am here using the term rather loosely: Mukherjee's is certainly a "postmodern" apocrypha. She does not pretend that her book actually recovers or is somehow inspired by a possibly forgotten or heretofore unknown Hawthornian text. Nonetheless, "people and their property often get separated" (5), as Beigh Masters remarks, and her author does not hesitate to "appropriate" that which used to be Hawthorne's exclusive property. Appropriating and "ironically 'doubling'"[15] a real work by Hawthorne, though, she works it into a "pseudo-Hawthornian" narrative that contains stuff Hawthorne might have—"has"—"left out" or "miswritten." This way, the unspoken and the unwritten in Hawthorne's letter(s) come to the fore in the rewrite. The latter is the *Letter*'s "futural other," to recall Joseph Riddel's phrase. Or, conversely, Hawthorne's *Letter* is, to Mukherjee's, the "prologue" written "before the fact, before the letter," awaiting—and now spectacularly receiving—its postmodern sequel. But this sequel does not pastiche or mimic the "style" of the precursor: Hawthorne provides mainly plot, characters, and, above all, a cultural mythology—quite a bit, actually. For, as it turns out, this is more than what an astoundingly inventive writer like Mukherjee needs to rewrite Hawthorne's story and, along with it, its transcultural and transhistorical problematics.

If Hawthorne supplies narrative materials, a story to retell, Thomas Pynchon may well be the one to furnish the literary tools and themes that Mukherjee makes her own and employs to "retool" Hawthorne: pastiche, dazzling amalgamation, geographic, geopolitical, and crosscultural dynamic of mysterious femininity. "Pynchon" stands for a whole modality of postmodern revision of the premodern history the *Letter* spans, for the generic functioning of the stylistic machine that rewrites history, literary and otherwise. This intertextual apparatus takes in and turns that (hi)story upside down and inside out, much as Pynchon's mysterious letter *V*, from his 1963 novel, "upsets" and repositions, according to Mukherjee's genuinely Borgesian imagination, Hawthorne's own *A*. As she tellingly writes about her character Hannah Easton, "her life is at the crossroads of many worlds. If Thomas Pynchon, perhaps one of the descendants of her failed suitor [Solomon Pynchon], had not already written V., I would call her a V., a woman who was everywhere, the encoder of a secret history" (60).

De-coding (rereading), re-encoding (rewriting) Hawthorne: this encoding frenzy permeates and links up the two major stories within Mukherjee's narrative. The "frame" and the "enframed" story are tightly interwoven and, together, worked into the novel's textually oversaturated fabric, which is in its turn modeled, half ironically half in earnest, after the MIT time-space, virtual reality-based computer grid.

Thus, Beigh Masters, a Massachusetts "asset-hunter," gets hired by a "Hollywood mogul," Bugs Kilken of Bel Air, to locate a famous gem called "The Emperor's Tear." Beigh finds the precious stone embedded, so to speak, in the bloody history of late seventeenth-century southern India. She is assisted in the search by her Hindu boyfriend, a computer wiz who is developing a software capable of "recapturing of past reality . . . [by] absorb[ing] my manuscript and all the documents, the travelogues and computerized East India records, the lavishly illustrated *namas*, or chronicles, of the emperors of the Mughal" (280). Accessing the past by virtual reality technology, Beigh witnesses crucial scenes of Indian history and, ultimately, tracks down the famous diamond.

This is the part sci-fi, part travel story, part thriller "outer edge" of Mukherjee's novel. I might point out, too, that the plot of this narrative also appears to allude to two well-known stories: Hermann Hesse's 1922 novel *Siddharta*, which revolves around the retrieval of a diamond and the Hindu culture this comes form, and possibly one of John Updike's own rewritings of Hawthorne's *Letter*, *S* (1988), where the woman protagonist joins a Hindu religious community in Arizona. But as I am suggesting here, the intertextual/rewriting operation is far more spectacular at a deeper level. There, Mukherjee manipulates Hawthorne to develop her own crossculturally/crosstextually allusive plot, or in her own words, "transcultural adumbrations" (*The Holder* 230). At this level, she feeds the *Letter* into her own rewriting machine, *The Holder*, in-scribing Hawthorne's characters into a (hi)story that, as Mukherjee insists, "was already rewriting [their] fate" (207). If the *Letter* recuperates an essential moment of North American history, the "story of [India's] Coromandel Coast" as chronicled by *The Holder* is "the story of North America turned inside out" (160). And this is exactly what Mukherjee's rewrite does: it turns its narrative "model" inside out, thereby uprooting and relocating its "insiders" and "outsiders" in what has come to be one of the most startling replies to Hawthorne and his world.

For all its cultural decenteredness, *The Holder* pivots on Mukherjee's mobile, ubiquitous Hannah Easton as Hester Prynne and on the imaginary New Salem of ancient India's Coromandel coast as the (Old) Salem of the "New" World. Indeed, one might ask, what is "new" and what is "old" here? What is the "model" and what is the "replica," the "prologue" and the "afterword," the rewritten and the rewrite? What happens to the "prototype"—to how we read the *Letter*—following its revisionary "misspelling" by Mukherjee? At any rate, Hawthorne, his book, and his universe supply the narrative chart, or, once again, the "grid" for mapping out the Indian territory based on the commonality ("coincidence") of a fundamental cultural and historical experience affecting both New England and India at the same time: colonization and the subsequent encounter between the British and the "Indian" natives, either Native Americans or Hindus. Like most of Mukherjee's women protagonists in *The Tiger's Daughter* (1971), *Wife*, *Darkness* (1985), *Jasmine*, and elsewhere, Hannah plays the role of the migrating female agent connecting the newly "discovered" Extreme West and Extreme West, two intertwined stories of conquest, acculturation, and desire. At both ends of the expanding British Empire, in the New England of John Hawthorne, Nathaniel's ancestor, and in India alike, she bumps against race-, gender-, and religion-based purist if not always Puritan orthodoxies. In New Salem, for example, she comes to be known as the Salem Bibi, the nonconformist white concubine of the fearless ruler of Devgad, Raja Singh, whose child she will actually bear—an ultimate yet proudly borne stigma. Thus, as Beigh seems to suggest, Hindustan may be seized as a vast Puritan analogy. It sets in motion similar mechanisms of exclusion, marginalization, and control as comparable "discourse operations"[16] of colonialism "write," in both cases, people into "subaltern" positions. The "Indian" becomes the culturally, ethnically, and racially ambiguous signifier or "metaphor"[17]—both critique-wielding and lending itself to critique—that Mukherjee uses to legitimate and deploy this analogy. Notably, though, this parallel entails no symmetry or cultural synonymy, blindness to the painfully actual differences. Mukherjee builds a sophisticated, quasi-Borgesian analogical narrative apparatus that reproduces and filters Indian history and mythology through the lenses of the *Letter* and, I should add, the 1682 *Narrative of the Captivity and Restoration of Mrs. Mary Rowlandson*.

As a matter of fact, the story of Rebecca Easton, Hannah's mother, which recapitulates the 1675 Native American uprising led by Metacomet, also known as King Philip, and Beigh's rendition of the episode devoted to Sita, Rama's wife, in the classical Hindu epic poem *Ramayana* are equally patterned after Mary Rowlandson's story. Now, as we recall, Siva's chastity is questioned in *Ramayana* by the people and Rama himself following her abduction by Ravanna, the demon-king of Lanka. After giving birth to Rama's two sons, Siva passes the trial of fire and exiles herself in the forest, where she eventually meets her courageous end (she will be swallowed by earth after refusing to take the fire test again). It is true, we do not have, as Beigh Masters reminds us, "Sita's version of captivity in Lanka" (177). We do not have her words, to be more precise. But we do have Hannah's, that is, the Salem Bibi's—Mukherjee's "apocryphal Hawthorne," that is. And Beigh goes on: "I know from her own [from Hannah's] captivity what Sita would have written." Thus, what Mukherjee's transculturally intertextual games of conversions, translations, adaptations, and permutations lay out is a polyphonic narrative where *Ramayana* is reinterpreted through—or "with"—the *Letter* and where, conversely, the latter is "contaminated" by Hindu epic literature, mythology, and history, and turned into the Salem Bibi story: Mukherjee's own book. To quote Beigh, here again an authorial alter-ego, underlying all this is "a hunger for connectedness, a belief that with sufficient passion and intelligences we can deconstruct the barriers of time and geography." This "deconstruction" may lead, she hopes, "circuitously, to Venn. And to the Salem Bibi and the tangled lines of India and New England" (11). Tangled and interrupted, hardly visible as they might have been rendered by a convulsive history, these lines are being retraced and woven into a coherent narrative of connectedness in *The Holder*. And what unifies, what holds together *The Holder*, I might say for one more time, is the Hawthornian narrative body—references, puns, allusions, and other intertexts with various degrees of visibility—shrewdly scattered throughout Mukherjee's novel. Definitely, *The Holder* is structurally marked by Hawthorne's presence. And, as observed above, the novel re-marks this "source" insistently as it unreels its own story.

Speaking of marks, one could pinpoint this presence by looking for how Mukherjee de-marcates—playfully repeats, reinscribes, or, on the contrary, blurs, dis-figures—the emblematic mark of the *Letter*: the Hawthornian, ambiguous, and dynamic *A*. Taking up the shifty symbolism of the letter, Mukherjee "disseminates" it all over her novel. At times, this operation is easily recognizable. Other times, though, one has to step back, distance oneself from the text to make out the contour of the purloined symbol. For, as Derrida insists in his critique of Lacan's interpretation of Poe's "Purloined Letter," the appropriated letter—or letters, literary works, that is—might not be hidden at all, but widely written across the body of the appropriating text, which may render it perhaps *too* re-markable, *too self-evident* to be seen and read ("The Purveyor of Truth" 176). At any rate, Mukherjee's "model" is, so to speak, marked for rewriting—and *The Holder* is marked as a rewrite—from the first to the last page. The novel begins, for example, with Beigh Masters reading *A and A*, the *Auctions and Acquisitions* magazine. Here, she comes across a story about a museum of antiquities located between (Old) Salem and Marblehead, a museum that has acquired a big gem. As she admits, it is not the stone itself that lures her, but the "inscription"—the "script" or original "intertext," I would add—in-scribed, marked on the gem, and in general anything having to do with Mughal India and the legendary Salem Bibi. More often than not, this in-scription is literally—I am tempted to say, "leterally"—performed on bodies and works as an exclusionary mark exactly like in Hawthorne. Scalped survivors of the King Philip upheaval display bodily stigmas that cast them out as much as many a "disreputable fellow with one of the several possible letters of the sinner's alphabet—Adulterer, Blasphemer, Thief, Incest breeder—branded to his forehead, or an Indian patch sewn to a woman's sleeve for miscegenation" (41).

But if Hester Prynne is forced, in the *Letter*, to wear the infamous veil, Hannah, one of her reincarnations in the *Holder*, takes up "needlework" on her own. This brings her fame and her author another opportunity to flaunt the intertextual makeup of the novel. One of Hannah's embroideries, for instance, plays in great detail upon the "rag of scarlet cloth" Hawthorne's authorial narrator discovers in the Custom-House in the introductory chapter of *The Scarlet Letter* (31). As we may recall, the "embroidery" (31) bearing the infamous "A" "had been twisted" around a "small roll of dingy paper . . . containing many particulars respecting the life and conversation of one Hester Prynne" (32)—the "groundwork of a tale" (33), the romance itself. Rolled around Hawthorne's own "roll," Mukherjee's tale and, within it, the *mise en abyme* motif of the cloth retextualize Hawthorne's text, dazzlingly complicating its cultural fabric. Hannah's "little embroidery" weaves together the West and the East. It features verses from Psalms "emblazoned" in colors "so tropical" that the "threads Hannah used had to have been brought over from a mysterious place with a musical name: Bandar Abbas, Batavia, Bimlipatam," and thus represents "one of the great colonial samplers" (Mukherjee 44). The needlepoint, which Hannah "took . . . with her to England and then to India" (47), we learn, "is a pure vision. It is the first native American response to a world that could be African or Indian or anything not American. It employs the same economy, the same apparently naive sophistication as the Mughal paintings that would later feature her." It was Thomas—Fitch, but it might as well have been Pynchon, I would add—who "framed her handiwork in the finest cherrywood left over from a chest he had made for the fearsome old magistrate, the twisted John Hathorne (whose excesses in the witch trials would so torment his descendant, Nathaniel Hawthorne)" (44–45).

This *textum*, this *textual* "vision" wrapped around Hawthorne and Pynchon, is a superb "embodiment of desire" à la *V*. It appears to body forth, illustrate ethnocentric and patriarchal paradigms by featuring the biblical lines about "desire" understood as the worship of true God, "heathens," and earthly "possessions." However, much like Mukherjee's reweaving of Hawthorne's narrative texture, what this embroidery does is overhaul this paradigm in a fundamentally political move: desire means uncensored physical desire where woman finds freedom and fulfillment through sexual initiative. Likewise, possession no longer designates "possession of the earth" by the true believers, but, again, and against both Hindu (Iyer 38) and Puritan patriarchal apprehensions, physical possession of the male partner—and a "heathen" partner at that.[18] Indeed, Hannah's work seems "like a clash of the sexes, a triumph of pioneer virility" (Mukherjee 43), with the proviso that "virility" becomes a feature of the female protagonist, while being a pioneer—a woman pioneer, more precisely—entails a rather nonimperial and noncolonial relation to the "unknown or the unexplored" (100).

True, Mukherjee does not cover up her character's inescapable "complicity . . . in imperialism" (Iyer 40). I would nevertheless argue that, through the same plagiaristic games, Mukherjee stresses Hannah's resistance to empire, which remains in the novel an essentially masculine, indeed masculinist project. Thus, the author lays strong emphasis on the conflict between Hannah-as-Hester Prynne, one of the novel's intertextual reincarnations of Hester, and one Cephus Prynne, the East India Company's Chief Factor (107) and "customs officer" (112). Obviously lifted from the same Hawthornian repertoire, the latter epitomizes the cynical colonizer and, generally speaking, the self-sufficient, monological story of gender- and race-based oppression *The Holder* seeks to revisit. Hannah, however, is mainly the female agent of this pluralist and enabling retelling where the imperial narrative of domination, acquisition, and assimilation is displaced through a narrative of interaction, "translation" (100, 118), and crosscultural, feminine solidarity. Revealingly, Mukherjee plays upon the identical motif of the stigmatizing letter(s) to mysteriously "write" Cephus Prynne's collective guilt all over his corpse. As we learn,

> Very little flesh remained [on the body when it was found], but for the tight skin of the forehead, upon which the letter *H* in a Roman script had been slashed. And on parts of the body the pariah dogs and buzzards and hyenas had not carried away, other letters were faintly discernible—an *A*, a *C*, an *E*—as though the Hindus or Muslims had thought by a promiscuous imitation of the English alphabet they were pointing the finger of guilt away from them, instead of directly at their hearts. (157)

Symbolically completing the circular trajectory of the purloined letter through history and stories, *The Holder* ends with—or rather *at*—its source, by re-marking its textual origin. Hannah, now called "Pearl," like Hester Prynne's daughter, sails back to New England to join her ostracized mother and is about to give birth to her own daughter, also named Pearl (Pearl Singh, after her father, the Raja). Hannah's Indian (Hindu) lover reiterates her mother's stigmatizing relationship with her Indian (Native American) husband and, of course, foreshadows Beigh's own relationship with Venn, the Indian immigrant. And here we are, come full circle; here is Hawthorne's letter sanctioning this transhistorical and transcultural analogy: Hannah returns to North America to find her mother wearing her "outmoded woolens with the shameful I"—"[I]t meant 'Indian lover'"—sewn in red to her sleeve (283). Remarkably, only nine years old when Hannah ("White Pearl"), Pearl ("Black Pearl"), and Rebecca Easton, the "Ur-Hester Prynne," get back to New England's Salem, and son of John Hathorne, the famous witchcraft judge, Joseph Hathorne is deeply affected by the stories White Pearl "related as she sewed" (284). He even "goes to sea" under the spell of these stories, apparently carrying on, rounding off, and rewriting a story for which his great-grandson, Nathaniel Hawthorne, was to provide the "model" ("preface")—retroactively as it were. Yet this is a paradox of which Mukherjee is fully aware, a paradox of literary history, of history itself, of time finally. "Time, O Time!" read the closing, re-markable lines of the novel, where Mukherjee re-inscribes her "model." "Time to tincture the lurid colors, time for the local understudies to learn their foreign lines, time only to touch and briefly bring alive the first letter of an alphabet of hope and of horror stretching out, and back to the uttermost shore" (285). Time, indeed, to revivify the "branded letters of sin: *E* for English, Extraordinary, Ethical" (127).

Time for irony, of course, but also time for "relettering" games that result in a "subversive alphabet" (54) in which "*A* is for Act . . . *B* is for Boldness . . . *C* is for Character . . . *D* is for Dissent, *E* is for Ecstasy, *F* is for Forage . . . [a]nd *I* is for . . . Indian lover," according to Hester, a friend of Hannah, or rather "Independence," as Hannah herself insists (54). The relation between this "subversive" cultural alphabet and Hawthorne's letter(s) is fairly obvious. Mukherjee's symbolic acronyms spell out and uphold a whole paradigm that Hawthorne's world—if not always Hawthorne's own story—tones down, represses, marks for control, stigmatization, and colonization: desire, sexuality in general, the female body and power, the "menacing," mysterious native, and so on.

Intertwined with, and growing from, this intertextual dialogue are other relations and tensions, where the politics of intertextuality in general and rewriting in particular come even more forcefully to the fore. First, a problematized, increasingly ambivalent rapport between center and margin, metropolis and colony, by virtue of which we get increasingly unsure which one comes first—is Old Salem a model for New Salem or vice versa? Do the "Indians" come before the Hindus, or the other way around? Mukherjee's postmodern rewriting of history disrupts linearity, priorities, cause-and-effect and model-and-copy narratives, which complicates the answer. Second, but in conjunction with this, what also obtains in *The Holder* is a new relation between the canonical "precursor" (Hawthorne)[19] and "imitator" (Mukherjee herself), through which the former Bengali, South Asian Canadian, Indian American, and—lately—American author reclaims the tradition of the American letters as hers and, for herself, a distinguished place in this tradition.

EPILOGUE

Rewriting Postmodernism

> Whenever I engage in discourse, I am using given meanings and values, changing them and giving them back. A community, a society, is always being constructed in discourse. . . . Postmodernism, then, for the moment, is a useful perspective and tactic. (Acker, *Bodies* 4–5)

> [I]t is from the perspective of (re)reading—closely connected with what we might call (re)writing—that the postmodern sensitivity to the phenomenon of hypertextuality can be better judged. (Calinescu, "Rewriting" 244)

A few years ago, British novelist Julian Barnes demanded, "There shall be no more novels which are really about other novels. No more 'modern versions,' reworkings, sequels or prequels" (99). Yet *Flaubert's Parrot*, the novel where he promulgates this ukase, rewrites—"parrots"—"Un coeur simple" and other Flaubertian pieces. It hardly "knits" its "own stuff," as Barnes recommends. One way or the other, the novel implies, rewriting is bound to happen, time and again. Authors such as John Hawkes, who retells in his 1971 novel *The Blood Oranges* Ford Madox Ford's *Good Soldier* so as "to preclude any further possible rewriting of Ford's novel" (Ziegler 69), struggle in vain. And how seriously are we to take Milan Kundera's character who proclaims, "If a person is still crazy enough to write novels nowadays and wants to protect them, he has to write them . . . in such a way that they cannot be retold"? Not very seriously, I think, for this passage is from *Immortality* (237–38), where Kundera rewrites Goethe (and Eckermann's *Gespräche* with Goethe), Musil, and Hemingway. Moreover, he rewrites himself, which results in texts similar to Raymond Carver's,[1] John Barth's, Philip Roth's, Kurt Vonnegut's, or Paul Auster's "crossreferenced" fictions.

In *Flaubert's Parrot*, *A History of the World in 10 1/2 Chapters*, and elsewhere, Barnes often debunks the myth of the "genuine" story or pure invention, untainted by other stories and storytelling techniques. The rewriting I study here constantly deflates this mimetic myth that fails to acknowledge the intertextual makeup and cultural construction of origins and originality, authors and authorship. What is more, read against Barnes's and others' works, such rewriting steps beyond mere aesthetic celebration of textual contamination; it does more than tell us that rewriting is inherent to writing. It also reveals with superior force that, whatever stuff one is knitting, the resulting text(ure) will be interwoven with the wider stuff—the *Stoff*, the "fabric"—of culture, social life, and politics.

To these complex imbrications and their consequences I want to turn now to strengthen, as I promised, the link between critical or "extensive" rewriting, on the one hand, postmodernism in general and postmodern politics in particular, on the other. As is well known, countless critics from Irving Howe and Charles Newman to Terry Eagleton, Fredric Jameson, and Valentine Cunningham, conservatives and radicals alike, have condemned postmodern politics (or lack thereof). Here, I take briefly on Eagleton and Jameson, among the most vocal detractors of postmodernism throughout the 80s and 90s, and use their rebuttal of postmodernism to bounce off my own point about it. More precisely, I want to throw light retrospectively, via Eagleton and Jameson, on my subject and approach from an ethical and political standpoint. In doing so, I intend to suggest how, by reconstructing postmodern poetics in terms of revisionist rewriting, one could recast postmodernism's politics in a more nuanced and encouraging way than it has been done. I am seeking neither a defense nor a *reparatio* of postmodernism, but an assessment, rather, of what the rewriting practices herein discussed accomplish from a broader perspective.

Taking stock of the "illusions of postmodernism," Eagleton submits that postmodernism's "rich body of work on racism and ethnicity, on the paranoia of identity-thinking, on the perils of totality and the fear of otherness: all this, along with its deepened insights into the cunning of power, would no doubt be of considerable value." But, he goes on, "its cultural relativism and moral conventionalism, its scepticism, pragmatism and localism, its distaste for ideas of solidarity and disciplined organization, its lack of any adequate theory of political agency: all these would tell heavily against it" (*Illusions* 134). Running along similar lines, Jameson's argument is well known and therefore requires no rehearsal. If I am bringing it up, rather expeditiously, along with Eagleton's, it is because it specifically represents—à la Lyotard but drawing different conclusions—"postmodernism" as "a rewriting and reworking of an older system," indeed a "prodigious rewriting operation" (*Postmodernism* xiv). Readers familiar with Jameson's critique of modernism might expect him to endorse this "rewriting operation." The trouble is, we gather, new "intellectuals" and "ideologues" (xiv) make use of the fashionable word to set in motion a "superficial" rewriting, to "recatalogue," repackage, and "transcode" yet hardly "change" the world. The term *postmodernism* is simply good for business, including intellectual business, insofar as it generates more "repackaging" of ideas, discourse. But the conceptual rewriting it appears to involve is, we are being told, delusive. As Jameson contends, this term works on the surface, merely as metadiscourse, as talk *about* postmodern society and culture, leaving old structures of control and commodification untouched.

What occurs at the metadiscursive level also takes place, according to Jameson, within literary discourse proper, in short stories, poems, and plays. The transition from modernism to postmodernism, his argument runs, boils down to the substitution of a "surface" model of literature and culture for a paradigm of "depth." The latter is defined, in passing, as "some vaster reality which replaces [the work of art] as its ultimate truth" (9). So far as modernist aesthetics goes, this "transcendent" (or "hermeneutical," as Jameson calls it) definition strikes me as too easy a target to detain us here. More relevant to my point is Jameson's use of his problematic mythology of "depth" to invalidate the allegedly "depthless" postmodern and come up with a straw-man model whose Baudrillardian bathos of "new depthlessness" (9) predictably results in "the death of the social," as Kroker and Cook put it (168–242), and in an equally lamentable "weakening of historicity" (Jameson, *Postmodernism* 6).

In fact, Jameson, Eagleton, and others ascertain postmodernism—entire postmodernism—as "weak" discourse, again, in a sense that has little to do with Vattimo's *pensiero debole*.[2] They ground their argument in postmodern "flatness," "weakness," or lack, lack, that is, of moral standards, political agency, historical depth, and, underlying all these negative categories, lack of subjectivity. The hollow, fragmented, and politically neutralized subject, the subject *as* lack, allegedly becomes *the* postmodern subject. Constituted around the brim of its inner void, this subject presumably manifests itself by perpetually enacting its inauthenticity. It emerges *as* an intertextual phenomenon, bricolage, agglutination of styles, expressions, bits and pieces of *other* cultural identities. There is, Jameson submits, a characteristic *form* for the intertextual emergence of the postmodern subject: "the disappearance of the individual subject, along with its formal consequence, the increasing unavailability of style, engender the well-nigh universal practice today of what may be called pastiche" (16).

Pastiche represents, in Jameson's views, more than a literary technique. It is, as in Baudrillard's vision of simulacral, "senseless repetition" (*America* 41, 1), also an ontological symptom. As such, along with the volatilization of the subject, it points to the contemporary vanishing of the real, history, and the possibility of social progress. In effect, critics such as Eagleton, Andrew Ross, and Jameson himself are very adamant about their point that pastiche bears witness to postmodernism's political bankruptcy: the demise, as reflected in pastiche, of the individual subject entails the crumbling of agency, which leads to political ineffectiveness or, worse, to "neoconservative" politics (Ross, *Universal Abandon*? 251). Like its formal(ist) relatives, parody, irony, and hybrids such as parodic irony, postmodern pastiche is "criticality that has been castrated" (Kuspit 56). This "impotency," Jameson argues, is most apparent in how pastiche applies itself to culture and history. Famously if hardly accurately, he calls pastiche "blank parody" (*Postmodernism* 17), "imitation of dead styles, speech through all the masks and voices stored up in the imaginary museum of a new global culture" and "random cannibalization of all the styles of the past" (18).

Postmodernism is, I think, a far more complex literary, cultural, and political phenomenon. Not all postmodern revisitations of past works, motifs, and styles are pastiche, as Susan Suleiman replies to Jameson in her feminist analysis of the "political status of postmodern intertextuality" (191). Nor are all pastiches flat, ahistorical, and apolitical. In fact, my own reading of *Ragtime*—a case of blank parody and main piece of evidence, we recall, in Jameson's case against the unsubstantial postmodern—emphasizes the historical and metahistorical dimension of postmodern intertextuality and extensive rewriting as a form of postmodern intertextuality in particular. I wish to restate here my sympathy for Linda Hutcheon's critique of Jameson's position. The latter fails, to my mind, to refute Hutcheon's interpretation of Doctorow's politics (*Postmodernism* 22–25). While articulating the "poetics" and the "politics" of postmodernism, Hutcheon manages—like McHale, Maltby, Varsava, Weisenburger, Frow, Cornis-Pope, and others—to prove that intertextuality, especially parody, and other "historiographic metafiction" techniques do not eschew the historical and the political. Quite the contrary. These forms can be "overtly historical and unavoidably political" (*Poetics* 23), suggesting that "Jameson is wrong about the lack of an oppositional strain in postmodernism" (Weisenburger, *Fables* 259). They confront the historical past and the political present. But they do it in a postmodern—and to postmodern writers the only possible—fashion: through other texts, more important, through those responsible, as I stressed in Part I, for the production of the past as *our* past, that is, for the narrative production of collective and personal identities. Postmodernism is not "ahistorical," but a rejection of "conclusive" (Hutcheon, "The Pastime" 59), totalizing (Marshall 150) views of history. The rejection involves, as Doctorow, Coover, or Auster shows, the problematizing and reconstruction through rewriting of dominant histories and fables of dominance.

Further, the rewrites examined denote that postmodernism *as* ideologically revisionist rewriting does not recycle the past's literary archive arbitrarily, as Jameson claims. Nor are this archive, its holdings, and their styles "dead," or "irrelevant" (Newman 87). Taking on Jameson precisely on this score, Jim Collins has rightly insisted that "The Post-Modernist aim is not . . . haphazard 'pastiche,' motivated only by perversity, but specific juxtapositions for particular purposes" (138). Revisionist postmodernism is, in my account, too, a fairly *discriminate* operation. It selects the bodies of literature it feeds off to attain specific objectives, as explained in Part I and exemplified throughout this book. It unfolds in response to precisely defined—aesthetic, social, political—conditions and picks out its "matrix" text according to the specifics of this response. What Tom LeClair notices with respect to intertextuality in the "system novels" also applies to this sort of rewriting: it "provide(s) the means to analyze and criticize the master ideologies of American and multinational cultures" (*The Art of Excess* 15–16) as embedded in certain texts. Toni Morrison's or Samuel R. Delany's engaging *The Scarlet Letter*—and *not* other texts—in a rewriterly dialogue purports to trade upon the critical potential of Hawthorne's woman outcast. Acker's own Hawthornian "pastiche is hardly a neutral mode" either (Brennan 251). *Blood and Guts* "rewrites the past in a new context" (Hutcheon, "The Pastime" 67), and this gesture is deeply consequential.

The context is indeed essential to extensive rewriting. Literary "models" are selected depending on the (re)writer's cultural positioning and program, as well as for the cultural-ideological potential of the rewritten. Acker's "peculiar rewriting" of romance "exploits the genre's inherent problematization of feminine identity and authority" (Elam 2, 147–62), let alone Hawthorne's specific plot. But it also displaces the *Letter* onto a politicized and politicizing milieu, likely to put a new, radical spin on issues of gender, desire, and control thereof. More than any other rewriter studied here, Acker proves—to further paraphrase one of Philippe Sollers's paraphrases—that rewriting is the continuation of politics by other means (Sollers 78): indeed, anything but "an irresponsible sport," as Borges describes, half seriously, half jestingly, his own rewrites (*Collected Fictions* 4). Coover, in his turn, chooses to redo Alger for the latter's symbolic participation in the American narrative furiously pushed during the McCarthy era, the epitome of which the Rosenbergs affair was. Reed uses Poe's fictional revelations to plough up contemporary structures of oppression and cultural enslaving, in a gesture parallel to Poe's exploration of his time's unconscious landscapes.

In doing so, Reed simultaneously "historicizes" Poe's psychoanalytic scenarios and dehistoricizes them, making them shed new light on the years of the "Camelot" administration. Even Leyner, probably the least "political" (re)writer analyzed here, reworks Hawthorne to take apart, by hyperbolic exaggeration, the languages, idioms, and encoding systems controlling the public representation of masculinity, consumption, and identity in contemporary America.

In brief, this sort of postmodern literature is "knit" together, in the very act of rewriting, with other discourses of our age and with a whole literary and cultural history vibrating in the present. Reweaving literary history, the revisionary or extensive rewrite recreates history. It cuts a cross-section through temporality and its cultural body, which questions the whole theory of postmodernism's historical "flatness." Curiously enough, Jameson seems to be dreaming about a "natural" modality of recapturing history by a purely referential gesture. But not only does revisionary rewriting show that such a gesture is fallacious; it also problematizes and recreates history through textual redistributions, suggesting ways to rewrite history as the rewrite works its way through extant bodies of writing. This progress strikes me as political since, again, such rewriting reshuffles cultural discourses that have partaken in the production of the texts subjected to rewriting.

For Eagleton, Jameson, and Baudrillard, postmodernity and rewriting practices such as those surveyed in this book betoken a "Xerox degree of culture" (Baudrillard, *Illusion* 74). Baudrillard's "Xerox degree" notion plays, of course, upon Roland Barthes's "zero degree of writing," and, in fact, what Baudrillard's phrase implies is the "zero degree of culture," the "zero" cultural "surplus" allegedley yielded by postmodernism. According to the French philosopher, the society in which we live is characteristically driven by a "recycling" mode that does not give rise to new, substantial cultural "value." All we do is "rewind modernity like a tape" (11), revise it feverishly. What comes out of this is a "retrospective apocalypse" that works like a "necrophagous cannibalism" (22) monomaniacally stuck in the past and "condemned to the infinite retrospective of all that has preceded us" (25). It must be so, Baudrillard contends, for history has left us a huge "dustbin," hence a big "waste" problem. Postmodernism, he says, has invented a way of dealing with such modern and modernist "leftover" ideologies, religions, ethnic conflicts, and all sorts of "grand narratives" (25–27): the "universal recycling of waste." "Topsy-turvy rewriting" (32) of history, the "rewriting of the past" (43) and the "retroactive," "anaphoric" or "anastrophic" (121) forms history is taking are our task. The "reappropriating [of] the works of the past" (25) is nowadays the defining technique in art and literature. But the "revisionism" (22) underlying this reappropriation, we learn, is "blanket" (22), superficial, nonideological (33). It is of a "transpolitical" (51) rather than political order, rendering the political obsolete. A symptom of the "age of recycling" and cloned "selfsame" [*le Même*] (*The Perfect Crime* 112), rewriting, retelling, and other sorts of cultural reappropriation operate at a zero degree of sociocultural and political involvement—the degree of simulation.

One recalls, though, that Barthes points up precisely this illusion of writing's neutrality. In my turn, throughout the book I have emphasized the presumptuousness of such Xerox degree of *re*writing, more precisely, of revisionary rewriting. It should be clear by now, mine is a more pragmatic, somehow "rational" since goals-oriented postmodernism. I cannot stress enough that, when read from the standpoint advocated in this book, rewriting cuts two ways. Reed, Johnson, Coover, and Acker prove that rewriting is a uniquely aesthetic performance as well as a means they purposefully use to rebuild and relocate identity, assign it new positions by raiding its former locales, dis-figuring and re-figuring its previous social, racial, national, and cultural figurations. Postmodernism *as* extensive, critical rewriting is a form of asserting, changing, and reasserting—renarrating—identity. Even its negative imaginary of surface and simulacra may be subsumed to a positive, "progressive" goal and may suggest a direction. In this view, the postmodern discourse rewriting engenders, the postmodernism I have "assumed" all along this inquiry, may be called "affirmative,"[3] as opposed to the more skeptical and apocalyptic version, which is, I admit, the glitzier. *My* "alternative" postmodernism is, simply put, enabling. The world it deploys is not necessarily gloomy, catastrophic, devoid of substance, hope, and agency. It is a world where literary discourse can still make a difference by instituting its difference, narrating its contentions, and asserting its discontents. Postmodern rewriting is not simply a sort of "bookishness." It is, to recall Ishmael Reed's polemical metaphor, "book keeping," too, a modality of setting up—and straight—the cultural accounts of society, its memory, and its struggles.

NOTES

PREFACE

1. Discussing postmodern rewriting, Matei Calinescu reminds us that "rewriting—in the broad sense of textual transformations leading to what Gérard Genette has called 'literature in the second degree'—is a relatively new and fashionable term for a number of very old techniques of literary composition" ("Rewriting" 243). Literary writing has been seized and practiced as "appropriating practice" or *re*writing for a long time (Plate, "Visions" vi; Walker 1). In fact, the classical notion of "topos" (or "locus") and the "existing stories" based on it have continuously called for "reformulat[ions] in a different narrative register and transformat[ions] during a process of 'rewriting'" (Barilli 13).

2. I should mention at least two works that promise to broaden our understanding of gender and rewriting: Sarah Appleton Aguiar and Mica Howe's forthcoming collection of essays *He Said, She Said: Rewriting the Male Text*, and Liedeke Plate's study of feminist "re-visions" ("Visions"). Marcel Cornis-Pope's *Narrative Innovation and Cultural Rewriting in the Cold War Era and After*, to come out soon, tackles similar issues.

PART I

1. In her excellent book on the feminine "revision" of American "narrative tradition," Nancy A. Walker also discusses, following Adrienne Rich, how women writers "resist" in their stories various "cultural mythologies" (4–9), chiefly, those that, deployed around issues of "authority," assign women socially marginal roles. I find her analyses of "revisionary, 'disobedient' narratives" (7) by Fanny Fern, Caroline Kirkland, Marilynne Robinson, and Margaret Atwood particularly insightful.

2. Reflecting "postmodernism's concern with the detachment of cultural forms from their historical roots, which makes possible the free integration of those forms into new contexts" (195), late twentieth-century recuperation of cultural forms like pastiche has, according to David Weir, "much in common with the dynamics of decadence" (194–95). I argue that rewriting, pastichelike or not, can be a vehicle for "progressive" criticism.

3. "[L]iterary symbiosis," David Cowart maintains, "is an important instrument of postmodern aesthetics, a brilliantly effective strategy not only for transforming the monuments of literary history but also for 'making it new' in

an age that notwithstanding its pose of superiority, remains troubled by the myth of originality" (3).

4. "The device of rewriting older texts, in whole or in part," Douwe Fokkema ventures, "may be motivated by the same necessity of making sense, now of obscure or half forgotten texts, whose meanings have been lost and which therefore are a burden of waste to those who are still aware of their existence" ("Conventions," Hoffmann 262). This can certainly be the case, for example, in D. M. Thomas's controversial 1981 novel *The White Hotel*, which reworks Anatoli Kuznetsov's *Babi Yar*. But what concerns me here is especially rewriting that takes up well-known, culturally central—by no means "forgotten"—works.

5. What I have in mind is the generative grammar concept. The "rewrite rule" is a principle or guideline for replacing a phrase or sentence, a linguistic structure in general, with a syntactically more developed enunciation.

6. Robert Kelly does not discuss rewrites per se in his book on "reverse tradition." But, notably, he "explores what happens, for example, when we read a Hawthorne novel with Nabokov in mind, a Charlotte Brontë novel with a consciousness touched by Toni Morrison" (5), *Benito Cereno after* Beckett, George Eliot *after The Woman Warrior*, and so on.

7. Michael Davidson uses the term *palimtext* to identify a defining—"intertextual" and "inter-discursive"—feature of postmodern writing. "The palimtext," he specifies, "is neither a genre not an object, but a writing-in-process that may make use of any number of textual sources. As its name implies the palimtext retains vestiges of prior writings out of which it emerges. Or more accurately, it is the still-visible record of its responses to those earlier writings" (78). As I claim, rewriting differs from the "palimtext" in that the rewrite presupposes a systematic, "intensive," often open reconstruction of the "vestiges."

8. "Transposition" is here taken in a sense close to Genette's. The critic writes that "[s]erious transformation, or *transposition*, is without any doubt the most important of all hypertextual practices . . . [it] can give rise to works of vast dimensions, such as *Faust* and *Ulysses*, whose textual amplitude and aesthetic and/or ideological ambition may mask or even completely obfuscate their hypertextual character, and this very procedure is linked to the diversity of the transformational procedures that it brings into play" (*Palimpsestes* 292) [trans. mine]. Another example of transposition Genette offers is Michel Tournier's novel *Vendredi*. Here, like in Coetzee's *Foe* and other rewrites of Defoe's novel, one could easily discern a narrative pattern that belabors ("transposes") *Robinson Crusoe*'s.

9. See Cynthia J. Smith's essay on "intertextuality as agent of representation" in *Tar Baby*.

10. I use the concept of dissent in the sense employed by Paul Maltby. Maltby distinguishes between an "introverted" and a "dissident" tendency in American postmodernism (Coover, Barthelme, Acker, Pynchon, Burroughs, DeLillo, Reed). "Ultimately," he points out, "the difference between these tendencies is best thought of as one of degree: the dissident tendency may be distinguished from the introverted by its *heightened perception* of the politics of language" (37). Regarding postmodern rewriting, one could say that dissident

rewriting is—and makes us—more aware of the politics of retextualization.

11. "I may have oversystematized *Ulysses*," Joyce told Beckett "with impressive modesty," as Richard Ellmann reports (715).

12. Addressing the "ideology of parody" in John Barth, John T. Matthews argues that the writer's dialogue with the history of narrative forms "rules out social or political involvement with the real" ("Intertextual Frameworks" 36).

13. "Critical rewriting" is, in my account, a narrative rewrite such as a story or novel that undertakes some sort of sociocultural critique. Marcel Cornis-Pope has also used this term to assess the superior involvement of the reader in a work's interpretation. Rewriting presents us, in this latter sense, with a more engaging, self-reflective, and deep-reaching kind of literary hermeneutics, a "critical practice that will turn *re-reading* into *(re)writing*, into self-conscious critical performances focused on the text's modes of signification, but also on their own interpretive and articulatory moves" (*Hermeneutic Desire* 25). Critical rewriting lays emphasis on the reader's initiative in the meaning-making process and demands an "active" "restructuring"—which Cornis-Pope calls "rewriting" (26)—of the work at hand.

14. To a certain extent, I set myself here in dialogue with Fredric Jameson's notion of "strong rewriting." In *The Political Unconscious*, Jameson differentiates between "weak" analyses (whether strictly textual or ethical) and interpretations "proper" that "seek a latent meaning behind a manifest one, or . . . rewrite the surface categories of a text in the stronger language of a more fundamental interpretive code" (59–60). Jameson seems to imply that "strong rewriting" makes more visible the ideological apparatus underlying the reorderings rewriting effectuates as the latter recasts the interpreted text according to the decoding system it uses (a certain "aesthetics," "conception of language," etc.). For example, one can do a "strong" rewriting of Balzac if one decides to rewrite *Sarrasine* à la Philippe Sollers (and thereby compose something like Barthes's *S/Z*) (18). Again, my own notion of extensive (polemical or revisionist) rewriting retains the critical-ideological dimension but is applied to fictional narrative, not to critical narrative, whose political unconscious Jameson wants to unearth. Finally, the opposition strong/weak has nothing to do with Italian philosopher Gianni Vattimo's distinction between "strong" and "weak thought," *il pensiero debole*, introduced by Vattimo and Pier Alto Rovatti in the homonymous anthology they edited in 1983. Weak thought, Vattimo says, is characteristic of postmodernism and its pluralistic-relativistic approach to epistemological and social theory. In contradistinction to *il pensiero debole*, strong thought aggressively promotes systemic reflection, totalizing and therefore totalitarian conceptualizing models that discount the force of "local" arguments and contradictions ("Bottle" 27).

15. There is, in point of fact, a third category of intertextual scholars: the "anti-intertextualists" (Plett 4). This class comprehends, we gather, scholars who are even more traditionalist than the traditionalists themselves and claim that the notion under discussion is a new terminological hat for what has all along been studied under the literary-historical and philological rubric of "influence" (Plett 4–5).

16. French critic Laurent Jenny has introduced a distinction somewhat reminiscent of Bloom's and Jameson's. He differentiates between "weak" and

"strong" intertextuality. The former, he suggests, is rather allusive, discontinuous, whereas the latter is more developed and explicit (257 passim). As far as I am concerned, strong intertextuality overlaps with intensive rewriting, namely, with the rewriting that impudently and repeatedly uncovers its literary roots. But I reserve the term *extensive* (and *critical*, *radical*, *oppositional*, etc.) to render justice to the cultural, transaesthetic impact of renarrativization. One could take *strong* or *critical* to be equivalent if one agrees with Jonathan Culler's observation: "Strength comes from a strategic positioning in the discourse of a culture, and to produce a strong discourse one must be an acute analyst of intertextuality" (*The Pursuit of Signs* 118).

17. See, e.g., Schweickart for a "feminist theory of reading" and a more detailed account of how a woman reader may "take control," from her own position, of the reading experience" (49).

18. Linda Hutcheon's work on postmodernism attempts to develop the necessary distinctions. She does not address rewriting per se, but almost all her contributions, from the early book on "narcissistic narrative" to the more recent study of the politics of irony, show constant interest in postmodern revisionism and its metadiscursive, self-reflective manifestations. Critics of postmodern fiction such as Jerome Klinkowitz, Matei Calinescu, Larry McCaffery, Brian McHale, Patrick O'Donnell, Paul Maltby, and Marcel Cornis-Pope have also paved the way of my project.

PART II

1. Many of Kleist's short stories and plays bring forward this haunting notion and its typically romantic variations (metempsychosis, resumption, the double, etc.). "The Beggarwoman of Locarno," for example, features a castle's room apparently haunted by the undead. "The Marquise of O-," "The Earthquake in Chile," "The Duel," "St. Cecilia or The Power of Music," and the play *Prince Frederick of Homburg* surprise the reader with spectacular escapes, conversions, recoveries, or discoveries of characters believed to be dead or irrevocably condemned to death. See Silz (87–172) for a full-fledged analysis of "Repetitions and Recoveries" in Kleist.

2. Postmodern critiques of modernity by Gianni Vattimo, Bruno Latour, and others are based on the fundamental notion of the eternal return of the same, which Nietzsche developed in his late works. As Vattimo notes, this idea "exposes the essence of modernity as the epoch in which Being is reduced to the *novum*" (*The End of Modernity* 168). In stressing the recursive logic of becoming (Nietzsche, *The Will to Power* 35, 330, 544, passim), Nietzsche and his followers bring to the fore a "resurgence of the past" essentially unacceptable and "incomprehensible to the moderns" (Latour 69), who prove unable to make out the "reversible" surfacing in the "progressive flow" (73). This is one of the major points of Doctorow's postmodern critique of ragtime modernism, considering that the novel's intertextuality makes Coalhouse into a "manifestation of Nietzsche's 'eternal reiteration of the same thing'" (Morris 106).

3. "Is the Alger story a Cinderella story?" Nackenoff asks (275). To my

mind, she is certainly right to respond that "the Alger narratives endure not simply because of their affinity with some kind of fairy-tale type" (7). For a more detailed answer, she refers us to Vladimir Propp's folk-tale morphology and Jameson's work on narrative and ideology in popular culture.

4. Talking about "historical consciousness" in Coover's novels, Balitas also uses Lévi-Strauss to show how cultural myth bridges contradictions and social fractures during crises (376).

5. Richard Poirier tells us that "Nixon is an expression, though a deformed one, of certain practices and inclinations that are recognizably American" (99).

6. Maltby tackles the Alger-Coover parallel, too (193). Also see, in this view, LeClair ("Robert Coover" 17), Poirier, Mazurek (39), Gallo (44), Ramage (60), Pearce (134), Walsh ("Narrative Inscription" 332), Ickstadt (355–66), and McCaffery (*Metafictional Muse* 92, 94). Likewise, in his Coover monograph, Cope argues that Coover's ironic and repeated "invocation" of Alger "in the course of Nixon's quest . . . is, perhaps, quietly subterranean, the most subtle summary of the whole journey through the American psyche upon which *The Public Burning* takes us" (112).

7. Also see Christine Brooke-Rose's comments on "palimpsest history" in contemporary fiction. While praising Fuentes, Márquez, Milorad Pavic, and Rushdie, Brooke-Rose contends that Pynchon, in *Gravity's Rainbow*, and Coover, in *The Public Burning*, "do not fully succeed in renewing the novel in this palimpsest way" (128). As my reading of Coover implies, I disagree with her verdict. Nor do I think that Coover exemplifies "American postmodernism['s] . . . concer[n] with the narcissistic relation of the author to his writing, which interests no one but himself" (128–29). His rewriting of Alger bears out a clear agenda.

8. See Vierek (65) and Walsh, "Narrative Inscription" (337), for a Bakhtinian reading of the carnivalesque in Coover's novel. Vierek insists on the circus, which she defines as "the metaphor Coover chooses to demonstrate the fusion of cultural concepts as well as a people's need for celebration of this type" (65).

9. Drawing upon Barthes's *Mythologies*, Stan Fogel defines *The Public Burning* as a "semiological dissection of American culture, denaturalizing the mythology that constitutes America collectively and individually" (191).

10. Christopher Tayler has pointed out, among other possible sources of *Timbuktu*, Kafka's "Investigations of a Dog." In Kafka's short story, the dog is the first-person and unlikely narrator (à la Tolstoy's "Kholstomer"), which is not the case in *Timbuktu*.

11. Quinn's pursuit of Stillman reminds Madeleine Sorapure of Poe, "The Man of the Crowd" (80).

12. See Nealon and Malmgren for the homology writer-detective in Auster, postmodern fiction, and language theory.

13. Auster himself declares that "the name Fanshawe is a direct reference" to Hawthorne's *Fanshawe* (*The Art of Hunger* 272).

14. See Alsen 245 and Swope for detailed analyses of Auster's reworking of Hawthorne's "Wakefield." Also see Chénetier, *Paul Auster* 114–15, for

Hawthorne's place in the "literary intertext" (114) of *Moon Palace.*

15. Chénetier invites us in his article "Paul Auster's Pseudonymous World" (34) to use Thoreau's "method" of "slow reading" to uncover the complexities of Auster's novels.

PART III

1. Reed takes issue in *Mumbo Jumbo* with what he calls the "Atonist" distortion of the Faustian model. Paragons of exclusivism and insensitivity (musical, sexual, cultural), the Atonists have allegedly purged this model of its original richness. They have reduced it to blind rationality (*Mumbo Jumbo* 90–91), "capitalism, imperialism, and the Faustian impulse" as "manifestations of uncontrolled desire" (also see Hume 513).

2. See Hedin (especially 181–82) for a theoretical introduction to a more analytical discussion of this complex phenomenon in nineteenth-century African American prose. The problem his article raises is how opposition can be imagined in texts that "encod[e] the very cultural relationships which, outside the texts, serve to shape them" (182). Addressing the important issue of black works' "intratextual audience," the critic shows how these works develop "both their sense of restriction and their strategies for coping with them" (182).

3. On Stowe's own "appropriation of th[e] narrative framework" of Josiah Henson's autobiography, see Mason I. Lowance Jr. 166–67. Aside from Reverend Henson's ghostwritten *Autobiography,* whose role as a source for Stowe's novels remains controversial to these days, Henry Bibb's *Narrative,* published two years before *Uncle Tom's Cabin,* and Bibb himself as an "informant" are other possible sources for Stowe. Thus, it is noteworthy that in her 9 July 1851 letter to Frederick Douglass, Stowe owns to be "very desirous . . . to gain information from one who has been an actual laborer on [a cotton plantation]." "Such a person as Henry Bibb, if in the country," she adds, "might give me just the kind of information I desire" (133).

4. These are correspondence fragments quoted by Winks in his Introduction to Henson (xxv–xxvi).

5. See Richard Yarborough's essay, "Strategies of Black Characterization," qtd. in Spillers 30.

6. See Norman Holland's explanation of "purloining," "that lovely, artificial word, so typically Poe-etic" (308).

7. Mitchell, Swille's son, tells his mother that the Sadists "want to make the South into their headquarters." He also refers to "Virginia as the Sadists' Canada" (*Flight* 127).

8. To my knowledge, Charles W. Chesnutt is the first African American writer to exploit southerners' chivalrous fantasies and passion for Walter Scott, "the literary idol of the South," as Chesnutt writes in *The House behind the Cedars* (108). His novel also draws an original parallel between slavery and feudal institutional codes. As Chesnutt argues in the beginning of the book's fifth chapter, "The Tournament," "the South before the war was essentially feudal, and Scott's novels of chivalry appealed forcefully to the feudal heart" (31). I

might also note that Dickens figures as a prominent author among other holdings of protagonist John Walden's library. As we know, Reed plays upon Dickens and Scott in several of his works, including *The Terrible Threes*, where one could find a reference to one General Walter Scott. Thus, Reed's intertextual revisionism has an important precursor in Chesnutt's critique of southern literary culture.

9. I am indebted to Thomas Foster for this association.

10. Kenneth Silverman is among those who have pointed up "denigrating . . . characterizations of blacks" (206–7) in Poe. The critic also notes that "Poe opposed abolition, and identified with slaveholding interests in the South, whom he felt northern writers misrepresented. Although in no way consumed with racial hatred, he considered blacks less than human" (207). On racial stereotypes in Poe's fiction and articles, see especially Dayan ("Amorous Bondage," "Romance and Race") and Rowe.

11. This name presents a quasi anagram of Edgar Allan Poe's and Edgar Lee Master's names. More than an innocent wordplay, its onomastic pattern sets forth a particular "politics of the proper name," to recall Derrida. The novel ironically refers to certain authors, "all white men with three names, dead many years" (*Flight* 117). It is *The Free-Lance Pallbearers* that first makes such a reference.

12. Aldon L. Nielsen points out that "While reading *Middle Passage*, one feels that Johnson's is a textual universe parallel to Melville's, that the characters from each author's fictions haunt one another's thoughts and actions, that the decades separating the fictions of Melville and Johnson are communicating passages in an intertextual maze" (159–60). For Melville's "parallel" characters, see Sarah Robbins 560.

13. Nielsen notes, "We read Melville within the text of Ralph Ellison's *Invisible Man*, but we must also read Melville differently because of Ellison's text. . . . We must read the texts that black writers inscribed between the lines of America's master texts, and we must read the echoes of those palimpsestic black texts in the writings of white readers" (24).

14. Johnson names Melville as a "source" of *Middle Passage* in an interview with Jonathan Little ("An Interview" 165).

15. We need, Johnson insists in an article, to acknowledge "that black American culture is not all of a piece but instead a *tissue* of history *interwoven* with all the diverse, global contributions that make the Republic a web of European, African, Eastern, and classical influences" ("Whole Sight" 4).

16. "[I]f there is such a thing as identity," Johnson argues, "I don't think that it's fixed or static; it's a process. I think it's dominated by change and transformation, more so than by any static qualities. It is many identities over the course of a lifetime. That identity, if it is anything at all, is several things, a tissue of very often contradictory things" ("An Interview" 161). Identity is "cumulative," in flow, and so is collective identity or community, for which the *Republic* is, of course, a transparent allegory. See Jablon (34–35) for a discussion of both identity forms in *Middle Passage*.

17. See Rushdy, "The Phenomenology of the Allmuseri," for an analysis of this relation and its treatment in Johnson's fiction.

18. Nielsen also talks about the transparent symbol of "the ship of state" (170–71), which changes its shape with each newcomer. Molly Abel Travis, in her turn, discerns in Johnson's vessel a "reversal of Plato's Republic," characterized as it is by "heterogeneity and flux" (188).

19. See more on this crucial connection and its bearings on "slave identity" in Rushdy, "The Properties of Desire" 80–98. The critic also compares *Middle Passage* and Reed's *Flight to Canada*, discussing how Johnson and Reed approach rewriting and property.

20. Analyzing Ellis's manifesto, Lott makes the important observation that "the parodic impulses of everyone from Reggie Hudlin to Lisa Jones both critique and keep alive the cultural nationalism they inherited." However, what Lott deems as a lack of "class critique" in Ellis's program makes him reluctant to fully accept that the NBA is "one of the only postmodernisms with a conscience" ("Response" 245), as Ellis implies. However, Gates considers Ellis's novel "at once socially engaged and artistically fresh" (from his blurb in *Platitudes* 1).

21. A sort of antiromantic reply to Goethe's *Werther*, to which *Home Repairs*' protagonist tellingly refers (167), the novel also seizes upon the epistolary genre to narrate the coming of age of an African American adolescent whose biography strikingly resembles Ellis's own biracial upbringing.

22. For more theoretical considerations on the subject, see Landow's chapter on "Collaborative Writing, Collaborative Authorship" in *Hypertext 2.0*.

23. Drawing upon Habermas's communication theory and defense of technological progress, Charles Ess talks about the "political computer" and the democratic possibilities in hypertextuality (Landow, *Hyper/text/theory* 225–67). Also in "The Politics of Hypertextuality" section of Landow's anthology (299–319), Moulthrop advocates hypertextual resistance in terms of the notion of "rhizome" Deleuze and Guattari have theorized in *A Thousand Plateaus*.

PART IV

1. John Cage's poems "Writing through the Cantos," like his *Writing for the Third Time through Finnegans Wake* and *Writing for the Fourth Time through Finnegans Wake*, recalls not only Louis Mink, whose influence Cage has acknowledged, but also Ferdinand de Saussure's anagrams. Editing and commenting on the latter in *Words upon Words*, Swiss critic Jean Starobinsky presents in detail Saussure's "anagrammatic" method. The method consists, Starobinsky explains, in identifying in ancient epic poems like the *Aeneid* letter patterns reconstituting names of central figures and themes such as gods and goddesses, which would correspond to Ezra Pound's own name in Cage.

2. See the title of Andrew Hultkrans's *Art Forum* article.

3. As we recall, Genette's *Palimpsestes* purports to study "hypertextuality." The critic defines it as "any relations connecting a B text—which I will call the *hypertext*—and a previous, A text, which I will call, of course, the *hypotext* and onto which the A text is being grafted in a way different from a critical commentary" (13) [trans. mine].

4. Leyner uses this metaphor throughout his work. A *Tooth Imprints* character, "virtuosic" attorney Susannah Levine observes that "[w]e're dealing with infinitely reflecting mirror images of fear—Chinese boxes of paranoia within boxes of paranoia" (202).

5. "I was one of those kids who would wake up really early and pick a volume of the encyclopedia and read it like a novel," Leyner confesses ("Talking with . . . Mark Leyner").

6. Also see Amerika and Olsen, "Smells" 2–4, passim for a plainer acknowledgment of Acker's influential position in the development of the avant-pop.

7. The name (title) of *Empire of the Senseless* "names" Nagisa Oshima's high-brow erotic movie *In the Realm of the Senses*.

8. Cornis-Pope indicates "androcentric realism" as a target of revisionist "narrative poetics" in contemporary fiction by women ("Contest" 194–95).

9. Following Foucault's *Use of Pleasure*, Rosolyn Diprose talks about "the body as the locus of one's ethos—where the body is constituted by a dynamic relation with the other bodies in a social context of power, desire and knowledge" (19).

10. Commenting on *Don Quixote*, Richard Walsh contends that "the purpose of Acker's plagiarism . . . is not polemical but expressive" since "it is not an attempt to hide behind other texts, but to appropriate them . . . a highly revisionary process" (*Novel Arguments* 153–54). This revision, however, is not limited to a formal overhaul of the "model," as I argue in my own reading of *Blood and Guts*. True, Acker "bends" former texts "to the purpose of her own thematic concerns" (154). But, as I note, these themes are politically relevant.

11. "I must write with the help of other texts," Acker insists (*Bodies* 100).

12. Theorizing the difference between plagiarism and parody, Linda Hutcheon reproduces the following mock classification from Alasdair Gray's 1981 novel *Lanark*, a postmodern plagiaristic narrative itself: "BLOCK PLAGIARISM, where someone else's work is printed as a distinct typographical unit, IMBEDDED PLAGIARISM, where stolen words are concealed within the body of the narrative, and DIFFUSE PLAGIARISM, where scenery, characters, actions or novel ideas have been stolen without the original words describing them" (qtd. in Hutcheon, *A Theory of Parody* 39). In Acker, rewriting once again appears as an "archigenre" since the writer resorts to all of these methods as well as parody and stylistic pastiche to revisit Hawthorne.

13. "Clearly Acker is engaging in social criticism by using the borrowed text as a touchstone for Janey's present reality. By attempting to assimilate Hawthorne's world, Janey tries to understand the forces of history that have led to what she sees as the near collapse of her society" (Phillips 175).

14. See Coombe (284–85) for new forms of authorial monopoly and recent functions of authorship in postmodern culture.

15. Low analyzes Mukherjee's notion of narrative mimicking in other stories and essays such as *The Middleman and Other Stories*, *Jasmine*, and *Wife*. The critic relates Mukherjee's essay "Mimicry and Reinvention" to Homi Bhabha's theory of mimicry as "imitative performance" that "disturbs an originary essence of identity by returning a *different* and strange image of the self" (Low 13).

16. "Colonialism (like its counterpart, racism) . . . is an operation of discourse, and as an operation of discourse it interpellates colonial subjects by incorporating them in a system of representation. They are always written by the same system of representation" (Tiffin and Lawson 3).

17. To Mukherjee, "Indianness is now a metaphor, a particular way of partially comprehending the world," as she writes in *Darkness* (qtd. in Iyer 29).

18. *The Holder*, Iyer observes, "also rewrites the Raj narrative popular in British literature. These colonial narratives often tell tales of forbidden relationships between white women and native men, which the English characters perceive as rape, and such alleged rape of the English woman is a central trope of these narratives. . . . In *The Holder of the World*, Mukherjee rewrites the Raj narrative by making the English woman (Hannah is seen as English in India) an agent in her sexual life rather than a passive subject" (42).

19. As Fakrul Alam maintains, "by inscribing Hawthorne into *The Holder of the World* . . . and by taking every opportunity to associate her novel with *The Scarlet Letter*, Bharati Mukherjee is making two points: she is asking her readers to place *The Holder of the World* in the tradition of American romance inaugurated by Hawthorne and is emphasizing the historical dimension of her novel" (129). Along the same lines, Nalini Iyer insists that, in taking on a "Great American Novel," Mukherjee "challenges the exclusivity of the American canon and interrogates the process of literary canon formation" (32) that tends to reinforce distinctions and disparities between "mainstream" and "marginal" ("postcolonial," "ethnic," "female") figures.

EPILOGUE

1. Raymond Carver is one of the writers who extensively "tinker" with their already published stories. Kundera, Nabokov, Roth, Pynchon, or Auster limit themselves to reiterating or alluding to characters and situations from their works. Hence, Carver may be the more "intensive" (self)rewriter.

2. Glenn Ward has used the conceptual binary "strong" versus "weak" to distinguish between varieties of postmodernisms—or rather different views of postmodernism. Referring to Jameson and other contributors to the journal *October*, Ward talks about critics who have stressed the "strong" or "radical" nature of postmodernism and critics who have seized it as a "weak," politically "impotent" cultural form (45–46).

3. I am borrowing the distinction between "affirmative" and "negative" postmodernism from Pauline Marie Rosenau's study of the postmodern paradigm's impact on social sciences. The Canadian critic differentiates between a "skeptical" and an "affirmative" postmodernism (15). Drawing from Heidegger and Nietzsche, the former and its proponents "offe[r] a pessimistic, negative, gloomy assessment, argue that the post-modern age is one of fragmentation, disintegration, malaise, meaningless, a vagueness or even absence of moral parameters and societal chaos . . . [a] period [in which] no social or political 'project' is worthy of commitment" (15). Contrary to this predominantly Continental, philosophical (epistemological) version is a "more indigenous" (North Ameri-

can) and "affirmative" sort of postmodern *Weltanschauung*, which does not rule out "struggle and resistance" (15). To clarify this distinction, Rosenau mentions Ben Agger, David Griffin, Hal Foster, Gerald Graff, and others who have felt the necessity to postulate a more "constructive," "revisionary," "radical," "dissident," "adversarial" (Maltby 14), "resistant," or "resistance" (Zavarzadeh and Morton 7) postmodernism. In my own interpretation, what I have called "extensive" or "revisionist" rewriting acquires a sociocultural relevance in *this* kind of postmodernism. Conversely, it is through the widespread practice of this type of rewriting that such a postmodernism comes into being.

BIBLIOGRAPHY

Acker, Kathy. *Blood and Guts in High School.* 1978. New York: Grove P, 1989.

———. *Bodies of Work: Essays.* London. New York: Serpent's Tail, 1997.

———. *Don Quixote. Which Was a Dream.* New York: Grove P, 1986.

———. *Empire of the Senseless.* New York: Grove P, 1988.

———. *Great Expectations.* 1982. New York: Grove Weidenfeld, 1989.

———. "In the Tradition of Cervantes, Sort Of." Interview by Lori Miller. *The New York Times Book Review.* Nov. 30, 1986: 10.

———. "The Path of Abjection: An Interview with Kathy Acker." McCaffery, *Some Other Frequency* 14–35.

Alam, Fakrul. *Bharati Mukherjee.* New York: Twayne Publishers. Prentice Hall International, 1996.

Alger, Horatio, Jr. *Fame and Fortune; or, The Progress of Richard Hunter.* Philadelphia: Porter and Coates, 1868.

———. *Struggling Upward and Other Works.* With an Introduction by Russel Crouse. New York: Crown Publishers, 1945.

Alsen, Eberhard. *Romantic Postmodernism in American Fiction.* Amsterdam-Atlanta, GA: Rodopi, 1996.

Amerika, Mark. "Tribute Kathy Acker." *American Book Review* 19.2 (Jan.–Feb. 1998): 4.

Amerika, Mark, and Lance Olsen. "Smells Like Avant-Pop: An Introduction, Of Sorts." Amerika and Olsen, *In Memoriam* 1–23.

Amerika, Mark, and Lance Olsen, eds. *In Memoriam to Postmodernism: Essays on the Avant-Pop.* San Diego: San Diego State UP, 1995.

Angenot, Marc. "Intertextualité, interdiscursivité, discours social." *Texte* 2 (1983): 101–112.

Anzaldua, Gloria. "Speaking in Tongues: A Letter to 3rd World Women Writers." Moraga and Anzaldua 165–173.

Appiah, Kwame Anthony, "Race." Lentricchia and McLaughlin 274–287.

Auster, Paul. *The Art of Hunger: Essays, Prefaces, Interviews, and* The Red Notebook. New York: Penguin, 1993.

———. *Hand to Mouth: A Chronicle of Early Failure.* New York: Henry Holt and Company, 1997.

———. *Leviathan.* New York: Viking, 1992.

———. *Moon Palace.* New York: Viking, 1989.

———. *The Music of Chance.* New York: Viking, 1990.

———. *The New York Trilogy: City of Glass, Ghosts, The Locked Room.* New York: Penguin, 1990.

———. *Timbuktu.* New York: Henry Holt and Company, 1999.

Austin, Doris Jean. Rev. of *Platitudes*, by Trey Ellis. *The New York Times Book Review* 19 Feb. 1989: 20.

Bakhtin, M. M./P. N. Medvedev. *The Formal Method in Literary Scholarship: A Critical Introduction to Sociological Poetics*. Trans. Albert J. Wehrle. Foreword by Wlad Godzich. Cambridge, MA, London, England: Harvard UP, 1985.

Bal, Mieke. *Narratology: Introduction to the Theory of Narrative*. Second Edition. Toronto, Buffalo, London: U of Toronto P, 1997.

Balitas, Vincent D. "Historical Consciousness in the Novels of Robert Coover. *Kwartalnik Neofilologiczny* 28. 3–4 (1981): 369–379.

Banks, Marva. "*Uncle Tom's Cabin* and the Antebellum Black Response." Machor 209–227.

Barilli, Renato. "My 'Long Infidelity' towards Calvino." Franco Ricci, ed. *Calvino Revisited.* Ottawa: Dovehouse, 1989.

Barnes, Julian. *Flaubert's Parrot.* New York: Random House, 1990.

Barone, Dennis, ed. *Beyond the Red Notebook: Essays on Paul Auster*. Philadelphia: U of Pennsylvania P, 1995.

———. "Introduction: Paul Auster and the Postmodern American Novel." Barone, *Beyond* 1–26.

Barth, John. *The Friday Book: Essays and Other Nonfiction*. New York: G. P. Putnam's Sons, 1984.

Barthes, Roland. *Image. Music. Text.* 1977. Essays selected and trans. by Stephen Heath. London: Fontana, 1984.

———. *Mythologies*. Trans. Annette Lavers. New York: Farrar, Straus and Giroux, 1993.

———. *S/Z*. Trans. Richard Miller. Preface by Richard Howard. New York: Hill and Wang, 1991.

———. et al. *Littérature et réalité*. Paris: Éd. du Seuil, 1982.

Baudrillard, Jean. *America*. Trans. Chris Turner. London. New York: Verso, 1988.

———. *The Illusion of the End*. Trans. Chris Turner. Stanford, CA: Stanford UP, 1994.

———. *The Perfect Crime*. Trans. Chris Turner. London. New York: Verso, 1998.

Beauchamp, Gorman. "Ragged Dick and the Fate of Respectability." *Michigan Quarterly Review* 31. 3 (Summer 1992): 324–345.

Beckett, Samuel. *How It Is*. Trans. from the French by the author. New York: Grove, 1964.

Bennett, Tony, and Janet Woollacott. *Bond and Beyond*. London: Macmillan, 1987.

Bernstein, Stephen. "Auster's Sublime Closure: *The Locked Room*." Barone, *Beyond* 88–106.

Bertens, Hans, and Douwe Fokkema. *International Postmodernism: Theory and Literary Practice*. Amsterdam/Philadelphia: John Benjamins Publishing Co., 1997.

Bhabha, Homi K., ed. *Nation and Narration*. London and New York: Routledge, 1990.

Bibb, Henry. *Narrative of the Adventures of Henry Bibb, an American Slave, Written by Himself.* 1850. With an Introduction by Lucius C. Matlack. Third Stereotype Edition. Miami, FL: Mnemosyne Publishing Co., Inc., 1969.

Blanchot, Maurice. *The Step Not Beyond.* Trans. of *Le Pas au-delà* by Maurice Blanchot. Trans. and with an introduction by Lycette Nelson. Albany: SUNY P, 1992.

Bleikasten, André. "'Cet affreux goût d'encre": Emma Bovary's Ghost in *Sanctuary.*" Gresset and Polk 36–56.

Bloom, Harold. *Agon: Towards a Theory of Revisionism.* New York: Oxford UP, 1982.

———. *The Anxiety of Influence: A Theory of Poetry.* New York: Oxford UP, 1973.

———. "Introduction." Hawthorne. *The Scarlet Letter* xi–xvi.

———. *A Map of Misreading.* New York: Oxford UP, 1975.

Boland, Eavan. "The Veil over the Future's Face." *Profession* (1997): 13–17.

Borges, Jorge Luis. *Collected Fictions.* Trans. Andrew Hurley. New York: Penguin, 1998.

———. *Ficciones.* Ed. and with an introduction by Anthony Kerrigan. New York: Grove P, 1962.

Brennan, Karen. "The Geography of Enunciation: Hysterical Pastiche in Kathy Acker's Fiction." *boundary 2* 21. 1 (Spring 1994): 243–268.

Brewer, Derek. "Retellings." Hahn and Lupack 9–34.

Brooke-Rose, Christine. "Palimpsest History." Eco, *Interpretation and Overinterpretation* 125–138.

Busby, Mark. "E. L. Doctorow's *Ragtime* and the Dialectics of Change." *Forum* 26. 3 (Summer 1985): 39–44.

Calinescu, Matei. *Five Faces of Modernity: Modernism, Avant-Garde, Decadence, Kitsch, Postmodernism.* 1977. Durham: Duke UP, 1995.

———. "Modernity, Modernism, Modernization: Variations on Modern Themes." *The Turn of the Century: Modernism and Modernity in Literature and the Arts.* Ed. Christian Berg, et al. Berlin, New York: Walter de Gruyter, 1995. 33–52.

———. *Rereading.* New Haven and London: Yale UP, 1993.

———. "Rewriting." Bertens and Fokkema 243–248.

———. "Secrecy in Fiction: Textual and Intertextual Secrets in Hawthorne and Updike." *Poetics Today* 15.3: 443–65.

Calvino, Italo. "Myth in the Narrative." Federman, *Surfiction* 75–84.

Campbell, Josie P. "Coalhouse Walker and the Model T Ford: Legerdemain in *Ragtime.*" *Journal of Popular Culture* 13.2 (Fall 1979): 302–309.

Carter, Angela. *Burning Your Boats: The Collected Short Stories.* With an Introduction by Salman Rushdie. New York: Penguin, 1995.

Certeau, Michel de. *Heterologies: Discourse on the Other.* Trans. by Brian Massumi. Foreword by Wlad Godzich. Minneapolis: U of Minnesota P, 1989.

———. *The Practice of Everyday Life.* 1984. Trans. Steven Rendall. Berkeley, Los Angeles, London: U of California P, 1988.

Chénetier, Marc. *Beyond Suspicion: New American Fiction Since 1960.* Trans. Elizabeth A. Houlding. Philadelphia: U of Pennsylvania P, 1996.

———. *Paul Auster as "the Wizard of Odds"*: Moon Palace. Paris: CNED. Didier-Érudition, 1996.

———. "Paul Auster's Pseudonymous World." Barone, *Beyond* 34–43.

Chesnutt, Charles W. *The House behind the Cedars*. 1900. Foreword by William L. Andrews. Athens: U of Georgia P, 1988.

Childers, Joseph, and Hentzi Gary, general eds. *The Columbia Dictionary of Modern Literary and Cultural Criticism*. New York: Columbia UP, 1995.

Choudhury, Romita. "'Is there a ghost, a zombie there?' Postcolonial intertextuality and Jean Rhys's *Wide Sargasso Sea*." *Textual Practice* 10. 2 (1992): 315–327.

Cixous, Hélène. *Three Steps on the Ladder of Writing*. Trans. Sarah Cornell and Susan Sellers. New York: Columbia UP, 1993.

Clayton, Jay, and Eric Rothstein, eds. *Influence and Intertextuality in Literary History*. Madison: U of Wisconsin P, 1991.

Coleman, James W. "Charles Johnson's Quest for Black Freedom in *Oxherding Tale*." *African American Review* 29. 4 (Winter 1995): 631–644.

Collins, Jim. *Uncommon Cultures: Popular Culture and Post-Modernism*. New York. London: Routledge, 1989.

Connor, Steven. "Rewriting Wrong: On the Ethics of Literary Revision." D'haen and Bertens, *Liminal Postmodernisms* 79–97.

Coombe, Rosemary J. *The Cultural Life of Intellectual Properties: Authorship, Appropriation, and the Law*. Durham and London: Duke UP, 1998.

Coover, Robert. "Les deux amours de Robert Coover: Cervantes and Beckett." *La Quinzaine littéraire* 421 (July 16–31): 19–20.

———. *A Political Fable*. New York: Viking, 1980.

———. *The Public Burning*. New York: Viking, 1977.

———. *The Universal Baseball Association, Inc., J. Henry Waugh, Prop*. New York and Scarborough, Ontario: Plume ed., 1971.

Coover Robert. "Robert Coover and His Own and Other Fictions. An Interview." With Larry McCaffery. *Genre* 14. 1 (Spring 1981): 45–63.

Cope, Jackson I. *Robert Coover's Fictions*. Baltimore and London: The Johns Hopkins UP, 1986.

Cornis-Pope, Marcel. "Contest vs. Mediation: Innovative Discursive Modes in Postmodern Fiction." *Violence and Mediation in Contemporary Culture*. Ed. Ronald Bogue and Marcel Cornis-Pope. Albany: SUNY P, 1996. 181–200.

———. "The Ethics of Reading in the Age of Multiculturalism." *College Literature*. 26. 2 (Spring 1999): 186–192.

———. *Hermeneutic Desire and Critical Rewriting: Narrative Interpretation in the Wake of Poststructuralism*. New York: St. Martin's P, 1992.

———. "Innovative Fiction and Cultural Representation." *American Book Review* 11. 1 (March–April 1989): 11–12.

———. "Narrative Innovation and Cultural Rewriting: The Pynchon-Morrison-Sukenick Connection." *Narrative and Culture*. Ed. Janice Carlisle and Daniel R. Schwarz. Athen: Georgia UP, 1994. 216–237.

———. "Self-Referentiality." Bertens and Fokkema 257–264.

———. "Systemic Transgression and Cultural Rewriting in Pynchon's Fiction." *Pynchon Notes* 28–29 (Spring-Fall 1991): 77–90.

Couturier, Maurice. *La Figure de l'auteur.* Paris: Éditions du Seuil, 1995.

Cowart, David. *Literary Symbiosis: The Reconfigured Text in Twentieth-Century Writing.* Athens and London: The U of Georgia P, 1993.

Culler, Jonathan. *The Pursuit of Signs.* Ithaca: Cornell UP, 1981.

Cunningham, Valentine. *In the Reading Goal: Postmodernity, Texts, and History.* Oxford UK and Cambridge USA: Blackwell, 1994.

Currie, Mark. *Postmodern Narrative Theory.* New York: St. Martin's P, 1998.

Davidson, Michael. "Palimtexts: Postmodern Poetry and the Material Text." Perloff 75–95.

Dawson, Anthony B. "*Ragtime* and the Movies: The Aura of the Duplicable." *Mosaic* 16/1–2 (1983): 205–214.

Dayan, Joan. "Amorous Bondage: Poe, Ladies, and Slaves." *American Literature* 66. 2 (June 1994): 239–274.

———. "Romance and Race." Emory Elliott, general ed. 89–109.

Deleuze, Gilles. *Difference and Repetition.* Trans. Paul Patton. New York: Columbia UP, 1994.

Derrida, Jacques. *La Dissémination.* Paris: Édition du Seuil, 1972.

———. *Glas.* Paris: Éditions Galilée, 1974.

———. *Positions.* Trans. and annotated by Alan Bass. 1981. Chicago: U of Chicago P, 1995.

———. "The Purveyor of Truth." Muller and Richardson 173–212.

D'haen, Theo, and Hans Bertens, eds. *Liminal Postmodernism: The Postmodern, the (Post-)Colonial, and the (Post) Feminist.* Amsterdam, Atlanta, GA: Rodopi, 1994.

———. *Narrative Turns and Minor Genres in Postmodernism.* Amsterdam, Atlanta, GA: Rodopi, 1995.

Diprose, Rosolyn. *The Bodies of Women: Ethics, embodiment, and sexual difference.* London, New York: Routledge, 1994.

Dix Shields, Douglas. "Kathy Acker's *Don Quixote*: Nomad Writing." *The Review of Contemporary Fiction* 9.3 (Fall 1989): 56–62.

Doctorow, E. L. *The Book of Daniel.* New York: Random House, 1971.

———. *Jack London, Hemingway, and the Constitution: Selected Essays, 1977–1992.* New York: Random House, 1993.

———. *Ragtime.* New York: Fawcett Crest, 1991.

Dodge, Trevor. Rev. of *The Tetherballs of Bougainville*, by Mark Leyner. *Review of Contemporary Fiction* 18.1 (Spring 1998): 226–227.

Dubrow, Heather. *Genre.* London, New York: Methuen, 1982.

Eagleton, Terry. *The Illusions of Postmodernism.* London: Blackwell, 1996.

———. *Literary Theory: An Introduction.* Second Edition. Minneapolis: The U of Minnesota P, 1996.

Eco, Umberto. *Postscript to the Name of the Rose.* New York and London: HBJ, 1984.

Ehrmann, Jacques. "The Death of Literature." Federman, *Surfiction* 229–253.

Elam, Diane. *Romancing the Postmodern.* London and New York: Routledge, 1992.

Elliott, Emory, general ed. *The Columbia History of the American Novel.* New York: Columbia UP, 1991.

Ellis, Trey. *Home Repairs*. New York: Simon and Schuster, 1993.
———. "The New Black Aesthetic." *Callaloo* 12.1 (Winter 1989): 233–243.
———. *Platitudes*. New York: Vintage, 1988.
———. "Response to NBA Critiques." *Callaloo* 12. 1 (Winter 1989): 250–251.
Ellmann, Richard. *James Joyce*. New York: Oxford UP, 1959.
Emerson, Ralph Waldo. "Thoreau." Thoreau 265–281.
Ess, Charles. "The Political Computer: Hypertext, Democracy, and Habermas." Landow, *Hyper/Text/Theory* 225–267.
Faber, Marion. "Michael Kohlhaas in New York: Kleist and E. L. Doctorow's *Ragtime. Heinrich von Kleist-Studien. Heinrich von Kleist Studies*. Ed. Alexej Ugrinsky. Berlin: Erich Schmidt Verlag, 1980. 147–156.
Favor, Martin J. "'Ain't Nothin' Like the Real Thing, Baby.' Trey Ellis' Search for New Black Voices." *Callaloo* 16.3 (Summer 1993): 694–705.
Federman, Raymond. *Critifiction: Postmodern Essays*. Albany: SUNY P, 1993.
———. *Double or Nothing: A Real Fictitious Discourse*. 1971. Third ed. Boulder, CO, Normal, IL: Fiction Collective Two, 1992.
———. ed. *Surfiction: Fiction Now . . . and Tomorrow*. Second Edition. Enlarged. Chicago: Swallow P, 1981.
Felman, Shoshana. "On Reading Poetry: Reflections on the Limits and Possibilities of Psychoanalytic Approaches." Muller and Richardson 133–156.
Fields, Annie, ed. *Life and Letters of Harriet Beecher Stowe*. Detroit: Gale Research Company. Book Tower, 1970.
Fleming, Richard, and Payne, Michael. *Criticism, History, and Intertextuality*. Lewisburg, PA: Bucknell UP. London, Toronto: Associated UP, 1988.
Fogel, Stan. "Richard Nixon by Robert Coover, Roland Barthes by Roland Barthes." *English Studies in Canada* 8.2 (June 1982): 187–202.
Fokkema, Douwe W. "Conventions of Reading among the Real Readers of Barthelme's *Snow White*." Hoffmann 261–272.
Foucault, Michel. *The Archaeology of Knowledge and the Discourse on Language*. Trans. from the French by A. M. Sheridan Smith. New York: Pantheon Books, 1972.
———. *Language, Counter-Memory, Practice: Selected Essays and Interviews*. 1977. Ed. with an introduction by Donald. F. Bouchard. Trans. from the French by Donald F. Bouchard and Sherry Simon. Ithaca, NY: Cornel UP, 1993.
———. *The Order of Things: An Archaeology of the Human Sciences: A Translation of* Les Mots and les choses. 1970. New York: Random House, Inc., 1994.
Foucault, Michel, et al. *Théorie d'ensemble*. Paris: Éditions du Seuil, 1968.
Fox, Robert Elliot. *Conscientious Sorcerers: The Black Postmodernist Fiction of Leroi Jones/Amiri Baraka, Ishmael Reed, and Samuel R. Delany*. New York: Greenwood P, 1987.
Freud, Sigmund. *On Creativity and the Unconscious: Papers on the Psychology of Art, Literature, Love, Religion*. Selected, with Introduction and Annotations by Benjamin Nelson. New York: Harper and Row, 1958.
Frick, Daniel E. "Coover's Secret Sharer? Richard Nixon in *The Public Burning*." *Critique* 37.2 (Winter 1996): 82–91.

Friedman, Ellen G. "'Now Eat Your Mind': An Introduction to the Works of Kathy Acker." *The Review of Contemporary Fiction* 9.3 (Fall 1989): 37–49.

Friedman, Susan Stanford. "'Weavings': Intertextuality and the (Re)Birth of the Author." Clayton and Rothstein 146–180.

Frow, John. "Intertextuality." *Marxism and Literary History.* London: Basil Blackwell, 1986. 125–169.

———. "Who Shot Frank Hardy? Intertextuality and Textual Politics." *Southern Review* 15. 1 (March 1982): 22–39.

Gado, Frank, ed. *First Person: Conversations on Writers and Writing with Glenway Wescott, John Dos Passos, Robert Penn Warren, John Updike, John Barth, Robert Coover.* Schenectady, NY: Union College P, 1973.

Gaggi, Silvio. *From Text to Hypertext: Decentering the Subject in Fiction, Film, the Visual Arts, and Electronic Media.* Philadelphia: U of Pennsylvania P, 1997.

Gallo, Louis. "Nixon and the 'House of Wax.' An Emblematic Episode in Coover's *The Public Burning. Critique* 23. 3 (Spring 1982): 43–51.

Gates, Henry Louis, Jr., ed. *Black Literature and Literary Theory.* New York and London: Methuen, 1984.

———. *The Signifying Monkey: A Theory of Afro-American Literary Criticism.* New York, Oxford: Oxford UP, 1988.

Geertz, Clifford. *The Interpretation of Cultures: Selected Essays.* New York: HarperCollins, 1973.

Genet, Jean. *Our Lady of the Flowers.* Trans. Bernard Frechtman. Introduction by Jean-Paul Sartre. New York: Grove P, 1963.

Genette, Gérard. *Palimpsestes: La littérature au second degré.* Paris: Éditions du Seuil, 1982.

Gerli, Michael E. *Refiguring Authority: Reading, Writing, and Rewriting in Cervantes.* Lexington: UP of Kentucky, 1995.

Geyh, Paula, Fred G. Leebron, Andrew Levy. *Postmodern American Fiction: A Norton Anthology.* London. New York: W. W. Norton, 1998.

Godard, Barbara. "Intertextuality." Irena R. Makaryk, general ed. and comp. *Encyclopedia of Contemporary Literary Theory: Approaches, Scholars, Terms.* Toronto, Buffalo, London: U of Toronto P, 1993.

Gordon, Lois. *Robert Coover: The Universal Fictionmaking Process.* Carbondale and Evansville: Southern Illinois UP, 1983.

Greenblatt, Stephen. "Culture." Lentricchia and McLaughlin 225–232.

———. *Shakespearean Negotiations: The Circulation of Social Energy in Renaissance England.* Berkeley: U of California P, 1988.

Gresset, Michel, and Noel Polk. *Intertextuality in Faulkner.* Jacskon, UP of Mississippi, 1985.

Guzlowski, John Z. "Coover's *The Public Burning*: Richard Nixon and the Politics of Experience." *Critique* 29. 1 (Fall 1987): 57–71.

Habermas, Jürgen. *Jürgen Habermas on Society and Politics: A Reader.* Steven Seidman, ed. Boston: Beacon P, 1987.

———. *The Structural Transformation of the Public Sphere: An Inquiry into a Category of Bourgeois Society.* Trans. Thomas Burger with the assistance of Frederick Lawrence. Cambridge, MA: The MIT P, 1989.

Hahn, Thomas, and Alan Lupack, eds. *Retelling Tales: Essays in Honor of Russell Peck*. Cambridge, UK, Rochester, NY: D. S. Brewer, 1997

Harper, Phillip Harper. *Framing the Margins: The Social Logic of Postmodern Culture*. New York. Oxford: Oxford UP, 1994.

Harpham, Geoffrey Galt. "E. L. Doctorow and the Technology of Narrative." *PMLA* 100. 1 (January 1985): 81–95.

Hartman, Geoffrey. *The Fate of Reading and Other Essays*. Chicago and London: Chicago UP, 1975.

———. *Saving the Text: Literature/Derrida/Philosophy*. Baltimore and London: The Johns Hopkins UP, 1981.

Hassan, Ihab. *Paracriticisms: Seven Speculations of the Times*. Urbana, Chicago, London: U of Illinois P, 1975.

———. *The Right Promethean Fire: Imagination, Science, and Cultural Change*. Urbana, Chicago, London: U of Illinois P, 1980.

Hawthorne, Nathaniel. *Collected Novels*. New York: Penguin, 1983.

———. *The Scarlet Letter*. With an Introduction by Harold Bloom. New York: Vintage Books/The Library of America, 1990.

———. *Tales and Sketches*. New York: The Library of America, 1996.

Hedin, Raymond. "Probable Readers, Possible Stories: The Limits of Nineteenth-Century Black Narrative." Machor 180–205.

Hendler, Glenn. "Pandering in the Public Sphere: Masculinity and the Market in Horatio Alger." 48.3 (Sept. 1996): 415–438.

Henson, Josiah. *An Autobiography of the Reverend Josiah Henson*. 1849. With an Introduction by Robin W. Winks. Reading, MA: Addison Wesley Publishing Company, 1969.

Herzogenrath, Bernd. *An Art of Desire: Reading Paul Auster*. Amsterdam, Atlanta, GA: Rodopi, 1999.

Hoffmann, Gerhard, ed. *Making Sense: The Role of the Reader in Contemporary American Fiction*. München: Wilhelm Fink Verlag, 1989.

Holland, Norman H. "Re-covering 'The Purloined Letter': Reading as a Personal Transaction." Muller and Richardson 307–322.

Hollander, John. *The Figure of Echo: A Mode of Allusion in Milton and After*. Berkeley: U of California P, 1981.

hooks, bell. *Yearnings: Race, Gender, and Cultural Politics*. Boston, MA: South End P, 1990.

Hulley, Kathleen. "Transgressing Genre: Kathy Acker's Intertext." O'Donnell and Davis, *Intertextuality* 171–190.

Hultkrans, Andrew. "Überwriter." *Art Forum* 34.1 (Sept. 95): 15–16, 106.

Hume, Kathryn. "Ishmael Reed and the Problematics of Control." *PMLA*. 108.3 (May 1993): 506–518.

Hutcheon, Linda. "'The Pastime of Past Time': Fiction, History, Historiographic Metafiction." Perloff 54–74.

———. *A Poetics of Postmodernism: History, Theory, Fiction*. New York and London: Routledge, 1995.

———. *The Politics of Postmodernism*. London and New York: Routledge, 1989.

———. *A Theory of Parody: The Teachings of Twentieth-Century Art Forms*. New York and London: Routledge, 1991.

Ickstadt, Heinz. "History, Fiction and the Designs of Robert Coover." *Amerikastudien* 28.3 (1983): 347–360.

Iser, Wolfgang. *The Implied Reader: Patterns of Communication in Prose Fiction from Bunyan to Beckett.* 1974. Baltimore and London: The Johns Hopkins UP, 1978.

Iyer, Nalini. "American/Indian: Metaphors of the Self in Bharati Mukherjee's *The Holder of the World.*" *Ariel* 27.4 (Oct. 1996): 29–44.

Jablon, Madelyn. *Black Metafiction: Self-Consciousness in African American Literature.* Iowa City: U of Iowa P, 1997.

Jacobs, Naomi. "Kathy Acker and the Plagiarized Self." *The Review of Contemporary Fiction* 9.3 (Fall 1989): 50–55.

James, Darius. *Negrophobia: An Urban Parable: A Novel.* New York: Citadel P, 1992.

Jameson, Fredric. *The Cultural Turn: Selected Writings on the Postmodern, 1983–1998.* London, New York: Verso, 1998.

———. *The Political Unconscious: Narrative as a Socially Symbolic Act.* 1981. Ithaca, New York: Cornell UP, 1994.

———. *Postmodernism, or, The Cultural Logic of Late Capitalism.* Durham: Duke UP, 1991.

Jenny, Laurent. "Stratégie de la forme." *Poétique* 27 (1976): 257–281.

Johnson, Charles. *Being and Race: Black Writing since 1970.* Bloomington and Indianapolis: Indiana UP, 1988.

———. *Faith and the Good Thing.* New York: Viking P, 1974.

———. "An Interview with Charles Johnson." By Jonathan Little. *Contemporary Literature* 34.2 (Summer 1993): 159–181.

———. *Middle Passage.* New York: Atheneum, 1990.

———. *Oxherding Tale.* Bloomington: Indiana UP, 1982.

———. "Whole Sight: Notes on New Black Fiction." *Callaloo* 7.3 (Fall 1984): 1–6. Special issue: Fiction. Charles Johnson, guest ed.

Joyce, James. *Ulysses.* New York: Random House, 1961.

Joyce, Michael. *Of Two Minds: Hypertext Pedagogy and Poltics.* Ann Arbor: The U of Michigan P, 1995.

Judy, Ronald A. T. "The New Black Aesthetic and W. E. B. Du Bois, or, Hephaestus, Limping." *The Massachusetts Review* 35.2 (Summer 1994): 249–282.

Kelly, Robert. *Reverse Tradition: Postmodern Fictions and the Nineteenth-Century Novel.* Cambridge, MA, London, England: 1993.

Kenner, Hugh. *A Homemade World: The American Modernist Writers.* New York: Morrow, 1975.

Kierkegaard, S. *Repetition: An Essay in Experimental Psychology.* Translated and with an introduction and notes by Walter Lowrie. With a bibliographical essay: "How Kierkegaard Got into English." Princeton: Princeton UP, 1941.

Kilcup, Karen L. "The Conversations of 'The Whole Family': Gender, Politics, and Aesthetics in Literary Tradition." *Soft Canons: American Women Writers and Masculine Tradition.* Karen L. Kilcup, ed. Iowa City: U of Iowa P, *1999.* 1–26.

Kleist, Heinrich von. *Michael Kohlhaas and the Marquise of O-.* Afterword by Thomas Mann. Trans. Martin Greenberg. London: Sphere Books, 1969.

Koelb, Clayton. "Incorporating the Text: Kleist's 'Michael Kohlhaas.'" *PMLA* 105. 5 (October 1990): 1098–1107.

Kolakowski, Leszek. *Modernity on Endless Trial.* Chicago and London: The U of Chicago P, 1990.

Kolodny, Annette. "Dancing through the Minefield: Some Observations on the Theory, Practice, and Politics of a Feminist Literary Criticism." Warhol and Herndl 97–116.

Krauss, Rosalind. "The Originality of the Avant-Garde: A Postmodern Repetition." *Art after Modernism: Rethinking Representation.* Edited and with an Introduction by Brian Wallis. Foreword by Marcia Tucker. New York: The Museum of Contemporary Art. Boston: David R. Godine, Publisher, Inc., 1984. 1988 ed. 13–30.

Kristeva, Julia. *Desire in Language: A Semiotic Approach to Literature and Art.* Ed. Leon S. Roudiez. Trans. Thomas Gora, Alice Jardine, and Leon S. Roudiez. New York: Columbia UP, 1980.

———. *Le Texte du roman: Approche sémiologique d'une structure transformationelle.* Second printing. The Hague. Paris: Mouton, 1976.

Kroeber, Karl. *Retelling/Rereading: The Fate of Storytelling in Modern Times.* New Brunswick, NJ: Rutgers UP, 1992.

Kroker, Arthur. David Cook. *The Postmodern Scene: Excremental Culture and Hyper-Aesthetics.* New York: St. Martin's P, 1988.

Kuhns, Richard. "The Strangeness of Justice: Reading Michael Kohlhaas." *New Literary History* 15. 1 (Autumn 1983): 73–91.

Kundera, Milan. *The Art of the Novel.* Trans. from the French by Linda Asher. New York: Harper and Row, 1988.

———. *Immortality.* Trans. from the Czech by Peter Kussi. New York: Grove Weidenfeld, 1991.

Kuspit, Donald. "The Contradictory Character of Postmodernism." Hugh Silverman, *Postmodernism* 53–68.

Landow, George P., ed. *Hyper/Text/Theory.* Baltimore, London: The Johns Hopkins UP, 1994.

———. *Hypertext 2.O: The Convergence of Contemporary Critical Theory and Technology.* Baltimore and London: The Johns Hopkins UP, 1997.

Latour, Bruno. *We Have Never Been Modern.* Trans. Catherine Porter. Cambridge, MA: Harvard UP, 1993.

LeClair, Tom. *The Art of Excess: Mastery in Contemporary American Fiction.* Urbana, Chicago: U of Illinois P, 1989.

———. "Robert Coover, *The Public Burning*, and the Art of Excess." *Critique* 23. 3 (Spring 1982): 5–28.

Lefevere, André. *Translation, Rewriting, and the Manipulation of Literary Fame.* London, New York: Routledge, 1992.

Leitch, Vincent B. *Cultural Criticism, Literary Theory, Poststructuralism.* New York: Columbia UP, 1992.

———. *Postmodernism: Local Effects, Global Flows.* Albany: SUNY P, 1996.

Lemeunier, Yves. "Visions of Poverty and the Poor in Alger's Novels." *All Men Are Created Equal: Ideologies, rêves et réalités*. Ed. and with a preface by Jean-Pierre Martin. Aix-en-Provence: Publications Université de Provence, 1983. 121–136.

Lentricchia, Frank. *Criticism and Social Change*. Chicago, London: The U of Chicago P, 1983.

Lentricchia, Frank, and Thomas McLaughlin, eds. *Critical Terms for Literary Study*. Second Edition. Chicago, London: The U of Chicago P, 1995.

Leyner, Mark. *Et Tu, Babe*. New York: Harmony Books, 1992.

———. "Geraldo, Eat Your Avant-Pop Heart Out." *New York Times* 21 Dec. 1997: (Op-Ed) Section 4.11.

———. "An Interview with Mark Leyner." By Alexander Laurence. http://www.altx.com/interviews/mark.leyner.html. *Online*.

———. *I Smell Esther Williams and Other Stories*. New York: Fiction Collective, 1983.

———. "Maximum, Flat-Out Drug Overkill: An Interview with Mark Leyner." By Larry McCaffery. McCaffery, *Some Other Frequency* 219–240.

———. *My Cousin, My Gastroenterologist*. New York: Harmony Books, 1990.

———. "Talking with . . . Mark Leyner: The Joy of Deliberately Getting Lost." Interview by Eric Levin. *Pics & Pans*. http://pathfinder.com?@@zUV8BacAk-GOk9liT/people/950424 /pages.html. *Online*.

———. *The Tetherballs of Bougainville: A Novel*. New York: Harmony Books, 1997.

———. *Tooth Imprints on a Corn Dog*. New York: Harmony Books, 1995.

Little, Jonathan. "Charles Johnson's Revolutionary *Oxherding Tale*." *Studies in American Fiction* 19.2 (Autumn 1991): 141–151.

Lott, Eric. "Hip-Hop Fiction." *The Nation* Dec. 19, 1988: 691–692.

———. "Response to Trey Ellis's 'The New Black Aesthetic.'" *Callaloo* 12.1 (Winter 1989): 244–246.

Low, Gail Ching-Liang. "In a Free State: Post-Colonialism and Postmodernism in Bharati Mukherjee's Fiction." *Women: A Cultural Review*. 4.1 (Spring 1993): 8–17.

Lowance, Mason, I., Jr. "Biblical Typology and the Allegorical Mode: The Prophetic Strain." *The Stowe Debate: Rhetorical Strategies in* Uncle Tom's Cabin. Edited by Mason I. Lowance Jr., Ellen E. Westbrook, R. C. DeProspero. Amherst: U of Massachusetts P, 1994. 159–184.

Lyotard, Jean-François. *The Inhuman: Reflections on Time*. Trans. Geoffrey Bennington and Rachel Bowlby. Stanford: Stanford UP, 1991.

McCaffery, Larry, ed. "13 Introductory Ways of Looking at a Post-Post-Modernist Aesthetic Phenomenon Called 'Avant-Pop.' Amerika and Olsen, *In Memoriam* 32–47.

———. *After Yesterday's Crash: The Avant-Pop Anthology*. New York: Penguin, 1995.

———. "Avant-Pop: Still Life after Yesterday's Crash." McCaffery, *After Yesterday's Crash* xi–xxxi.

———. *The Metafictional Muse: The Works of Robert Coover, Donald Barthelme, and William Gass*. Pittsburgh: The U of Pittsburgh P, 1982.

———. *Some Other Frequency: Interviews with Innovative American Authors.* Philadelphia: U of Pennsylvania P, 1996.

McGee, Patrick. *Ishmael Reed and the Ends of Race.* New York: St. Martin's P, 1997.

McHale, Brian. *Constructing Postmodernism.* London, New York: Routledge, 1992.

———. *Postmodernist Fiction.* London, New York: Methuen, 1987.

Machor, James L., ed. *Readers in History: Nineteenth-Century American Literature and the Contexts of Response.* Baltimore, London: The Johns Hopkins UP, 1993.

Malmgren, Carl. "Detecting/Writing the Real: Paul Auster's *City of Glass.*" D'haen and Bertens, *Narrative Turns* 177–200.

Maltby, Paul. *Dissident Postmodernists: Barthelme, Coover, Pynchon.* Philadelphia: U of Pennsylvania P, 1991.

Marshall, Brenda K. *Teaching the Postmodern: Fiction and Theory.* New York, London: Routledge, 1992.

Martin, Richard. "Ishmael Reed: Re-Writing America." *Kwartalnik Neofilologiczny* 33 (1986): 499–511.

Matlack, Lucius C. Introduction to Bibb. Bibb i–xiv.

Matthews, John T. "Intertextual Frameworks: The Ideology of Parody in John Barth." O'Donnell and Davis, eds. 35–57.

———. "Intertextuality and Originality: Hawthorne, Faulkner, Updike." Gresset and Polk 144–157.

Mazurek, Raymond A. "Metafiction, the Historical Novel, and Coover's *The Public Burning.*" *Critique* 23.3 (Spring 1982): 29–41.

Merleau-Ponty, Maurice. *Sense and Non-Sense.* Trans. and with a Preface by Hubert L. Dreyfus and Patricia Allen Dreyfus. Evanston, IL: Northwestern UP, 1964.

Miller, J. Hillis. *Fiction and Repetition: Seven English Novels.* Cambridge, MA: Harvard UP, 1982.

———. "Laying Down the Law in Literature: The Example of Kleist." *Deconstruction and the Possibility of Justice.* Ed. Drucilla Cornell et al. London, New York: Routledge, 1992. 305–329.

Miller, Karl. *Doubles: Studies in Literary History.* Oxford: Oxford UP, 1985.

Miller, Nancy K. *Subject to Change: Reading Feminist Writing.* New York: Columbia UP, 1988.

Miller, Owen. "Intertextual Identity." *Identity of the Literary Text.* Mario J. Valdés and Owen Miller, eds. *Identity of the Literary Text.* Toronto, Buffalo, London: U of Toronto P, 1985.

Moraga, Cheeríe, and Gloria Anzaldua, eds. *This Bridge Called My Back: Writings by Radical Women of Color.* Forward Toni Cade Bambara. New York: Kitchen Table: Women of Color P, 1983.

Moraru, Christian. "Mimesis and Anamnesis: Deconstruction of Metaphysics and Reconstruction of Psyche." Ronald Bogue and Mihai I. Spariosu, eds. *The Play of the Self.* Albany: SUNY P, 1994. 23–38.

———. *Poetica Reflectarii.* Bucharest: Univers P, 1990.

———. "'Zonal' Ethics: *Gravity's Rainbow,* Dislodged Subjects, and Infernal

Technology." *Canadian Review of Comparative Literature* 24.2 (Jun. 1997): 263–281.

Morgan, Thaïs. "The Space of Intertextuality." O'Donnell and Davis, *Intertextuality* 239–279.

Morris, Christopher D. *Models of Misrepresentation: On the Fiction of E. L. Doctorow*. Jackson, London: UP of Mississippi, 1991.

Morrison, Toni. *Playing in the Dark: Whiteness and Literary Imagination*. Cambridge, MA, London, England: Harvard UP, 1992.

Moulthrop, Stuart. "Rhizome and Resistance: Hypertext and the Dreams of a New Culture." Landow, *Hyper/Text/Theory* 299–319.

Mowitt, John. *Text: The Genealogy of an Antidisciplinary Object*. Durham and London: Duke UP, 1992.

Mukherjee, Bharati. *The Holder of the World*. 1993. New York: Fawcett Columbine, 1994.

Muller, John P., and William J. Richardson, eds. *The Purloined Poe: Lacan, Derrida, and Psychoanalytic Reading*. Baltimore, London: The Johns Hopkins UP, 1988.

Nackenoff, Carol. *The Fictional Republic: Horatio Alger and American Political Discourse*. New York, Oxford: Oxford UP, 1994.

Nealon, Jeffrey. "Work of the Detective, Work of the Writer: Paul Auster's *City of Glass*." *Modern Fiction Studies* 42.1 (Spring 1996): 91–110.

Neumeyer, Peter F. "E. L. Doctorow, Kleist, and the Ascendancy of Things." *The CEA Critic* 39.4 (May 1977): 17–21.

Newman, Charles. *The Postmodern Aura: The Act of Fiction in the Age of Inflation*. With a Preface by Gerald Graff. Evanston, IL: Northwestern UP, 1985.

Nielsen, Aldon, L. *Writing between the Lines: Race and Intertextuality*. Athens, London: The U of Georgia P, 1994.

Nietzsche, Friedrich. *Unzeigemässe Betrachtungen: Unmodern Observations*. William Arrowsmith, general ed. New Haven, London: Yale UP, 1990.

———. *The Will to Power*. A New Translation by Walter Kaufmann and R. J. Hollingdale. Ed., with commentary, by Walter Kaufman and with facsimilies of the original manuscript. New York: Vintage Books, 1968.

O'Donnell, Patrick, and Robert Con Davis. "Introduction: Intertext and Contemporary American Fiction." O'Donnell and Davis, *Intertextuality* ix–xxii.

O'Donnell, Patrick, and Robert Con Davis, eds. *Intertextuality and Contemporary American Fiction*. Baltimore, London: The Johns Hopkins UP, 1989.

Ong, Walter J. *Orality and Literacy: The Technologizing of the Word*. 1982. London, New York: Routledge, 1999.

Pearce, Richard. "The Circus, the Clown, and Coover's *Public Burning*." Robert A. Collins and Howard D. Pearce, eds. *The Scope of the Fantastic—Culture, Biography, Themes, Children's Literature: Selected Essays from the First International Conference on the Fantastic in Literature and Film*. Westport, CT, London, England: Greenwood P, 1980.

Perloff, Marjorie, ed. *Postmodern Genres*. Norman, London: U of Oklahoma P, 1989.

Pfister, Manfred. "How Postmodern Is Intertextuality?" Plett 207–224.

Phillips, Rod. "Purloined Letters: *The Scarlet Letter* in Kathy Acker's *Blood and Guts in High School.*" *Critique* 35.3 (Spring 1994): 173–180.

Plate, Liedeke. "Negotiating Identity in the Margin: The Estraging Case of *Mary Reilly.*" *The Comparatist* 22 (1998): 168–180.

———. "Visions and Re-Visions: Female Authorship and the Act of Rewriting." Diss. Indiana U, 1995.

Plett, Heinrich F., ed. *Intertextuality.* Berlin, New York: Walter de Gruyter, 1991.

Poirier, Richard. "Horatio Alger in the White House: Richard Nixon as Hero." *Harper's Magazine* 245.1468 (Sept. 1972): 96–104.

Potter, Russell A. *Spectacular Vernaculars: Hip-Hop and the Politics of Postmodernism.* Albany: SUNY P, 1995.

Probyn, Elspeth. *Sexing the Self: Gendered Positions in Cultural Studies.* London, New York: Routledge, 1993.

Pucci, Joseph. *The Full-Knowing Reader: Allusion and the Power of the Reader in the Western Literary Tradition.* New Haven, London: Yale UP, 1998.

Pynchon, Thomas. *The Crying of Lot 49.* 1965. New York: HarperCollins, 1999.

Ramage, John. "Myth and Monomyth in Coover's *The Public Burning.*" *Critique* 23.3 (Spring 1982): 52–68.

Readings, Bill, and Bennet Schaber. *Postmodernism across the Ages: Essays for a Postmodernity That Wasn't Born Yesterday.* Syracuse: Syracuse UP, 1993.

Reed, Ishmael. *19 Necromancers from Now.* Ishmael Reed, ed. Garden City, New York: Doubleday, 1970.

———. *Conversations with Ishmael Reed.* Bruce Dick and Amritjit Singh, eds. Jackson: U of Mississippi P, 1995.

———. *Flight to Canada.* New York: Random House, 1976.

———. "Interview with Ishmael Reed" (Peter Nazareth). *Iowa Review* 13.2 (Spring 1982): 131–171.

———. "An Interview with Ishmael Reed." *Review of Contemporary Fiction* 4.2 (Summer 1984): 176–187.

———. "Ishmael Reed." Bellamy, Joe David. *The New Fiction: Interviews with Innovative American Writers.* Urbana, Chicago: U of Illinois P, 1974. 130–141.

———. *Mumbo Jumbo.* Garden City, New York: Doubleday and Company, Inc., 1972.

Rich, Adrienne. *On Lies, Secrets, and Silence: Selected Prose 1966–1978.* New York: W. W. Norton and Company, 1979.

Riddel, Joseph N. *Purloined Letters: Originality and Repetition in American Literature.* Ed. Mark Bauerlein. Baton Rouge, London: Louisiana State UP, 1995.

Robbins, Bruce. *Feeling Global: Internationalism in Distress.* New York, London: New York UP, 1999.

Robbins, Sarah. "Gendering the History of the Antislavery Narrative: Juxtaposing *Uncle Tom's Cabin* and *Benito Cereno*, *Beloved* and *Middle Passage.* *American Quarterly* 49.3 (Sept. 1997): 531–573.

Roberson, Matthew M. "Raymond Federman's Supreme Pla(y)giarism: *Take It or Leave It.*" *New Novel Review* 5.1 (Fall 1998): 37–61.

Rosenau, Pauline Marie. *Post-Modernism and the Social Sciences: Insights, Inroads, and Intrusions*. Princeton, NJ: Princeton UP, 1992.

Ross, Andrew. *No Respect: Intellectuals and Popular Culture*. New York, London: Routledge, 1989.

———. *Universal Abandon? The Politics of Postmodernism*. Minneapolis: U of Minnesota P, 1988.

Roudiez, Leon S. "Introduction." Kristeva, *Desire in Language* 1–20.

Rowe, John Carlos. "Poe, Antebellum Slavery, and Modern Criticism." Ed. Richard Kopley. *Poe's Pym: Critical Explorations*. Durham: Duke UP, 1992. 117–138.

Royar, Robert Delius. "Consumer Paradise or Puritan Hell: Which Do You Choose?" http://www.morehead-st.edu/people/r.royar/hawthorn.htm. *Online*. Mar. 5, 1998.

Rucker, Mary E. "Science and Art in Hawthorne's 'The Birth-mark.'" *Nineteenth-Century Literature* 41.4 (Mar. 1987): 445–461.

Rushdy, Ashraf H. A. "The Phenomenology of the Allmuseri: Charles Johnson and the Subject of the Narrative of Slavery." *African American Review* 26.3 (Fall 1992): 373–394.

———. "The Properties of Desire: Forms of Slave Identity in Charles Johnson's *Middle Passage*." *Arizona Quarterly* 50.2 (Summer 1994): 73–108.

Russo, Adelaide M. "An Exchange of Tokens: Michel Leiris, Marcel Duchamp, and Jacques Derrida." Fleming and Payne 77–97.

Said, Edward W. *The World, the Text, and the Critic*. Cambridge, MA: Harvard UP, 1983.

Sartre, Jean-Paul. *Saint Genet: Comédien et martyr*. Paris: Gallimard, NRF, 1952.

Schiff, James A. "Contemporary Retellings: *A Thousand Acres* as the Latest *Lear*." *Critique* 39.4 (Summer 1998): 367–381.

———. *Updike's Version: Rewriting* The Scarlet Letter. Columbia and London: U of Missouri P, 1992.

Scholes, Robert. *Fabulation and Metafiction*. Urbana, Chicago, London: U of Illinois P, 1979.

———. *Protocols of Reading*. New Haven, London: Yale UP, 1989.

Schwartz, Hillel. *The Culture of the Copy: Striking Likenesses, Unreasonable Facsimiles*. New York: Zone Books, 1996.

Schweickart, Patrocinio P. "Reading Ourselves: Toward a Feminist Theory of Reading." Ed. Elizabeth A. Flynn and Patrocinio P. Schweickart. *Gender and Reading: Essays on Readers, Texts, and Contexts*. Baltimore, London: The Johns Hopkins UP, 1986. 31–62.

Sciolino, Martina. "Confessions of a Kleptoparasite." *The Review of Contemporary Fiction* 9.3 (Fall 1989): 63–67.

Scott III, Daniel M. "Interrogating Identity: Appropriation and Transformation in *Middle Passage*." *African American Review* 29.4 (Winter 1995): 645–655.

Silverman, Hugh., ed. "Introduction: The Philosophy of Postmodernism." Hugh Silverman, *Postmodernism* 1–9.

———. *Postmodernism: Philosophy and the Arts*. New York, London: Routledge, 1990.

Silverman, Kenneth. *Edgar A. Poe: Mournful and Never-Ending Remembrance.* New York: HarperCollins Publishers, 1981.

Silz, Walter. *Heinrich von Kleist: Studies in His Works and Literary Characters.* Philadelphia: U of Pennsylvania P, 1961.

Slethaug, Gordon E. *The Play of the Double in Postmodern American Fiction.* Carbondale, Edwardsville: Southern Illinois UP, 1993.

Smith, Cynthia J. "Intertextuality as Agent of Representation in Toni Morrison's *Tar Baby.*" *Genre* 27 (Fall 1994): 165–182.

Smith, Duncan. "Michael Kohlhaas and *Ragtime*: The Hopeful Text and the Dispairing Story." *Wissenschaftliche Zeitschrift der Wilhelm-Pieck-Universität Rostock* 31.8 (1982): 3–7.

Snead, James A. "European pedigrees/African contagions: nationality, narrative and community in Tutuloa, Achebe, and Reed. Bhabha 231–249.

———. "Repetition as a Figure of Black Culture." Ed. Gates Jr. *Black Literature and Literary Theory.* 59–80.

Sollers, Philippe. "Écriture et révolution. Entretien de Jacques Henric avec Philippe Sollers." Foucault et al. 67–79.

Sorapure, Madeleine. "The Detective and the Author: *City of Glass.*" Barone, *Beyond* 71–87.

Spanos, William V. *Repetitions: The Postmodern Occasion in Literature and Culture.* Baton Rouge, London: Louisiana State UP, 1987.

Spillers, Hortense J. "Changing the Letter: The Yokes, the Jokes of Discourse, or, Mrs. Stowe, Mr. Reed." *Slavery and the Literary Imagination: Selected Papers from the English Institute, 1987.* New Series, no. 13. Ed. Deborah E. McDowell and Arnold Rampersad. Baltimore, London: The Johns Hopkins UP, 1989. 25–61.

Steiner, George. *Babel: Aspects of Language and Translation.* Third Edition. Oxford, New York: Oxford UP, 1998.

Stonehill, Brian. *The Self-Conscious Novel: Artifice in Fiction from Joyce to Pynchon.* Philadelphia: U of Pennsylvania P, 1988.

Stowe, Harriet Beecher. *Life and Letters of Harriet Beecher Stowe.* Ed. Annie Fields. Detroit: Gale Research Company, Book Tower, 1970.

Sukenick, Ronald. *The Death of the Novel and Other Stories.* New York: The Dial P, Inc., 1969.

———. "The New Tradition in Fiction." Federman, *Surfiction* 35–45.

Suleiman, Susan Rubin. *Subversive Intent: Gender, Politics, and the Avant-Garde.* Cambridge, MA, London, England: Harvard UP, 1990.

Sussman, Henry. *The Aesthetic Contract: Statutes of Art and Intellectual Work in Modernity.* Stanford: Stanford UP, 1997.

Swope, Richard. "Postmodern Detective Fiction: Hawthorne's 'Wakefield' and Other Missing Persons." *Critique* 39.3 (Spring 1998): 207–227.

Tate, Allen. "The Angelic Imagination." *Edgar Allan Poe: Critical Assessments.* Volume IV. *Poe in the Twentieth Century.* Ed. Graham Clarke. Mountfield, East Sussex: Helm Information, 1991. 192–205.

Tate, Greg. "'Cult-Nats Meet Freaky-Deke: The Return of the Black Aesthetic." *Village Voice Literary Supplement* (Dec. 1986): 5–8.

Tayler, Christopher. "Dog as Trope." Rev. of *Timbuktu* by Paul Auster. *Times Literary Supplement* 28 May 1999: 22.

Thieme, John, ed. *The Arnold Anthology of Post-Colonial Literatures in English*. London: Arnold, 1996.

Thoreau, Henry David. *Walden*. With Ralph Waldo Emerson's Essay on Thoreau. Introduced by Christopher Bigsby. London: J. M. Dent and Sons Ltd. Rutland, Vermont: Charles E. Tuttle, 1992.

Tiffin, Chris, and Alan Lawson, eds. *De-Scribing Empire: Post-colonialism and textuality*. London, New York: Routledge, 1994.

Todorov. Tzvetan. *Poétique de la prose*. Paris: Éditions du Seuil, 1971.

———. "Présentation." Barthes et al. 5–10.

Travis, Molly Abel. "*Beloved* and *Middle Passage*: Race, Narrative, and the Critic's Essentialism." *Narrative* 2.3 (Oct. 1994): 179–200.

Trotter, David. "A Horse Is Being Beaten: Modernism and Popular Fiction." Kevin J. Dettmar, *Rereading the New: A Backward Glance at Modernism*. Ann Arbor: The U of Michigan P, 1992. 199–220.

Vattimo, Gianni. "Bottle, Net, Truth, Revolution, Terrorism, Philosophy." *Denver Quarterly* 16.4 (Winter 1982): 24–34.

———. *The End of Modernity: Nihilism and Hermeneutics in Postmodern Culture*. Trans. and with an Introduction by Jon R. Snyder. Baltimore: Johns Hopkins UP, 1988.

Vierek, Elisabeth. "The Clown Knew It All Along: The Medium Was the Message." *Delta* 28 (June 1989): 63–81.

Walker, Nancy. *The Disobedient Writer: Women and Narrative Tradition*. Austin: U of Texas P, 1995.

Wallace, David Foster. "Tri-Stan: I Sold Sissee Nar to Ecko." McCaffery, *After Yesterday's Crash* 232–245.

Walsh, Richard. "'A Man's Story Is His Gris-Gris': Cultural Slavery, Literary Emancipation and Ishmael Reed's *Flight to Canada*." *Journal of American Studies* 27.1 (1993): 51–71.

———. "Narrative Inscription, History and the Reader in Robert Coover's *The Public Burning*." *Studies in the Novel* 25.3 (Fall 1993): 332–346.

———. *Novel Arguments: Reading Innovative American Fiction*. Cambridge, England, New York: Cambridge UP, 1995.

Ward, Glenn. *Teach Yourself Postmodernism*. NTC Publishing Group: Lincolnwood, IL, 1997.

Warhol, Robyn R., and Diane Price Herndl, eds. *Feminisms: An Anthology of Literary Theory and Criticism*. 1991. New Brunswick, N.J.: Rutgers UP, 1996.

———. "Introduction." Warton and Still 1–44.

Waugh, Patricia. *Metafiction: The Theory and Practice of Self-Conscious Fiction*. London, New York: Routledge, 1984.

———. *Practising Postmodernism/ Reading Modernism*. London, New York: Edward Arnold, 1992.

Weir, David. *Decadence and the Making of Modernism*. Amherst: U of Massachusetts P, 1995.

Weisenburger, Steven. *Fables of Subversion: Satire and the American Novel, 1930–1980*. Athens, London: The U of Georgia P, 1995.

———. "Inside *Moon Palace*." Barone, *Beyond* 129–142.

Weixlmann, Joe. "Ishmael Reed's Raven." *The Review of Contemporary Fiction* 4.2 (Summer 1984): 205–208.

———. "Politics, Piracy, and Other Games: Slavery and Liberation in *Flight to Canada*." *MELUS* 6.3 (1979): 41–50.

West, Cornel. "Black Culture and Postmodernism." Ed. Barbara Kruger and Phil Mariani. *Remaking History*. Seattle: Bay P, 1989. 87–96.

Wexelblatt, Robert. "Thomas Hobbes and Michael Kohlhaas." *Southern Humanities Review* 18.2 (Spring 1984): 109–128.

Widdowson, Peter. *Literature*. London, New York: Routledge, 1999.

Winks, Robin W. Introduction to Henson. Henson i–xxxiv.

Woodmansee, Martha. "On the Author Effect: Recovering Collectivity." Woodmansee and Jaszi 15–28.

Woodmansee, Martha, and Peter Jaszi, eds. *The Construction of Authorship: Textual Appropriation in Law and Literature*. Durham, London: Duke UP, 1994.

Worton, Michael, and Judith Still, eds. *Intertextuality: Theory and Practice*. Manchester: Manchester UP, 1990.

Yarbrough, Stephen R. *After Rhetoric: The Study of Discourse beyond Language and Culture*. Carbondale, Edwardsville: Southern Illinois UP, 1999.

Yen, Alfred C. "The Interdisciplinary Future of Copyright Theory." Woodmansee and Jaszi 159–173.

Zavarzadeh, Mas'ud, Donald Morton. *Theory, (P)ostmodernity, Opposition: An "Other" Introduction to Literary and Cultural Theory*. Washington, D.C.: Maisonneuve P, 1991.

Ziegler, Heide. "Love's Labours Won: The Erotics of Contemporary Parody." O'Donnell and Davis, *Intertextuality* 58–71.

Žižek, Slavoj. *Enjoy Your Symptom: Jacques Lacan in Hollywood and Out*. New York, London: Routledge, 1992.

———. *Looking Awry: An Introduction to Jacques Lacan through Popular Culture*. 1991. Cambridge, MA, London: MIT P, 1993.

INDEX